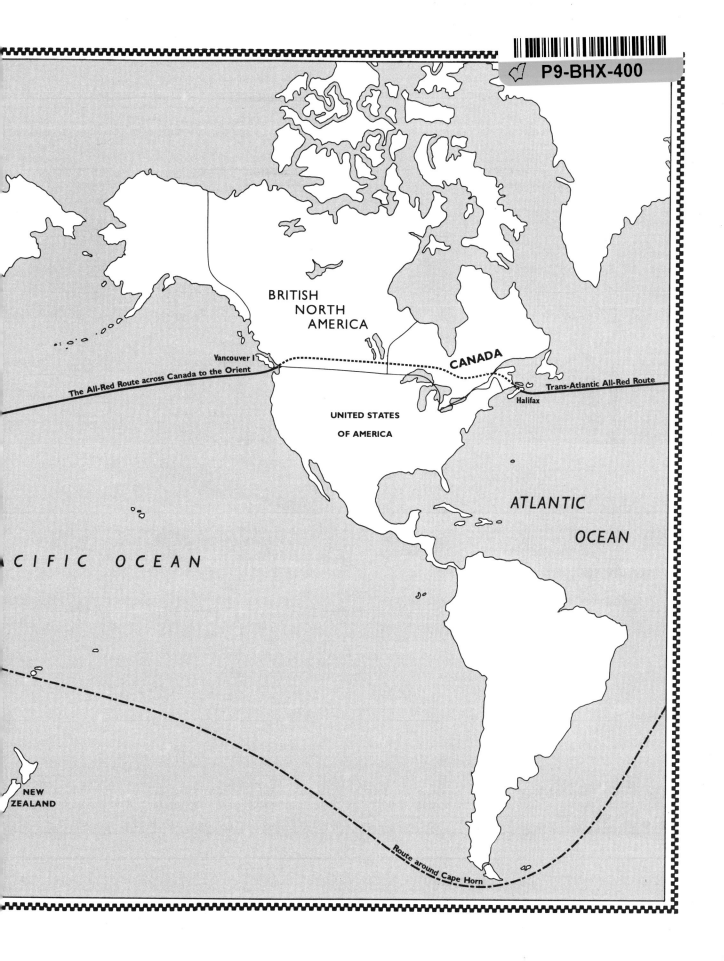

BRITISH
NORTH
AMERICA

CANADA

Vancouver I

The All-Red Route across Canada to the Orient

Trans-Atlantic All-Red Route

Halifax

UNITED STATES
OF AMERICA

ATLANTIC

OCEAN

PACIFIC OCEAN

NEW
ZEALAND

Route around Cape Horn

THE ASIAN DREAM

THE ASIAN DREAM

THE PACIFIC RIM AND CANADA'S NATIONAL RAILWAY

DONALD MACKAY

Donald MacKay

Douglas & McIntyre
Vancouver/Toronto

Other books by
Donald MacKay

The Lumberjacks
Anticosti
Scotland Farewell
Empire of Wood
Heritage Lost

Douglas & McIntyre Ltd., 1615 Venables Street,
Vancouver, British Columbia V5L 2H1

Canadian Cataloguing in Publication Data

MacKay, Donald, 1925–
    The Asian dream

    Includes index.
    Bibliography: p.
    ISBN 0-88894-501-9
    ISBN 0-88894-528-0 (Presentation Edition)

    1. Canadian National Railways–History.
2. Merchant marine–Canada–History. 3.
Chinese–Canada. 4. Japanese–Canada.
I. Title.
HE2810.G7M24 1986 385'.0971 C86-091153-5

Design: Barbara Hodgson and Heather Griblin
Map research: Anthony Clegg; map artwork, David Gay
Frontispiece photograph: CN Roundhouse, Turcot Yard, Montreal
Printed and bound in Canada by D. W. Friesen & Sons Ltd.

Contents

"It must be recognized that Pacific Asia is the least familiar to Canadians of all the world's great zones of civilization. Furthermore, Western perceptions of the 'Far East,' which have always been shrouded in ignorance and myths, have failed to keep pace with the tremendous changes in progress, particularly in contemporary China and Japan."

Report of the Standing Senate Committee
on Foreign Relations, Ottawa, 1973

Introduction

THE DRAMATIC GROWTH IN Canada's trans-Pacific trade during the past decade is the latest, and most promising, chapter in a story almost 500 years old. When John Cabot sailed the *Matthew* through the North Atlantic fog to Newfoundland in the spring of 1497 it was not a new land he was seeking but trade with the opulent old empire of Cathay, which Marco Polo had visited via ancient caravan routes a century earlier. During the next 350 years many ships and lives were lost in the fruitless drive to find a northwest passage through Arctic waters to the Orient. By the seventeenth century it had become apparent that an Arctic route was virtually impassable, and the realists who ran the Hudson's Bay Company, having been granted the right to continue the search, sensibly opted to trade in beaver furs instead of spices. The overland route to the West, they discovered, consisted of waterways unfit for anything grander than a canoe or small boat, and the formidable Rocky Mountains barred the path to the shores of the Pacific. Not until the 1830s and England's invention of the steam railway did a new generation of adventurers grasp the possibilities of a North American "land bridge" from the Atlantic to the Pacific to link up with ships bound for China and Japan. Rather than an Arctic sea lane, the northwest passage would be an overland system of steel rails. This book is the story of Canadian National Railways, heir to two pioneer railways that pushed their way through northwestern Canada to the Pacific; it tells of the people whose vision enabled the lines to span the continent and of those who later extended the resulting commerce to the Asian Pacific.

The story began to take shape in the 1860s when a transcontinental railway was needed to bind together the new federation of British Colonies and keep the West out of the hands of the Americans. It seemed likely that the builder would be the Grand

Trunk Railway Company, Canada's first major railroad which already stretched from the Atlantic to the western border of Ontario. But the Grand Trunk's British shareholders, eager for profit, were dubious of such a visionary scheme, and the honour of laying rails from the Atlantic to the British Columbia coast fell by default to a newcomer, the Canadian Pacific Railway Syndicate.

Much has been written about the CPR, and with good reason, but in the end the Canadian West was opened not by one railway but by three, the others being the oft-forgotten Grand Trunk Pacific, a late-blooming offshoot of the Grand Trunk Railway Company, and the Canadian Northern Railway, built by two former Ontario farm boys. Both lines have passed into history now; they were nationalized some sixty years ago and amalgamated into the publicly owned Canadian National Railways, which uses their routes to this day. Their lives were brief, hectic and terminated by near bankruptcy; but between them they unlocked the northwest, where the CPR did not run, and helped turn the West into one of the world's great granaries. They were responsible for the birth of hundreds of communities, among them the port of Prince Rupert, which seventy years ago was meant to be a gateway to the Orient but only now is beginning to fulfill its destined role. Although dependent on others to develop Pacific trade, they laid down routes which enable present-day commerce to be conducted with the countries of the western Pacific Rim, as the Far East is now called.

The Pacific Rim, or Pacific Basin, properly speaking includes Russia, which has been Canada's leading grain customer in recent years, and Indo-China, which because of long years of war has been slow to develop trade patterns. Although some people would include countries whose shores are far from Pacific waters, such as India, Sri Lanka or even Pakistan, for the purposes of this book I have taken the Asian Pacific Rim to mean China, South Korea, Taiwan, Hong Kong, Australia, New Zealand, the six members of the Association of South East Asian Nations (ASEAN) — Malaysia, Indonesia, Thailand, the Philippines, Brunei and Singapore — and the scattered string of islands including Micronesia, Polynesia and Melanesia which make up Oceania.

These Pacific countries vary enormously in size, density of population, industrial development, politics, language, religion, culture and stability. At one extreme, Japan, with few natural resources of its own, has built a market economy and industrial base second only to the United States. On the other hand China, a country of tremendous potential, has the resources to make it relatively self-sufficient but suffers a striking lack of industrial development. At various stages in between are the ASEAN bloc and the so-called NICS (newly industrializing countries): South Korea, Taiwan and Hong Kong. With the exception of the prosperous city state of Singapore, the ASEAN have natural resources but lack development whereas the resource-poor NICS are successfully emulating Japan in buying raw materials abroad and selling their finished products. Japan and the NICS have turned the Asian Pacific into the world's most dynamic region in terms of trade and economic growth, and the Pacific Ocean into the world's number one trade route. The Asian Pacific has overtaken western Europe as Canada's second largest trading region (though it is a poor second to the United States which accounts for nearly three quarters of Canada's trade). While it would be pointless to exaggerate the impact of trans-Pacific trade, given that overwhelming attachment to the United States, or to expect too much of the future, the recent Macdonald Commission report on Canada's prospects was optimistic: "There are a number of reasons to believe that Canada's economic relations with the Asia Pacific rim will continue to strengthen and diversify in the decades ahead. The single most important of these reasons is the relatively high growth rates projected for the region and, particularly, for the 'newly' and 'nearly' industrializing economies of East and South East Asia. The growth in output and trade of these countries is likely to continue to outpace significantly that of Canada's trading partners, the United States and Western Europe."

Meantime, the present multi-billion-dollar level of trans-Pacific trade is the closest Canada has ever come to realizing the old dream that has run through its history like a silken thread through homespun weave. Largely as a result of demand from the Asian Pacific, new industries have been born in the three westernmost provinces. Bulk exports that were once confined to grain now include coal, sulphur and potash. British Columbia exports more goods to the Asian Pacific than to the United States. Vancouver has become one of the world's busiest ports. Prince Rupert, after decades of stagnation, has been transformed into a major coal, grain and lumber port. For CN, the only railway with two terminals on the Canadian west coast — one in Vancouver and one in Prince Rupert — this trade accounted for almost a quarter of its total earnings in 1984, for the movement of bulk traffic has revolutionized railroading in western Canada.

Precisely 150 years ago CN's earliest ancestor, the tiny Champlain and St. Lawrence, Canada's first steam railway, was opened to facilitate exports of produce from Montreal to New England. The success of that railway and others like it gave birth to plans for lines to the Pacific coast, to unite a new nation and open a route to the Far East. The first of these aims proved easier to achieve than the second, but despite many disappointments, as the dream of easy Oriental riches gave way to reality, the notion that Canada was destined to become a Pacific as well as an Atlantic nation has survived. Now more than any time in the past, Canada's future is linked with what may well be the century of the Pacific.

THE ASIAN DREAM

1 QUEST FOR AN ALL-RED ROUTE

AMID THE MIGHTY FORESTS and rivers of the New World, Canada's first railway seemed little more than a toy. Its diminutive engine, named Dorchester after a colonial administrator but affectionately known as Kitten, was built in England for a tamer landscape. Weighing not much more than six tons, it was 162 inches long, roofless, and its source of energy was a cord of wood in the tender.

When its owners, the Champlain and St. Lawrence Railroad, opened their line for business near Montreal on 21 July 1836 — a ceremony enlivened by the presence of Governor General Lord Gosford, 300 guests and the music of a regimental band — the engine had just enough strength to pull two cars; the rest were hauled by teams of horses. The Champlain and St. Lawrence was what was known as a portage railway, conveying passengers and freight from the St. Lawrence River to the Richelieu River fourteen and a half miles away. The track was made of pinewood topped with strips of iron that had a nasty tendency to spring up and strike the undercarriage, but the engine managed to make the run in a little under an hour. The horses took a bit longer. Whatever its shortcomings, Kitten heralded the advent of Canada's railway age, Britain's gift to the world in the 1820s, and encouraged people to dream of linking the Atlantic to the Pacific with the new steam technology. As the engines grew stronger they freed men from dependence on the speed and stamina of their own legs or those of horses.

Of course there had been a time, and within living memory at that, when people had believed the Pacific could be reached by a water route, such as one of those depicted in the wildly inaccurate

The Champlain and St. Lawrence, Canada's first public railway. Artist Sheriff Scott's impression of the inaugural festivities at Laprairie, on the south bank of the St. Lawrence opposite Montreal, 21 July 1836. *Courtesy CN*

maps of the sixteenth century, which ended somewhere on the British Columbia coast. Capt. James Cook had put an end to that notion in 1778. With secret instructions from the British Admiralty to seek "a northern passage by sea from the Pacific to the Atlantic Ocean," he sailed as far north as the Bering Strait and found no trace of one. Although the search for a passage through the Arctic seas was to continue, the Scottish explorer Alexander Mackenzie demonstrated in 1793 that there was a viable land route when he became the first white man to penetrate the Rocky Mountains and reach the Pacific at Bella Coola Inlet, just missing an encounter with Capt. George Vancouver who had been there by ship.

Forty years later when the editor of the *Toronto Patriot*, Thomas Dalton, suggested a transportation system consisting of the new steam trains, augmented by canals and steamboats, he was merely reviving the dream of a northwest passage by land. Sir John Smyth, an English poet and visionary who had settled in Toronto, proposed a "land bridge" to supplant the tedious sea voyage around the Cape of Good Hope, or the dangerous trip through the Roaring Forties around Cape Horn, there being as yet no Suez Canal. Since western British North America was as little known as Africa, apart from a fringe of coastal British Columbia, Dalton and Smyth might as well have been suggesting a balloon trip to China. Only a few years later did a series of pamphlets appear that people took seriously. They were written in the late 1840s by hardheaded British army engineers like Maj. Robert Carmichael-Smyth of the 93rd Highland Regiment and Col. Sir Richard Bonnycastle who wrote a book called *Canada and the Canadians*. "We shall yet place an iron belt from the Atlantic to the Pacific," said Bonnycastle, "a railroad from Halifax to Nootka Sound, and thus reach China in a pleasure voyage."

It was a time when British North America, having achieved a considerable degree of self-determination and weathered a threat by a group of Montreal businessmen to join Canada to the United States, was entering a new era. The northern colonies, unlike those to the south, would use their new independence for the greater

George Stephenson's Rocket, the world's first railway engine, hauled fourteen coal cars at four miles an hour in 1828 in the north of England. *Courtesy CN*

glory of the Mother Country as well as for their own advancement. Carmichael-Smyth wrote:

This national highway from the Atlantic to the Pacific is the great link required to unite in one chain the whole English race. It will be the means of enabling vessels steaming from our magnificent colonies — from New Zealand, Van Diemen's Lands, New South Wales, New Holland, from Borneo, the West Coast of China, from the Sandwich Islands, and from a thousand other places — all carrying the rich products of the East to land them at the commencement of the West — to be forwarded and distributed throughout our North American provinces and delivered within thirty days to the ports of Great Britain.

Carmichael-Smyth, like other pamphleteers such as Lt. Millington Synge in his *Canada in 1848* and F. A. Wilson and A. B. Richards in *Britain Redeemed and Canada Preserved*, was anticipating the

Although the Champlain and St. Lawrence
Railway was a toy compared with later trains,
an artist's inaccurate sketch at the time
possibly overdid that impression. *Courtesy CN*

imperial advantages of what came to be called an "all-red route"
across British North America, red being the colour used by map-
makers to designate the United Kingdom and her distant colonies.
Trade could be improved between Britain and Asia, and soldiers
sped out to police it by a railway from Halifax to a British port on
the west coast from whence ships could sail on to the Orient. By
this time hopes of finding the long-sought northwest sea passage
via the Arctic had been virtually abandoned after Sir John Franklin's expedition in two specially outfitted ships met with disaster
in 1847.

The British railway mania, having spread through Europe and
into the eastern United States, which was soon to boast 2000
miles of track, had infected the colonies of Nova Scotia, New
Brunswick and particularly the united provinces of Upper and
Lower Canada. Canadians in the past had been content to ship
their timber and farm produce by water until winter came each
November to paralyze the waterways. With the success of the
Champlain and St. Lawrence, which carried passengers, flour,
meal, pork, beef and timber from Montreal to St-Jean, Quebec,
from whence they were floated down Lake Champlain by steamer
into the United States, other portage railways had been opened.
The *Gazette* of Montreal and the *Toronto Patriot* extolled the merits
of the railway over the canals that Canadians had been building at
such great expense.

Lord Durham, in his report recommending the union of Canada, which was to shape the future of the country, had strongly
recommended a railway between the maritime provinces and Quebec, and in Halifax Nova Scotia's most popular politician, Joseph
Howe, was trying to interest the imperial government in a scheme

called the European and North American Railway. Conceived by the railway pioneer John A. Poor in Boston, it would have linked Portland, Maine, via New Brunswick and Nova Scotia, to England. Passengers reaching a Nova Scotia port would have been taken by steamer across the Atlantic to Galway, Ireland, across Ireland by train, across the Irish sea by ferry to Liverpool, and hence to London by train. The British government showed no interest, but it promised to guarantee a construction loan if an "intercolonial railway" were built to connect the maritime colonies and the province of Canada. "I am neither a prophet nor the son of a prophet," Howe told a Halifax audience, "but I believe that many in this room will live to hear the whistle of the steam engine in the passes of the Rocky Mountains and make the journey from Halifax to the Pacific in five or six days."

In England a group called the Canadian Land and Railway Association petitioned the imperial government to build a railway devised by a highly respected London civil engineer, Alexander Doull. The first professionally detailed plan for a transcontinental line, it would have run from Halifax to Montreal, as Lord Durham wished, then northwestward along the forbidding north shore of Lake Superior, still largely terra incognita, across the prairies, through a pass in the Rocky Mountains, and down to the mouth of the Fraser. It was in many ways like the route followed by the Canadian National Railways to this day.

After the opening of the Champlain and St. Lawrence, more than thirty railway charters were granted by the government, but by the end of the 1840s Canada had less than 100 miles of track. It took the Railway Guarantee Act at the end of the decade to get major construction started by encouraging any railway more than 75 miles long to borrow money.

In Toronto a mining promoter, lawyer and former cavalryman, Allan Macdonell, swore that if the Egyptians could build pyramids Canadians should be able to build a railway across 3000 miles of unexplored forest, prairies, rock and rivers. He had visited the north shore of Lake Superior by boat and had not been discouraged by talk that it was impossible terrain for a railway. With the backing of Toronto businessmen and politicians he solicited the government of the province of Canada for a charter to build the Lake Superior and Pacific Railway: "The shortest, cheapest and safest communication for Europe and all Asia; not only are the United States but the whole of Europe aroused to the importance of securing the immense trade of China and the East Indies," Macdonell said. "Should the United States construct a railway

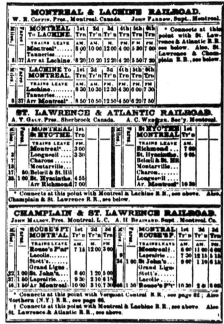

A Typical Page from the "American Railway Guide for the United States" of January, 1852, Same Size as the Original

In the late 1840s a 46-mile ride on the Champlain and St. Lawrence cost $1.50.
Courtesy CN

The Champlain and St. Lawrence was commemorated in the currency of 1837.
Courtesy CN

Prince Rupert of the Rhine, son of the King of Bohemia, cousin of King Charles II of England, and first governor of the Hudson's Bay Company. *Courtesy Public Archives of Canada /C 4299*

through the territory, England might soon feel how precarious is her active and energetic rival." The government turned him down, but reaction from the United States convinced Macdonell he was on the right track. Said the *New York Tribune* of 27 March 1851:

A route through British America is in some respects even preferable to that through our own territory. Having its Atlantic seaport at Halifax and its Pacific depot near Vancouver's Island, it would inevitably draw to it the commerce of Europe, Asia and the United States, so thus, British America, from a mere colonial dependency, would assume a controlling rank in the world. To her, other nations would be tributary, and in vain would the United States attempt to be her rival; for we could never dispute with her the possession of the Asiatic commerce, or the power which that commerce confers.

Two years later Macdonell tried again, and at the same time a Montreal group of politicians and businessmen sought to build a "Northern Pacific Railway" from Quebec to Sault Ste. Marie, Ontario, from whence it would head south into Michigan and west through United States and British territory. Both schemes were turned down by a provincial government whose reluctance to encourage a western railway was attributable to the absence of financial support from the government in London.

Another obstacle was the fact that most of the two million square miles of British North America west of the Great Lakes was ruled by neither government but by the Hudson's Bay Company. For almost two centuries this had been the largest privately controlled territory in the world, awarded in 1670 by King Charles II of England to "the Governor and Company of Adventurers of England trading into Hudson's Bay," partly in recompense for failure to find a northwest sea route to the Orient. Instead of trading with Asia they were dealing with the tribes of North America. The company, whose first governor was the king's cousin, Prince Rupert, and whose original territory was called Rupert's Land, held the key to the northwest from the 90th parallel to the Pacific. But when, in 1854, Sir Richard Broun urged the Hudson's Bay Company to participate in a project called the Imperial British American Main Trunk Railway, Ocean Ferry and Freehold Land Company, it declined. Mindful of Indian wars in the United States, it wanted neither railway nor settlement to disturb the fur trade and the peaceful coexistence built up over the years with native tribes.

At all events, there was no population in the West to support a railroad. Beyond the Ottawa Valley the land lay empty; apart from Indian bands and Hudson's Bay trading posts there were few people between Fort Garry on the Red River and Victoria on Vancouver Island. If there were to be a transcontinental railway it would be built because of imperial priorities for communication and trade with the Orient, and the need to assert Britain's ownership of the northern half of North America.

Meanwhile, the railway boom came to what is now Quebec and Ontario during the early 1850s in a wave of prosperity to which railway construction contributed its share. In eight years 2000 miles of track were built, all of it on the southern fringe of Canada and much of it operated by the Grand Trunk Railway Company of Canada, which, despite its name and the fact that one fifth of its financing came from the government of Canada, was owned in England. Which is not to say it was not deeply involved in Canadian politics; from the start it had friends, and even senior employees, in high places.

For example, there was Francis Hincks, who came from Ireland and who was a joint premier of Canada when work on the Grand Trunk began. Hincks had launched the boom by drafting the country's first railway policy, the Railway Guarantee Act of 1849. He gained the backing of two City of London firms acting as financial agents for the Canada Government — Baring Brothers and Company and Glyn Mills and Company, the latter known as "the railway bank" — and the support of Peto, Brassey, Betts and Jackson who had built half the railways in England and Europe and were to build the Grand Trunk. In the process Hincks did not go unrewarded, having acquired 1000 shares in the company he was using his political office to promote.

Then there was the Grand Trunk's first president, John Ross, who also happened to be the Solicitor General of Canada. Ross at times got his hats mixed up, forgetful of whether it was Canada or the Grand Trunk he was representing. Another powerful politician, Georges-Etienne Cartier, who wrote the Grand Trunk charter, served as the company's chief solicitor while he was co-premier and chairman of the government's Railway Committee.

It was this mix of public and private function that prompted one of the Grand Trunk's harshest critics, George Brown, the Liberal politician and editor of the *Toronto Globe*, to complain that it was the Grand Trunk, not the government, that really ran Canada. "The Grand Trunk governs Canada at the present moment," said the *Globe* on 22 April 1857. "Its power is para-

Beaver, moose, and a fox: the insignia of the Hudson's Bay Company. *Courtesy Hudson's Bay Company*

19

mount. The Ministry are mere puppets in its hands and dance whatever tune the Company pipes." Even if this was an exaggeration, there could be no doubt that for thirty years the Grand Trunk was Canada's foremost railway. Its prospectus, glowing with more superlatives and questionable information than is common even in such documents, claimed it would be "the most comprehensive system of railways in the world." Admitting that it would, in fact, run no more than 800 miles at first, it declaimed:

> The American railroads now in course of construction place the Grand Trunk line in the most direct communication with the arterial lines to the Great West and to the Mississippi, a region whose advance in population and in wealth has been regarded as almost fabulous, and yet those resources are still very partially developed.
>
> Commencing at the debouchure of the three largest lakes in the world, the Grand Trunk Railway of Canada pours the accumulating traffic throughout the entire length of Canada [Ontario and Quebec]. . . . The whole future traffic between the western regions and the east, including Lower Canada, parts of the state of Vermont and New Hampshire, the whole of the state of Maine and the provinces of New Brunswick, Nova Scotia, Prince Edward Island and Newfoundland, must therefore pass over the Grand Trunk Railway.
>
> This great and comprehensive scheme of railway communication throughout the most wealthy, populous and important colonial dependency of Great Britain is now offered as a new project to the public. It comes with the guarantee of the government of Canada. . . .

Building the line proved a long, tough job, but by 27 October 1856 the main link, 334 miles between Montreal and Toronto, was ready for traffic. People turned out from miles around to cheer the first train, a high-stacked woodburning locomotive hauling seven yellow coaches at an average speed of thirty miles an hour. Within eight years from the time it was chartered in 1852 the Grand Trunk built or otherwise acquired 1000 miles of track, extending from Sarnia, on the southwestern Ontario border with Michigan, through Toronto, Montreal and on down the south shore of the St. Lawrence to a point east of Quebec City. There, at Rivière-du-Loup, it stopped abruptly, far short of the neighbouring colony of New Brunswick. It was hoped that some day this might be the jumping-off place for the intercolonial railway that would connect

Canada with Nova Scotia. In the meantime, to secure a winter port on the Atlantic, the Grand Trunk leased a 300-mile Canadian–U.S. railway, known either as the Atlantic and St. Lawrence or the St. Lawrence and Atlantic, depending on which side of the border you were on, that joined Montreal to Portland, Maine.

Other railways were built in the 1850s, notably the American-financed Great Western from Hamilton to Windsor, Ontario, but the Grand Trunk was the backbone of the colony and the ideal candidate to build a railway to the Pacific coast. As its name implied it was Canada's main line, an iron corridor through the eastern forests, linking towns and settlements along waterways which had traditionally carried lumber and farm produce.

As early as 1853 the *Railway Times* in England predicted it would be the first, perhaps in all of North America, to reach the west coast. There were rumours that the imperial government was considering the British navy station of Esquimalt on Vancouver Island as the terminus of a railway vital to the defence of the Empire and a gateway to British possessions and trade with Asia. By building such a railway the Grand Trunk was bound to profit by cutting many weeks off the sea voyage from Liverpool or London to the Orient. "Nothing would serve the Grand Trunk Company so much as the opening of the western prairies," said the *Morning Chronicle* of Halifax. The *Times* of London argued that "the construction of the railway would not merely open to cultivation a large territory of British North America hitherto almost unexplored but would open passage to the China seas and to all possessions in the East Indies . . . that a railway will inevitably be made is as certain as that now is the time to undertake it." But for the next three decades the hope of building a railway to the Pacific through British North America would be as elusive as a mirage.

The Grand Trunk's attitude was ambivalent. As its president, John Ross, told the House of Commons committee hearings in London looking into the future of the Hudson's Bay Company's northwest territories, the Grand Trunk was certainly interested, but as businessmen they wanted the West reasonably settled before the railway was built. Until that time, Ross would be content with "a good, broad, open road."

Expert witnesses at these London hearings in 1857 insisted that the only sensible course would be to avoid the thousand miles of rocky, forested, unpopulated and unexplored territory north of Lake Superior and run south of the lake into Michigan and Minnesota before pushing west through British North America. Appealing as it did to commercial rather than visionary political and

John Ross, the Grand Trunk Railway's first president, believed his company should build a line to the Pacific but only after there was sufficient population to support it. *Courtesy CN*

Great Western Railway, the Grand Trunk's principal rival in the 1850s in western Ontario. *Courtesy CN*

imperial instincts, this argument was popular with the absentee management and shareholders of the Grand Trunk in London.

The two arguments — either an all-British route or one that passed through the United States — were embodied in the reports of two separate expeditions sent out to explore the territory in the late 1850s. Capt. John Palliser, the Irish adventurer commissioned by the Colonial Office, opposed an all-British route and favoured one via St. Paul, Minnesota. On the other hand, the expedition commissioned by the government of Canada and led by Professor H. Y. Hind of the University of Toronto and a civil engineer from Trois-Rivières, Quebec, S. J. Dawson, favoured a line north of Lake Superior. Dawson set out to prove his point by building a rough wagon road through it. Sandford Fleming, then a young man commencing the career which was to make him one of Canada's most illustrious engineers, supported Hind. His "Practical Observations on the Construction of a Continuous Line of Railway from Canada to the Pacific Ocean on British Territory" was a bible for railway promotors long before Fleming became the chief engineer of the Canadian Pacific Railway in the 1880s.

Along with the question of when and where the railway should be built was the rivalry — in the end more apparent than real — between the Americans and British over who would build the first railway to the Pacific. The hearings in London into the future of the Hudson's Bay territory aroused public interest. One unsolicited proposal, addressed to John A. Macdonald, then attorney general of Canada and not yet convinced of the importance of a railway to the Pacific, warned that the Americans by constructing a route from St. Louis to California, "will completely shut us out and become sole master of the traffic and territory."

In the heyday of the clipper ships around Cape Horn the race to fetch tea, silk and spices from the Orient went to the fastest. In a race to build a railway to the Pacific the prize would be nothing less than mastery of trade with Asia, or so it seemed to Asa Whitney of New York. Grown rich in the China trade, he had been trying since 1842 to interest the American Congress in a Pacific railway. George Wilkes, another New York trader, was trying to promote his "Project of a National Railroad from the Atlantic to the Pacific Ocean, for the purpose of obtaining a short route to Oregon and the Indies." In the 1850s Americans were concerned the British would get there first. Isaac I. Stevens, an army engineer who had surveyed an all-American rail route from the Great Lakes to the Washington Territory, of which he was governor, warned that the Grand Trunk might well build a line to the coast before the Americans could do so.

"England is suddenly about to become a rival for a great continental communication with the Pacific," said the *New York Herald*. "There is every reason to believe that before very long Great Britain will have taken some steps to consolidate her colonies by a magnificent scheme for a railroad built on this continent." The *Boston Evening Transcript*, reflecting the fears of New England railwaymen eager to link their eastern lines with the west coast, went further. "While Congress is postponing the consideration of the Pacific railway from May to December, and from December till May, Great Britain has her railway to the Pacific already commenced. . . . Let anyone who doubts the joint ability of the Canadian and English governments to accomplish so great an enterprise take down the map and look at the line of the Grand Trunk, already connecting the Atlantic with the lakes, and then look at the comparatively short [sic] distance from Lake Superior to Vancouver Island."

Suddenly the financially struggling Grand Trunk was being regarded, at least in the United States where its power and prestige was held in higher esteem than it was in Canada, as a threat to American rail lines. Since the United States already had 30,000 miles of railroads in the East and was a generation ahead of the British in settling the West, this concern that the British would beat them to the Pacific seems strange, unless seen as a campaign to get a reluctant Congress to back a transcontinental American railway. At the same time there were certainly politicians and railway moguls, particularly at St. Paul in the new Territory of Minnesota, where Red River colony settlers frequently came to trade, who coveted the great plains held by the Hudson's Bay

Company and were excited by the gold discoveries on the Fraser River. William B. Ogden of the Minnesota and Pacific Railroad, for example, envisaged "a great chain of railroads embracing the Grand Trunk . . . a road on Canadian soil to the Pacific along a route near the fiftieth parallel."

That the Canadian government was worried was clear from the instructions given to its delegate at the Hudson's Bay Company hearings, Chief Justice W. H. Draper:

> His Excellency [the Governor General] feels it particularly necessary that the importance of securing the North West Territory against the sudden and unauthorized influx of immigration from the United States side, should be strongly pressed. He fears that the continued vacancy of this great tract, with a boundary not marked on the soil itself, may lead to further loss and injury both to England and to Canada. He wishes you to urge the expediency of marking out the limits, and so protecting the frontier of the lands above Lake Superior, about the Red River, and thence to the Pacific, as effectually to secure them against violent seizure or irregular settlement, until the advancing tide of emigrants from Canada and the United Kingdom may fairly flow into them and occupy them as subjects of the Queen on behalf of the British Empire.

For Draper the way to secure the West for the Crown was to build a railway. "I hope to see, or at least that my children will see, a railway wholly on British territory from the Atlantic to the Pacific Ocean," he told the committee in London. "There is very serious apprehension that if something is not done, that territory will in some way or another cease to be a British territory."

In 1858, the year British Columbia became a crown colony, Confederation for the first time became government policy. It was a concept that included a railroad linking Halifax to Montreal, and then in good time, Montreal and Toronto with the west coast. Who was to build it? In the absence of initiative on the part of the Grand Trunk, the irrepressible Macdonell, having failed twice to obtain a charter, had finally been given his chance. The aim of his North West Transportation, Navigation and Railway Company was to open a wagon road and telegraph line to the Red River at Fort Garry, and from there to the Fraser River, with the idea that it would eventually become the route of a railway. Unfortunately, as the legislators had always suspected, Macdonell could not raise the money, though he himself blamed the Hudson's Bay Company for his failure.

The obvious candidate to build a Pacific railway was still the Grand Trunk, but it had all it could do to keep its existing service running, being close to bankruptcy and chronically short of working capital and rolling stock. There had been too much "politics." Too much of the $50 million invested in the Grand Trunk since 1854 had gone to enrich the contractors. After five years of full-scale operations, the Grand Trunk was still not making enough money to begin paying off the heavy interest charges on its borrowing. One of the larger shareholders, a Lancashire businessman named H. C. Chapman, coming out to investigate the railroad, commented sourly: "I am quite satisfied that the Grand Trunk has not begun to be managed as a commercial carrying company. . . ." Anthony Trollope, the English novelist on a visit to Canada, was not so sure: "The whole property seems to be involved in ruin; and yet the line is one of the grandest commercial conceptions that was ever carried out on the face of the globe. . . ." The Grand Trunk's afflictions were investigated by the government auditor, John Langton, who decided there must be more capital if the Grand Trunk was to survive. Since the government was not prepared to help, it was fortunate that Baring and Glyn were in no mood to lose their investment. "We consider ourselves invested with a security and a trust," said George C. Glyn, a Grand Trunk director, "which we hold to be to the advantage of all. We will prevent, except under the most extraordinary and unexpected circumstances, the closing of the lines." President Ross resigned, along with most of his officers. To replace him, Baring and Glyn sent out their own man, a young English railwayman named Edward Watkin.

2 A NORTHWEST PASSAGE BY RAIL

"Neither of us would die, if we could help it, 'until we had looked upon the waters of the Pacific from the windows of a British railway carriage.' "

Edward Watkin, recalling his vow with Leonard Tilley*

IN THE DRAMA of Canadian Confederation, Edward Watkin was one of those supporting actors thrown up by history to advance the plot and act as catalyst. It was he, for example, who was responsible for the buying out of the Hudson's Bay Company, thereby unlocking its hold on the West and opening the way for a railway to the Pacific. A promoter in the Victorian tradition, melding business and politics, personal ambition and patriotism, Watkin's photograph, taken in his mid-forties, suggests a man of impatient will, an impression supported by his own writings and those of his colleagues. He could be charming, but made enemies because of his ebullient, even brash, convictions which he expressed in a manner many considered insensitive and autocratic. In Canada he frequently attacked government finance and trade policies. It was sometimes difficult to know whether he was working for the Grand Trunk, the British government, or for himself.

Born of a prosperous merchant family in Manchester, Watkin learned his trade at the London and Northwestern Railway. At the time he was hired to take over Grand Trunk operations he had served six years as general manager of the Manchester, Sheffield and Lincolnshire and had gained some insight into North Ameri-

---

*Edward William Watkin was president of The Grand Trunk Railway Company of Canada from 1862 to 1868. Leonard Tilley was one of the Fathers of Confederation.

Built in 1882 the Grand Trunk Railway's No. 235 had the sort of power needed by a country preparing to open up the Far West. *Courtesy CN*

The first locomotive built by the Grand Trunk Railway at its Point St Charles Shops, Montreal, in 1859. It pulled the royal train carrying the Prince of Wales and the Colonial Secretary, the Duke of Newcastle, in 1860. *Courtesy CN*

can ways when a group of shareholders sent him out to repair the affairs of the bankrupt Erie Railroad.

As a Liberal member of parliament and the Manchester city council, Watkin had a reputation as a man of imperial vision who believed in the unity of what were, after all, Britain's oldest colonies. He felt British North America had been neglected, and was pleased when the new colonial secretary, the Duke of Newcastle, toured Canada in the company of the Prince of Wales, the future King Edward VII, in 1860. During this, the first formal royal visit to the colony, the prince opened the mile-long Victoria Bridge at Montreal, one of the greatest engineering feats of the century but a great drain on the Grand Trunk finances. Watkin was acquainted with the Duke, since both had been members of parliament in neighbouring ridings, and shared similar views of empire.

Watkin's own opinion appeared in the *Illustrated London News* just before he took over the Canadian operations of the Grand Trunk. He wrote:

Our augmenting interests in the East demand, for reasons both of Empire and of trade, access to Asia less dangerous than by Cape Horn, less circuitous even than by Panama, less dependent than by Suez and the Red Sea. We say then, "Establish an unbroken line of road and railway from the Atlantic to the Pacific through British territory." Such a great highway would give shorter distances by both sea and land, with an immense saving of time. . . . For Japan, for China, for the whole Asiatic Archipelago, and for Australia, such a route must become the great highway to and from Europe; and whatever nation possesses that highway must wield of necessity the commercial sceptre of the world.

By his own account, Watkin accepted the thankless task of Superintending Commissioner of the Grand Trunk so as to be able to play a part in the future of British North America. Paying a call on the colonial secretary before sailing for Montreal, he found Newcastle eager that the maritime provinces be served by the Grand Trunk, whose easternmost flank in Canada was still hanging in the air at Rivière-du-Loup with not enough revenue to support it. As a member, along with his employers Baring and Glyn and the Duke himself, of the British North America Association, which lobbied in England for Canadian interests, Watkin had been one of those working to secure such a link, which was to be called The Intercolonial Railway.

Sir Edward Watkin helped to open the West for Confederation but failed to build a Grand Trunk line to the Pacific. *Courtesy CN*

Newcastle suggested that Watkin, in addition to his duties as chief troubleshooter for the Grand Trunk, become an unofficial, unpaid imperial government agent to promote the Intercolonial — and while he was at it to investigate ways and means of developing a communication system right across the continent to the Pacific. Trade and flag being closely intertwined, it was typical of Watkin — and the times — that the two tasks be linked. Although one was on behalf of a private commercial railway and the other a task on behalf of the imperial government, they were considered not only compatible but even complementary. As Watkin told Thomas Baring, who had taken over the chairmanship of the Grand Trunk the better to protect the British investment, extending the railway to the Atlantic and then, eventually, to the Pacific would unite the colonies and ensure a profitable future for a company whose existing market was patently too small.

"This line [The Grand Trunk] both as regards its length, its work, and its alliances with third parties, is both too extensive and too expensive for Canada of today," Watkin told Baring in November 1860, "and left, as it is, dependent mainly upon the development and industry on its own line, and upon the increase of the traffic of the west, it cannot be expected, for years to come, to emancipate itself throughout from the load of obligations connected with it." On the other hand, there was a solution in which the Grand Trunk could play its role. "Try to realize . . . a main through railway, on which the first thousand miles belong to the Grand Trunk Company, from the shores of the Atlantic to those of the Pacific, made just within — as regards the northwestern and unexplored district — the corn-growing latitude. The result of this Empire would be beyond calculation; it would be something, in fact, to distinguish the age itself; and the doing of it would make the fortune of the Grand Trunk."

From a commercial view there was little to recommend such a railway. Only about 23,000 Europeans lived west of Lake Superior, mostly on Vancouver Island. Even in the province of Canada there was insufficient population to make the Grand Trunk pay, whereas in England the railways were assured of sufficient population between towns to contribute freight and passenger income. It was one of Watkin's tasks to correct the imbalance between capital structure and revenue, and on his arrival in Montreal, early in August 1861, this he set out to do. He overhauled rolling stock, revitalized the traffic department to increase cash flow, and worked out ways to get a reluctant Canadian government to aid a railway which, writing home to his wife, he called "an organized mess."

A month after his arrival, Watkin changed roles and went to the maritime provinces to pursue Newcastle's aim of linking Halifax to Canada with an intercolonial line. The eastern provinces had almost 300 miles of railway but, despite the efforts of Joseph Howe and others, had failed to persuade the imperial government to extend it through northern New Brunswick to join the Grand Trunk system in Quebec. There had always been some reason, it seemed, why the government could not help, whether it was the inroads made on the imperial treasury by the Crimean war or the cost of the Indian Mutiny. Watkin made the acquaintance of both Howe in Nova Scotia and Leonard Tilley, the premier of New Brunswick. Writing in his memoirs, Watkin recalled: "I found Mr. Tilley fully alive to the initial importance of the construction of this arterial Railway — initial in the sense that, without it, discussions in reference to the fiscal, or the political, federation, or the absolute union, under one Parliament, of all the Provinces, was vain. I found, also, that Mr. Tilley had ardently embraced the great idea — to be realized some day, distant though that day might be

As engines gained power and speed, the bowler hats of the crew gave way to more practical head gear. The distinctive high stack was phased out as railways switched from wood to coal. *Courtesy CN*

— of a great British nation, planted, forever, under the Crown, and extending from the Atlantic to the Pacific."

In late September they all attended a railway conference in Quebec City with delegates from the province of Canada. They arranged to go to London in a body to meet the cabinet, though prospects for an eastern intercolonial line, let alone one to the Pacific, did not look promising. "Certainly, in 1861, this great idea seemed like a mere dream of the uncertain future," Watkin wrote, "Blocked by wide stretches of half-explored country; dependent upon approaches through United States territory; each province enforcing its separate and differing tariffs, the one against the other through its separate custom house. It was not a matter of surprise to find a growing gravitation toward the United States, based, alike, on augmenting trade and augmenting prejudices. Amongst party politicians at home [in England] there was, at this time, of 1861, little adhesion to the idea of a Colonial Empire." The "adhesion," however, was improving, due to the outbreak of the American Civil War. There were fears that the Northerners, inflamed by British sympathy for the Confederates of the south, might cut off the Grand Trunk route to Portland, Maine, and with it Montreal's winter access to England. The War Office began to take an interest and urge an all-British line from Halifax to Montreal. Jingoist American newspapers, such as the *New York Herald*, were showing hostility towards British North American colonies.

Charles J. Brydges, managing director of the Grand Trunk from 1862 to 1874. *Courtesy CN*

"When they are annexed to this republic, which is only a matter of time — a question which may receive its solution before the termination of the present year — we will show them how to act as an independent party and assert the dignity and freedom of the Anglo Saxon race," said the newspaper in mid-July.

When Watkin returned to England late that year he found a warmer welcome and was able to arrange meetings with the Prime Minister, Lord Palmerston, as well as Newcastle. It was at this time that the Intercolonial Railway, without which the British government was not disposed to turn its attention to a Pacific railway, began to materialize, though it would be 1876 before it was completed.

In the spring of 1862 Watkin was back in Montreal to assist at the passage of the Grand Trunk Arrangements Act which reaffirmed the fact that the Grand Trunk was controlled in London. Under this act the Canadian government provided financial aid, though not to the company's satisfaction because it meant that the Grand Trunk had to proceed with very limited funds. While removing the Grand Trunk from Canadian party politics and ensuring its position as a purely British commercial enterprise, the new act militated against the company's sharing with the government the task of building a line to the Pacific.

Watkin, appointed president of the Grand Trunk that year, gave himself more time for his empire-building by hiring as general manager Charles J. Brydges, a young Englishman who had been chief executive of the Great Western, the Grand Trunk's competitor. An ambitious man, he was to influence government policy both as an officer of Grand Trunk and later as general manager of the Intercolonial Railway.

Watkin, believing he had done all he could to make the Intercolonial a reality, now devoted his energies to a route to the Pacific. As he told a London meeting: "Men's minds are turning again to the idea of the French Jesuits of two hundred years ago, of a road to the East, over what is now British Territory throughout, to the waters of the Pacific."

The lure of the West, having faded during the years since the Palliser and Hind expeditions, drew fresh attention when an expedition of 115 people travelled in Red River carts across the prairies in 1862 by way of St. Paul, Fort Garry and the fur trader's trail to the Yellowhead Pass and down the Thompson and Fraser rivers. These people, calling themselves "The Overlanders," were seeking gold and were the first to travel the overland "northwest passage" apart from explorers and fur traders. That same year the British

Overland Transit Company applied for a charter to establish a route of stage coaches and steamers from the Grand Trunk rail-head in western Ontario. Meant to get passengers to the Pacific in twelve days, it collapsed for lack of money. It was also the year Viscount Milton and Dr. W. B. Cheadle set out from the Red River to the Pacific on their expedition of hunting and exploration which was to capture the British imagination. They wrote a romantic report which urged the end of the Hudson's Bay Company monopoly and the opening up of the West. According to Milton and Cheadle:

> We have attempted to show that the original idea of the French Canadians was the right one and that the true Northwest Passage is by land, along the fertile belt of the Saskatchewan, leading through British Columbia to the splendid harbour of Esquimalt and the great coal fields of Vancouver Island, which offer every advantage for the production and supply of a merchant fleet, thence to India, China and Japan. . . . Millions of money and hundreds of lives have been lost in the search for a Northwest Passage by sea. Discovered at last, it has proved useless. The Northwest Passage by land is the real highway to the Pacific; let us hope that our countrymen gained the glory of the former brilliant achievement, valueless to commerce, so they may be the first to establish a railway across the Continent of America, and reap the solid advantages which the realization of the old dream has failed to afford.

Faced with the inability of the Grand Trunk to build a line to the Pacific, and the disinclination of the imperial government to participate, the government of Canada took a more modest

Long before the Canadian Northern Railway and the Grand Trunk Pacific built branches through the northern prairies, freight was hauled by wagon trains over trails made by fur traders early in the nineteenth century.
Courtesy CN

Henry Pelham, MP, fifth Duke of Newcastle-under-Lyme, Secretary of State for the Colonies 1859–64, wanted an "all-red route."
Courtesy Public Archives of Canada/PA 121301

approach. In the spring of 1862 it decided that a telegraph line, a cheaper, faster way of establishing sovereignty over western British North America, was the short-term answer. Moreover, it would answer the continual refrain from London that imperial expenditure must have an imperial objective, because London was planning an undersea cable to Halifax which could be linked with an overland telegraph system, if one could be built. The Canada government also wanted a road over which to carry mail, since the fastest service then available was the Hudson's Bay Company winter dog teams that ran in relays from Fort Garry to Fort Edmonton.

In this role as entrepreneur and go-between, and in an effort to get a basic transcontinental communication system started, Watkin proposed to the Duke of Newcastle that an Atlantic and Pacific Transit and Telegraph Company be established. It was to consist of a telegraph wire from Halifax to New Westminster, the capital of the British Columbia crown colony, to be followed later with a road, and then a railway. Since the co-operation of the Hudson's Bay Company, which controlled much of the route, would be crucial, Newcastle put the question to that company. According to Watkin, the response of the Hudson's Bay governor, the crusty Henry H. Berens, was not promising. "What! Sequestor our very tap-root! Take away the fertile lands where our buffalo feed! Let in all kinds of people to squat and settle and frighten away the fur-bearing animals they don't hunt and kill! Impossible. Destruction — extinction — of our time-honoured industry. If these gentlemen are so patriotic, why don't they buy us out?" This proposal was rather unfair to Berens, who had already agreed to give up a strip of Hudson's Bay land between the Red River and the Rockies — a total of 13,000 square miles — for a telegraph line. Watkin and his masters evidently wanted considerably more — enough potentially saleable land to help defray construction costs.

The expectation that the Hudson's Bay Company would sooner or later have to give up its territorial rights was hardly new, for as early as 1857 the Select Committee of the British House of Commons on the future of the British North America West had said: "It is essential to meet the just and reasonable wishes of Canada to be enabled to annex to her territory such portion of the land in her neighbourhood as may be available to her for the purposes of settlement — with which lands she is willing to open and maintain communications, and for which she will provide the means of local administration. . . . Your Committee trust that there will be no difficulty in effecting arrangements as between Her Majesty's

Government and the Hudson's Bay Company, by which these districts may be ceded to Canada on equitable principles."

During the next four months Watkin tried to raise the million and a half pounds sterling the Hudson's Bay Company named as its price for control of the West. Although Newcastle had given his personal support, there was no indication the government as a whole had, or would. Baring wanted nothing to do with it, suspecting that Newcastle was using Watkin as a pawn in a geopolitical chess game. "If the Duke wants these great efforts to be made, he must make them on behalf of the government," said Baring. "He must not leave private persons to take the risk of Imperial work." Without Baring's support, Glyn would not provide assistance, which accounts for the slightly desperate note that began to creep into the Watkin letters to Baring seeking support for his Telegraph and Transit Company. "You must really help me in that Pacific matter," wrote Watkin. "The Pacific affair is part of our Policy — the success of it will make — believe me — a vast difference in the value of your Grand Trunk property."

There were several reasons why Watkin persisted. He had a relish for grand schemes. His reputation was at stake. He was now president of the Grand Trunk, and not merely a troubleshooter, and he was convinced that the Grand Trunk's destiny, like that of Canada, was linked with the West. He believed, rightly as it turned out, that if he could get no financial support from Baring, Glyn or Newcastle he could find it elsewhere and that in the end either the imperial government or the government of Canada would, for the national good, take over the Hudson's Bay Company territories themselves.

Still unsure of where funding would come from, on 1 December 1862 Watkin went to the Hudson's Bay Company headquarters in Fenchurch Street, London, to meet with officials of that august organization, including Governor Berens. "The room was the 'Courtroom,' dark and dirty," recalled Watkin. "A faded green cloth, old chairs, almost black, and a fine portrait of Prince Rupert. . . . Mr. Berens, an old man and obstinate, bearing a name to be found in the earliest lists of Hudson's Bay shareholders, was somewhat insulting in his manner. We took it patiently."

Berens himself complained that the proposals put to him were far too vague, and that he had no clear idea as to who were the parties actually trying to buy the Hudson's Bay Company. Watkin received some reassurance of support when Newcastle told him that William Gladstone, the future prime minister, had written to say, "Your Pacific scheme will be one of the grandest affairs ever

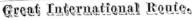

Great International Route.

GRAND TRUNK
Broad Gauge Railway.

1377 MILES UNDER ONE MANAGEMENT!

THE GREAT DIRECT CANADIAN

MAIL AND EXPRESS ROUTE

BETWEEN THE

Eastern and Western States.

THE CHEAPEST AND BEST ROUTE TO ALL POINTS EAST AND WEST,

Close Connections made with all Connecting Lines, and Through Tickets issued to all important points.

☞ For San Francisco, Sacramento, Salt Lake City, Omaha, and intermediate places on the Pacific Railway, the Grand Trunk is the most direct route.

Splendid Palace Sleeping Cars are now run between Chicago and Sarnia without change.

From Passengers holding Through Tickets, American Money is received, at par, for Sleeping Berths and Refreshments.

BE SURE AND ASK FOR TICKETS VIA THE GRAND TRUNK RAILWAY.
C. J. BRYDGES, MANAGING DIRECTOR.

achieved, and I hope it will be completed in your time. It shall have my hearty support." But by late spring it had become clear that the imperial government would spend no money on a Hudson's Bay takeover. The Duke of Newcastle began to ease himself out of the picture as gracefully as he could, leaving Watkin to carry on alone. In a statement to parliament designed to divorce the government from the scheme, Newcastle said merely that Watkin was "a gentleman of great experience, knowledge and energy, who was constantly travelling between Canada and this country, to inquire whether it would be possible to effect a communication across that Continent. This gentleman — Mr. Watkin — had returned with considerable information, and I had suggested to him to place himself in communication with persons in the commercial world who might be willing to undertake the carrying out of such a communication."

Funding would have to come from private sources, so Watkin turned to the newly founded International Financial Society, a group of London-based entrepreneurs looking for just such a project. By the summer a deal between the Society and the Hudson's Bay Company had been concluded and a new board installed, though its primary business continued to be fur trading. "Thus, after a long and continuous period of industry and investigation — a grave game of chess with the Hudson's Bay Company — many anxieties and a great pecuniary risk, surmounted without the expected help of our Government, the battle was won," wrote Watkin in his memoirs.

He was contemplating not only a telegraph line but a railway as well, though not an all-British route. "At that time, 1863, the best route for a railway to the Pacific was to commence at Halifax, to strike across to the Grand Trunk Railway at Rivière-du-Loup, 106 miles east of Quebec, then to follow the Grand Trunk system to Sarnia; to extend that system to Chicago; to use, under a treaty of naturalization, the United States lines from Chicago to St. Paul; to build a line from St. Paul to Fort Garry by English and American capital; and then to extend the line to the Tete Jaune [Yellowhead] Pass, there to meet a railway through British Columbia starting from the Pacific."

In July a prospectus was issued stating that capital had been fixed at two million pounds sterling for the reorganized Hudson's Bay Company. "With the view of providing the means of telegraphic and postal communication between Canada and British Columbia, across the Company's territory, and thereby of connecting the Atlantic and Pacific oceans by an exclusively British

Route. . . . one of the first objectives of the Company will be to examine the facilities and consider the best means for carrying out this important work; and there can be little doubt that it will be successfully executed either by the Hudson's Bay Company itself, or with their aid and sanction."

Watkin was supposed to visit the Red River settlement to consult with Hudson's Bay officials on the best way of proceeding with a telegraph line, but things began to fall apart. Watkin had been expecting — it was even mentioned in the prospectus — that the government of Canada would at least back the scheme to the extent of guaranteeing part of the share issue. But when the government decided that the plan was too vague Watkin's enthusiasm began to flag. He cancelled plans to proceed to the Red River.

Not that the project died right away. Watkin tried to interest the Montreal Telegraph Company and the United States Telegraph Company. As for an eventual railway, in September Brydges reported from St. Paul, Minnesota, with Watkin-like optimism, that he was "safe in saying that negotiations, which are now in progress . . . will result in the actual construction of that line of railway [north from St. Paul to Fort Garry] before very long and that steps will immediately be taken to continue the line across to the Pacific coast."

Prime Minister Sir John A. Macdonald; indifference turned to determination to promote a railway to the west coast. *Courtesy Public Archives of Canada /C 5327*

Hopes persisted right into 1864, the *Victoria Colonist* reporting on 5 January that "Mr. Brydges, the Grand Trunk Manager, has just returned from England with assurances of British Capitalist approval of a telegraph line, with a railway line to follow." Dr. John Rae, the Scottish physician and explorer who had mapped 1700 miles of the Arctic on behalf of the Hudson's Bay Company in the effort to find a northwest sea passage, was commissioned to examine the Yellowhead Pass and the Fraser River as far as Prince George, then called Fort George. But the sad fact was that Watkin was getting nowhere. In those days even John A. Macdonald, the man eventually responsible for ramming a line to the Pacific, was uninterested. "The country itself is of no present value to Canada," said Macdonald, who was then finance minister. "We have unoccupied land enough to absorb the immigration for many years."

Watkin's work at the Grand Trunk, as opposed to his personal efforts to build a communication system to the west coast, had grown firmer fruit. He and Brydges had built up traffic, reorganized financing, increased net earnings, and managed to turn the shaky company around, if not actually to make it wealthy. He laid plans to replace iron rails with steel, change broad gauge to standard, and replace wood with coal as locomotive fuel. He projected a line from Sarnia, and neighbouring Port Huron in Michigan, to Chicago, though this was not to be completed until 1882, thus improving the railway's income by carrying produce from the Midwest to the Atlantic at Portland. Watkin and Brydges also introduced a "first" into North American railways which was to play an important part in promoting overseas trade. Traditionally the railways had handled overseas freight only to and from a seaport, the shipper himself being responsible for carriage by sea. In 1863 the Grand Trunk, with its new "through bills of lading," took responsibility for freight by sea as well as by land.

Three years after Watkin had assumed the presidency of the company, traffic had increased by 50 per cent. The worst of the debts were paid, and credit had been restored to the point where Canadian banks were again prepared to lend substantial amounts to buy much-needed equipment. But his successes were to be undermined by bad luck and the poor business conditions following the U.S. civil war. With inflation and the unstable American dollar, the Grand Trunk, doing business on both sides of the border, suffered the consequences. Unable to reduce operating costs, Watkin tried to get American railways to co-operate in raising rates but was rebuffed. To the chronically impatient stockholders in England, whatever else Watkin may have done he was not providing the dividends that had somehow failed to match the promise of the prospectus issued when the Grand Trunk was born.

Watkin's response in 1867 resembled that of a man staking everything on one roll of the dice. Whether to break out of an unsatisfactory economic situation in the East, or to assure British autonomy and a Grand Trunk market in the West, time was running out. The United States Congress had already passed bills to ensure that the Union Pacific would, after all, beat any British effort to build the first railway across the continent. The Northern Pacific Railroad, starting to build a line from Duluth, Minnesota, at the southwestern tip of Lake Superior, to Tacoma on Puget Sound in Washington Territory, had launched a propaganda campaign against Canada's efforts to complete a Pacific railway on its own. "Enough is known of the geography and topography of Western British America," it said, "to make certain that the Northern Pacific Railroad cannot be rivalled by any transcontinental line in that direction."

It was Watkin's belief that if the Canadians did not build their western railroad soon, the Northern Pacific would do it first with a line up into British territory. Given the American expansionist mood, which prompted U.S. Secretary of State W. H. Seward to

Grand Trunk maintenance crew on a hand-operated speeder aided by a man with a pole. Such crews were called gandy dancers. *Courtesy CN*

say in 1867 that "nature" had intended the whole of the continent to be American, Watkin was concerned when he learned that an American group, using English front men, was trying to buy out the Hudson's Bay Company in order to colonize Rupert's Land. This the Canadian government resolutely refused to permit, and a firm Canadian policy to build a railway coast-to-coast began to take shape.

In the spring of 1867 Watkin appeared before the Grand Trunk shareholders in London to say the time had come for a complete reorganization, recapitalization, and a merging with competitors such as the Great Western to prepare for an expansive future. Although he did not invoke it in so many words, the vision of a Grand Trunk railway to the west coast lurked behind his statements, and this was not what the shareholders wanted to hear. They had invested in hopes of a healthy return, not an expansion of the railway into empty regions where there could be no profit. If the Canadian government desired a Pacific line let them build one, but not at the expense of British shareholders.

Sir Henry W. Tyler. During his twenty-three years as president, the Grand Trunk tracks doubled to nearly 5000 miles, but he refused to build to the west coast. *Courtesy CN*

The rebellion against Watkin was led by a former army engineer, Capt. Henry W. Tyler, Chief Inspector of Railways in Britain, who did not believe a coast-to-coast railway could pay its way. One had only to look at the demographic figures: three quarters of the population of British North America — three and a half million — lived in what is now Ontario and Quebec. It was there that efforts should be concentrated, not in the empty distances west of Lake Superior. Tyler declared that while the Grand Trunk certainly had a future, he for one did not have much confidence in its current management.

He found an ally of sorts in Brydges. While not agreeing completely that a railway to the coast was a bad thing — he had been too deeply involved in Watkin's plans for that — he opposed an all-British line. "I have no belief myself in any line of railway running to Fort Garry, for a long time to come, through British territory," Brydges said. "I am quite clear that railways from Fort Garry around the north shore of Lake Superior and Lake Nipissing cannot be built except at frightful cost, and when built cannot be worked successfully in winter, and if it could be worked would have no traffic to carry on it."

On the eve of Confederation, with his dream of a transcontinental railroad under attack, Watkin fought back, trying to describe to an audience of shareholders who had never been to Canada the difficulties which had bedeviled efforts to achieve earning power: the business recession; the poor harvest; the detrimental effects of the end of the reciprocity treaty with the United States; the necessity of competing with the low rates of waterborne traffic on the St. Lawrence River system, which paralleled the Grand Trunk tracks.

Defeated by Grand Trunk shareholders who, as he saw it, put dividends before the greater good of British North America, the now-ailing Watkin was succeeded in 1869 by Richard Potter, chairman of the Great Western in England. Potter had helped Watkin in taking over control of the Hudson's Bay Company, most of whose territory was in turn taken over by the federal government after Confederation. Watkin was knighted for his service to the crown, but just how important his role actually was is not easy to assess. He had wrested control of the Hudson's Bay Company from the old fur traders and imposed up-to-date management, removing a major impediment to Confederation. Certainly he brought to Canada a strong vision, not then generally shared, of a united nation, linked by rail from coast to coast. With or without the Grand Trunk, a railway from ocean to ocean was now Canadian national policy, without which Confederation would have little practical value. But for all the activity of the previous twenty years, ideas on how a western line might be built were still surprisingly vague — except for those of a few men like Sandford Fleming, or the less well known Alfred Waddington.

Waddington, one of those Englishmen imaginative to the point of eccentricity who has made the Empire so interesting, had turned up in British Columbia during the gold rush and got himself elected to the legislature. He caught the railway mania and for more than a decade, at his own expense, devoted himself to planning a railway running from the Ottawa Valley, north around Lake Superior, through the prairies into Yellowhead Pass, and then on to the wild and lonely Bute Inlet, a fiord facing the north shore of Vancouver Island, 200 miles north of Victoria. While not a trained surveyor, his route had a lot to recommend it and was praised by Fleming, who was soon to embark on a more professional survey for the government over much of the same route.

In his pamphlet "Overland Route through British North America, or the Shortest and Speediest Road to the East," Waddington asserted that England was losing her Asian trade to the United States and might also forfeit Australia and New Zealand. He warned that British interests would lose out to the Americans when the Union Pacific, then nearing completion, would "connect with the splendid steamers already subsidized by the American Government and running between San Francisco, Japan, China and the Sandwich Islands."

Having failed to engage British interest, Waddington, who was then in his seventies and something of a character in his home town of Victoria, petitioned the government of Canada for a charter to build what he called the Canada Pacific Railway, thus suggesting the name, at least, for the company which was to become world famous. Since negotiations were already proceeding to bring British Columbia into Confederation and link it to the East with a railway, his proposal attracted entrepreneurs eager to partake of a bonanza unequalled since the Grand Trunk and Great Western Railway boom of the 1850s. Among them was Jay Cooke, the Philadelphia financier, who now controlled the Northern Pacific. Egged on by W. B. Ogden of Minnesota, a founder of the line, Cooke had visions of running the first railway through British territory to the coast and even annexing it to the United States. But when Cooke sent a delegation to Ottawa it met with a cool reception, for Sir John A. Macdonald, now prime minister, had reason to be worried.

Early in 1870 Macdonald had received a letter from Brydges, whose business brought him into frequent contact with American railway men, warning "that there is some political action at the bottom of this, and that the United States government at Washington are anxious to take advantage of the organization of the Northern Pacific Railway to prevent your getting control, for Canada, of the Hudson's Bay Territory." If there was any doubt of the American threat, the recent United States Senate Committee Report on Pacific Railroads had removed it:

> The line of the Northern Pacific runs for 1500 miles near the British possessions and when built will drain the agricultural products of the rich Saskatchewan and Red River, districts east of the mountains, and the gold country of the Fraser, Thompson and Kootenay Rivers west of the mountains . . . the opening by us first of a Northern Pacific Railroad seals the destiny of the British possessions west of the 91st meridian. They will become so Americanized in interests and feelings that they will in effect be severed from the new Dominion and the question of their annexation will be a question of time.

"It is quite evident to me," Macdonald told Brydges, "that the United States government are resolved to do all they can short of war to get possession of the western territory, and we must make immediate and vigorous steps to counteract them. One of the first things to be done is to show unmistakenly our resolve to build the Pacific Railway."

Having promised British Columbia a railway if it came into Confederation — as it did in 1871 — Macdonald's government boldly took over responsibility for the project (as well as for the intercolonial line promised the Maritimes) and commissioned the Canadian Pacific Survey long before they had any idea what company, if any, would eventually take it over as a commercial proposition. Sandford Fleming, now chief engineer of the Intercolonial, and who had been one of the first in Canada to use the term "all-red route," was the Canadian Pacific's chief engineer, holding both jobs simultaneously. Under him laboured hundreds of surveyors, engineers, chainmen, Indian guides, axemen and cooks who during the decade of the survey were to explore for the first time the Canadian Shield and British Columbia's "sea of mountains."

Starting things off with a survey of his own in 1872, Fleming covered 5300 miles from Halifax to the west coast. It was one of those historic expeditions, carried out by a professional, that brings reality to vision, and Macdonald, who had now staked his career on an all-Canada route, was relieved when Fleming found no reason why a railway could not be built around the top of Lake Superior, despite the objections of Grand Trunk men and others. As the expedition secretary, the Reverend George M. Grant, put it in his account *Ocean to Ocean*, "We are satisfied that the rugged and hitherto unknown country extending from the Upper Ottawa to the Red River of the North, is not, as it has always been represented on maps executed by our neighbours and copied by ourselves, impracticable for a railway; but entirely the reverse."

From Fort Garry, Fleming followed the Carlton Trail up to Fort Carlton in Saskatchewan and along the pleasantly wooded North Saskatchewan River valley to Fort Edmonton and the foothills above the Athabaska River to the Yellowhead Pass, whose easy grades had made it the trail of the fur traders. He had commended Waddington's route to Bute Inlet, and also considered a northwesterly line from Yellowhead to the mouth of the Skeena River, but his preference lay in a southwesterly route down the Thompson and Fraser rivers to Burrard Inlet. There, where the city of Vancouver now stands, the chronicler of Fleming's journey became eloquent at the thought that Canada was to become a Pacific, as well as an Atlantic, nation. "All this country is a single colony of the British Empire," Grant wrote, "and this colony is dreaming magnificent dreams of a future when it shall be the Greater Britain, and the highway across which the fabrics and products of Asia shall be carried."

Having committed himself to the vast project, Macdonald sought a company to carry it out. At the Grand Trunk Watkin was long gone, and Brydges, the general manager, was of no help; in fact, when he was approached by a Toronto syndicate to head up a western railway company, he declined on grounds the scheme would never work. In 1871 Macdonald turned to the one man in Canada who seemed to have the financial power to take the project off his hands.

Sir Hugh Allan was one of those many nineteenth-century Scots who in their youth came to North America to make their future. Now with his Gaelic-Gothic mansion, Ravenscrag, on the slopes of Mount Royal, and a commercial empire which included a local Quebec railway, a bank, and coal, iron and wheat interests as well as Canada's principal shipping line, the Montreal Ocean Steamship Company, which he had started a decade earlier with four ships, Allan was the richest man in Canada. Although his success was partly due to the existence of the Grand Trunk, without whose

Sir Sandford Fleming blazed trails for several major Canadian railways, invented Standard Time, and designed Canada's first postage stamp. *Courtesy CN*

services he could hardly have built his wealth, the railway constituted a monopoly whose English caution vexed his Scottish exuberance.

Informed by Francis Hincks, the original promoter of the Grand Trunk, who had popped up again as Macdonald's finance minister, that the Northern Pacific was pursuing plans to build a railway in western Canada, Allan got in touch with Macdonald. What did the government propose? Not much, Macdonald told him, until the question could be debated in parliament. Waddington's application for a charter was still pending; meanwhile Allan would be at liberty to make his own proposals. Unfortunately Macdonald failed to make clear that Americans were not invited to participate, and within three months Allan began negotiations with Cooke.

Waddington faded out of the picture and died the next year, having aided Cooke and Allan who, like the Grand Trunk, wanted a line that would make ready money by running south rather than north around the Great Lakes. For Brydges this Canadian-American alliance was ominous. Unable to partake in a western railway himself, he wanted to ensure that whoever built it would be compatible with the Grand Trunk and he had reason to fear the Northern Pacific would not be. He began to disrupt Allan's plans, invoking the old fear of American annexation, and advising the money merchants in London, where Cooke looked for funds, of just what was going on.

With the backing of Georges-Etienne Cartier, still the company solicitor and still a powerful voice in the Macdonald cabinet, Brydges convinced Senator David L. Macpherson of Toronto, a contractor who had done very well out of the Grand Trunk, to form a rival all-Canadian company to seek a western charter. This was to be called the Interoceanic Railway Company and was committed to Macdonald's all-Canada route north of the Great Lakes. Macdonald, having encouraged Allan in the first place, now persuaded him to break off relations with the Americans. Allan then was awarded the charter, whereupon both Allan and Cooke got into trouble.

Having overextended itself, Cooke's Northern Pacific went bankrupt, his influence and impact on the economy being such that the collapse helped start the long recession in North America which continued through most of the 1870s. It was to be some time before the Northern Pacific recovered under new management and went on to build through the United States to the Oregon coast, and by then its dream of a western Canada route was reduced to a couple of north-south branch lines insinuated into Manitoba and British Columbia. Allan had distanced himself enough from the Americans to escape injury from the Cooke crash but failed to escape Canada's "Pacific Scandal" the same year.

Allan thought nothing of bribing politicians to further his railway ambitions in that era of buccaneer business, but unlike others he was caught. The Liberals accused Allan and Macdonald of making a deal whereby, in exchange for a Pacific railway charter, Allan contributed $350,000 to the Conservative war chest that put Macdonald back into power in 1872. Macdonald was forced out of office and a somewhat chastened Allan surrendered his railway charter. The first serious effort to build a Pacific railway had ended in failure, but it had ensured that the railway, when it came, would be free of American domination.

Five years were to pass before Macdonald got back into office to pursue a national policy which included a railway to the Pacific. Meanwhile, under Fleming's direction the survey crept across the rock and around the lakes and through the boreal forest of northern Ontario while forty separate parties searched for the best route in British Columbia. At one time 800 men were on the survey, often suffering hardships rarely experienced except in warfare. Huge areas of the country never before seen by a white man were revealed. The survey chiefs, being of independent mind, favoured routes that had little to do with the one preferred by Fleming through the Yellowhead Pass and south to the mouth of the Fraser River. Some liked the Waddington route to Bute Inlet, which for a while looked certain to be chosen. Others liked a more northern route to the coast, through Pine Pass or the Peace River Pass to the mouth of the Skeena. Preliminary construction got underway in bits and pieces. In 1875, not far from Fort William at the northwest tip of Lake Superior, the first sod was turned amid the pine, spruce and rock of the very region the Grand Trunk had always insisted was no place to build a railway.

For several years relatively little work was done despite the promise that British Columbia would get a railway if it joined Confederation. There were arguments as to which pass in the Rockies should be used, which point on the coast would become the terminus, and questions whether a disappointed British Columbia intended to remain in Confederation or join the United States. On 27 September 1877 London's *Pall Mall Gazette* complained:

> It is impossible to admit the pretensions of the Dominion government that this is merely a Canadian question, and that it must be

settled between the Parliament of Ottawa and a few thousand settlers in British Columbia. The Pacific Province is equal in area to the German Empire. Its ports are upon the most direct line between Europe and the Far East. Victoria, the chief town of Vancouver's Island, is no more than twenty-one days sail from Hong Kong, and it has been calculated that were the Trans-Continental Railway opened, the communication between Southampton and the Chinese ports might be shortened by fifteen or twenty days. At any rate, the time must come when the trade of these Pacific colonies with Japan and China will become a most important element in the world's commerce; and the childish narrow-minded trickery of the Canadians is unconsciously diverting the future stream of wealth and power from the British Empire to the American Republic.

Not until 1879, twelve years after Confederation, was the railway project restored to vibrant life. The depression was over, and Sir John A. Macdonald, back in power, was in a hurry: "Until this great work is completed, our Dominion is little more than a geographical expression," he said. "We have as much interest in British Columbia as in Australia, and no more. The railway, once finished, we become one great united country with a large interprovincial trade and a common interest."

The dream of shorter, quicker access to the wealth of Pacific Asia was exerting its old fascination. Macdonald had been encouraged by overtures from the recently established Japanese trading company, Mitsubishi, which had interests in shipping and wanted the Canadian government to subsidize a steamship service, but he felt the time would not be ripe until a transcontinental railway was completed. Charles Tupper, the minister of railways, appealed to the imagination of parliamentarians in Ottawa, picturing "an Imperial Highway across the Continent of America entirely on British soil . . . a new and important route from England to Australia, to India and to all the dependencies of Great Britain in the Pacific as also to China and Japan."

In 1880 Macdonald and Tupper sailed to England in search of a syndicate prepared to build and operate a railway. There were talks with the Brassey and Baring and Glyn groups which had built the Grand Trunk with so little government support, and with a shadowy European syndicate led by a former employee of the American Jay Cooke. Tupper claimed to have extended an invitation, once more, to the Grand Trunk, at a meeting in the House of Commons restaurant in London with Henry Tyler. In his memoirs

The lure of the Orient, rather than the opening up of the West, was the initial motive for building a transcontinental railway. Hong Kong, little more than a fishing village when the British annexed it in the 1830s Opium War, by the 1880s had become a major entrepôt. *Courtesy CN (Hong Kong)*

Tupper asserts that Tyler refused to consider putting the proposal to his board unless the government agreed to drop its policy of an "all-red route" north around Lake Superior and opt for the easier, more lucrative run south around the lakes through American territory and up to Winnipeg. The Grand Trunk president claimed later that while he had met Tupper no such invitation was given; but whatever happened the outcome was much the same: the Grand Trunk lost its last chance to pioneer a railway to the Pacific.

With the success of the rival Canadian Pacific Railway a few years later, Tyler came to regret the Grand Trunk's timidity, but popular wisdom supported him at the time. A Toronto newspaper, the *Bystander*, called the western railway "a mad undertaking." The *Times* of London called Macdonald's northern route "the pauper the rest of the family will have to support." The *New York Herald* predicted that because of the harsh climate the railway would have to close down four months every winter and could not hope for any return on its investment for half a century. There were rumours the Macdonald mission to London had failed, but when Macdonald's supporters turned out to welcome him back to Montreal one September afternoon in 1880 they found him far from disappointed. He had found his man — George Stephen — the entrepreneur he had failed to find in Hugh Allan.

Headed by Stephen, president of the Bank of Montreal, the Canadian Pacific Railway Syndicate took up the challenge the Grand Trunk had declined. With the promise of a $25-million grant and 25 million acres of virgin land, which could be sold off as financing was needed, the syndicate signed a contract that autumn to complete and operate a railway to the Pacific. The government would finish construction of two of the toughest stretches, those between Lake Superior and the prairies, and west-ward from Kamloops to Yale in British Columbia.

Having every expectation that the venture would fail and that the Grand Trunk would be able to pick up the pieces, Tyler concentrated on improving the Grand Trunk in the East. Although the *Canadian Monthly and National Review* had dismissed the Grand Trunk as "an object of perennial promise and perpetual disap-pointment," Tyler was making progress. The completion of the government's Intercolonial Railway linking Nova Scotia with Que-bec had ensured that the Grand Trunk tracks to Rivière-du-Loup would no longer be a perpetual money loser. The Grand Trunk's line to Chicago, via Sarnia and Port Huron, Michigan — the Grand Trunk Western Railroad Company — was finally opened, capturing a third of Midwest America's meat and wheat traffic between Chicago and New England. The Grand Trunk was now earning a quarter of its revenue from its United States operation, one fifth of its total mileage.

Fearful that the Canadian Pacific would gobble up existing eastern Canadian lines, the Grand Trunk absorbed a variety of railways — sixteen all told. These included the Great Western, the Grand Trunk's Ontario rival for the American market, the Mid-land, the Northern, and the pioneer portage railway, the Cham-plain and St. Lawrence. By now the Grand Trunk's main line between Portland, Maine, and Chicago was fed by a network of branch lines and it operated on 3000 miles of track. To provide faster movement of traffic it was double tracking the line between Montreal and Toronto. Such was the health of the Grand Trunk in 1883 that Tyler was able to tell the shareholders in London, "so long as the Grand Trunk was in debt and hardly able to pay its debenture interest, the concern was a discredit to Canada, but now it is on a sound and solid basis."

At the same time, the Grand Trunk was taking another look at expanding to the west itself. A great deal of correspondence was exchanged with the Manitoba government about a railway to Sault Ste. Marie, Ontario, then along the south shore of Lake Superior to Duluth, Minnesota, and on northwestward to Winnipeg, but nothing came of it. Amid growing competition from the CPR, Tyler went on the attack, telling a Grand Trunk shareholders meeting in 1885:

Their most serious troubles and difficulties will really begin when they have their lines finished from ocean to ocean. You may form some idea of what it will be to work a railway for 3,000 miles with very little population upon it, with a very severe climate to contend against and with all sorts of disadvantages much greater than those we labour under. . . . It appears to me that the best thing for them and for us, and for the Government — and I think it will come sooner or later — would be that the Canadian Pacific Company should be taken over by the Canadian Government, and when that happy time arrives there will be an end to undue competition and the Grand Trunk properties will all be glad to help the Government in any way it can in making as little loss as possible in working the Canadian Pacific Railway.

By the late 1880s the Canadian Pacific Railway was more or less complete, with tracks from Atlantic tidewater at Saint John, New Brunswick, to the Pacific, though not literally an "all-red route" because its eastern leg from Quebec to New Brunswick lay through the State of Maine. In the West it ran neither through Yellowhead Pass nor to Bute Inlet, but in a change of plans it took a more direct route from Calgary and pushed up the heavy grades of Kicking Horse Pass, 200 miles south of Yellowhead, and down the Fraser to Burrard Inlet where it gave birth to the city of Vancouver.

One of the first to ride the new line was Sir Edward Watkin, now almost seventy but eager to fulfill his vow, made a quarter of a century earlier, to look upon the Pacific "from the windows of a British railway carriage." It was not, as he would have wished, a Grand Trunk car, nor did he live to see the Grand Trunk complete its own line — the Grand Trunk Pacific — to the west coast from Winnipeg nearly thirty years later through the pass he had suggested, the Yellowhead. "This will probably be my last visit to this country," Sir Edward told a reporter for the *Montreal Gazette*, "and my only object in it was to see the Canadian Pacific Railway. I suggested the idea long ago, and brought a good deal of influence to bear on the matter but others took it up and carried out the idea a good deal more ably, I have no doubt, than I could have done."

Sir Edward was a disappointed man. "The old Grand Trunk proprietors feel that their early pioneer services to Canada, and their heavy sacrifices, have rather been ignored in competition, than recognized, by the Canadian Pacific not being an extension of the Grand Trunk system," he wrote in his memoirs. "Had I remained in office as president of the Grand Trunk undoubtedly I should have laboured hard to bring about such a consummation, which undoubtedly would have economised capital and hastened

the completion of the great inter-oceanic work." ⎯⎯,
had felt a new hand had been needed to pioneer the western line,
one free of eastern debt and commitments, unhampered by the
demands of British shareholders.

In its early years the Canadian Pacific Railway was as much a
political as a commercial venture, something not to the taste of the
British shareholders of the Grand Trunk. As the proud stepfather
of the Canadian Pacific Railway, Prime Minister Macdonald, in a
triumphal tour of the West, told a Winnipeg audience that the
railway had brought security to Canada and to the Empire, particularly to the Asian colonies, and all could now count on a "rich
trade" with the Orient. The Canadian Pacific Railway had begun
to solicit traffic in Japan and China, and the first cargo to be
carried by a CPR train, in the summer of 1886, consisted of
17,000 half-chests of tea brought by the 800-ton *W. B. Flint* from
Yokohama. Six other vessels arrived that year with tea for Toronto,
Montreal, Chicago and New York.

Within two years a score of ships were bringing goods to
Canada every year. In 1889 the CPR signed a contract with the
British government for a monthly mail service from Vancouver to
Hong Kong, Yokohama and Shanghai, honouring Stephen's vow
that the CPR would not be complete "until we have an ocean
connection with Japan and China." His successor, William Corne-
lius Van Horne, began the first regular Canadian steamship service
between Vancouver, China and Japan with the Empress ships. In
1891 his second-in-command and fellow-American, Thomas
Shaughnessy, spent four months in the Orient establishing the
foothold that was to serve the CPR well during the depression of
the 1890s when, as Tyler had expected, it might have foundered as
did 156 railways in the United States.

Ironically, one casualty of that depression was Tyler himself. In
eighteen years as president of the Grand Trunk he had seen his
railway mature into a viable transportation system with nearly
5000 miles of track. But unlike Van Horne he had neither the silk,
tea and spices of the Orient nor, more importantly, the support of
a doting Conservative government, to see him through the lean
years. This meant little or nothing to the British shareholders, who
now numbered 20,000, and in May 1895 Tyler resigned along with
his entire board.

Tyler's successor, Sir Charles Rivers Wilson, had been comp-
troller-general of the British National Debt and a director of the
Suez Canal Company in Egypt where he had reorganized that
country's chaotic finances. He knew little about railways and less

about North America. Supported by a new board consisting of gentlemen of the old school, like Col. Frederick Firebrace, Lord Welby and Sir Henry Mather Jackson, one might have expected this retired civil servant to be content with consolidating Tyler's considerable gains. That he actually found himself presiding over the largest, most spectacular, and ultimately disastrous, project the Grand Trunk ever attempted was largely due to the fact that he hired Charles Melville Hays as his right-hand man in Canada.

3 A STRUGGLE FOR SUPREMACY

WHEN GRAND TRUNK CHAIRMAN and president Sir Charles Rivers Wilson asked his friend J. P. Morgan, the financier, to recommend someone to compete with the Americans then running the Canadian Pacific Railway, Morgan mentioned Charles Melville Hays. Thus it was, on a cold and snowy New Year's Day in 1896, that Hays arrived in Montreal. His arrival was typical of the man. His terms of employment stated that January first was the day he was to start work, and though it was New Year's Day he scrupulously complied, to the surprise of employees used to a more leisurely British approach.

At the age of thirty-nine Hays had mastered the difficult art of making a railway go. Like all railroaders in those days he had been educated on the job, leaving high school in Rock Island, Illinois, when he was seventeen to become a clerk in the passenger department of the Atlantic and Pacific in St. Louis, and in his early thirties Hays had become vice-president and general manager for the Wabash, St. Louis and Pacific, which he rescued from bankruptcy. A stocky, dapper man with a neat beard and keen eyes, Hays had been nicknamed "the Little American." The *Railway Age Gazette* described him as "very self-possessed, seldom showing irritation or anger, and his capacity for work seemed unlimited." Independent of mind, blunt of manner, headlong in his enthusiasms, Hays, in Montreal, and the cautious, diplomatic Rivers Wilson, in London, were a study in contrast. In the beginning, at least, the young Midwest booster and the aging British civil service mandarin got on well, even when Hays showed a tendency to run things his own way without the Board's knowledge or consent. In the end this acquiescence was to contribute to unfortunate results.

In 1905, Charles Melville Hays (left), accompanied by Grand Trunk Pacific general manager Frank Morse (right), travelled 700 miles by horse and buggy to find the best route across the prairies for the Grand Trunk Pacific. *Courtesy CN*

53

Sir Charles Rivers Wilson, president of the Grand Trunk Railway from 1895 to 1909, knew a lot about finances and canals but little about railways. *Courtesy CN*

In his knowledge of railways, his taste for grand enterprise and his personal ambition, Hays was the American counterpart of Edward Watkin, and like Watkin a generation earlier Hays set about chopping down deadwood. Although the Grand Trunk was highly respected in the United States, he found it considerably less esteemed in Canada and he was impatient to get it reorganized, profitable, and running on time. One story passed down from those days gives some indication of the ruthless dispatch with which he went about achieving his goals.

One of those bosses who is always first into the office, Hays failed one morning to find the senior official he wanted. He came back again, and then again, to find the man still absent. Finally when the employee came in he was told to report to Hays.

"Don't you find it necessary to come down earlier?" asked Hays.

"Oh, no," replied the dignified official, "I can get through my work like this all right."

"Indeed!" said Hays. "Then I think we might safely dispense with your office altogether."

Hays hired many Americans and imposed a faster, more informal style. Whereas interdepartmental business, even in head office, had been by letter, now officials were encouraged to walk into Hays's office whenever they had problems. Having set out to secure fresh business, he found few things too small to claim his attention. For example, he discovered that the railway had been losing the business of the ubiquitous touring theatre companies because it had no cars big enough to transport sixty-foot scenery flats. To accommodate them he ordered some special cars. He speeded up the program of replacing ten-ton freight cars, more suitable to England than the great distances of Canada, with the thirty-tonners common in the United States.

Customers could no longer count on trains being late, and when they were Hays demanded a satisfactory explanation. He improved grades to speed the flow of freight, replaced hand brakes with the new vacuum brakes so that trains could travel safely at higher speeds, introduced automatic couplers, and rebuilt the suspension bridge into the United States over the Niagara River. Despite pressure from London to channel profits into dividends, Hays tried to seed earnings back into the railway. To spot the weak links in the system, he reorganized the gathering of statistics. He reduced operating expenses by 10 per cent and managed to produce dividends on junior shares that had never paid before. This naturally pleased the shareholders and the Board in London, but Hays knew this state of affairs would not last unless the Grand Trunk could expand, and expansion lay only in the West.

The Grand Trunk had a third of Canada's railway mileage, all of it in the East. Although its western terminus in the United States was in Chicago, in Canada the Grand Trunk ran no farther west than North Bay. So far as the West was concerned, the Grand Trunk was no more than a feeder line, picking up or delivering freight from the Canadian Pacific Railway.

There was talk of securing running rights over CPR tracks so as to get access to western sources of revenue, and of expanding from Chicago up into Winnipeg and from there westward. Nothing came of these ideas so in August 1900, when the Southern Pacific presidency fell vacant, Hays accepted the position and moved back to the United States. This hiatus lasted only eighteen months, and after a falling-out with the new owners of the Southern Pacific, Hays came back to the Grand Trunk early in 1902, more convinced than ever that the future must lie in the West. Concentrated as it was in Ontario and Quebec, the Grand Trunk was boxed in.

"The Grand Trunk is in this ridiculous position from a business stand point," Hays said, "of gathering up traffic from the largest and most prosperous portion of Canada, taking it to North Bay, our connection with the Canadian Pacific, and from there giving it to the Canadian Pacific to haul across the country. . . . Now we have another rival in that same territory which is competing with us to a certain extent now, that brings grain down to the lake [Superior] and conveys it by water from Port Arthur and Fort William [Thunder Bay] to our Ontario ports."

The new rival was the Canadian Northern Railway. In five years it had grown from a shoestring start in Manitoba into a major enterprise on the northern prairies, hauling grain to the Lakehead and providing transportation to 130 new communities in vast areas where the CPR did not run. It was a remarkable railway, reflecting the characters of the two men who built it. In an age when the major railway men were Britons or Americans, William Mackenzie and Donald Mann were home-grown Canadians who had learned their railroading in rough and tumble construction camps.

Mackenzie, the president and financial wizard of Canadian Northern, and the senior and more urbane of the two, had left the family farm at Kirkfield, Ontario, by the traditional escape route, schoolteaching. Having little patience or aptitude for teaching he drifted into storekeeping, lumbering and railroad contracting, first in Ontario for various local lines, and then for the CPR. He

Charles Melville Hays introduced American methods into operations of the British-owned Grand Trunk Railway. *Courtesy CN*

Sir Donald Mann, a farmer's son and one-time blacksmith, ran the construction side of Mackenzie Mann and Company and helped his partner, William Mackenzie, build an unusual railway. *Courtesy CN*

became president of the Toronto street railway system and the money-making Brazilian Traction Company (Brascan) in South America. A Conservative in politics and an elder of the Presbyterian Church, he liked to install pianos in his construction camps and gather the men around to sing hymns on a Sunday night. He ran for parliament but was never elected.

Vice-president Mann, born on a farm in Acton, Ontario, looked the part of a railway contractor, burly, bearded and blunt, though he had studied for the Methodist ministry and practised spiritualism. He started out as a blacksmith, sliding into railway construction, knocking around a good deal, and doing railway work in China. A Liberal in politics, thereby nicely balancing the odds for Canadian Northern whoever was in power in Ottawa, Mann ran the construction side of Mackenzie Mann & Company Limited.

Having met on a job for the CPR in the Rockies (while engaged in mule trading), the two men combined forces during construction of the CPR line across Maine from Quebec to New Brunswick. They realized the potential of the northern prairies, then being advertised by government immigration posters as "Canada's 1,000-mile farm" or "The Last Best West," referring to the fact that the American West was filling up and land that cost $60 an acre there could be had for $5 in Canada. In 1896 they bought their first railway, taking up an option on the dormant Lake Manitoba Railway and Canal Company, which guaranteed them a government land grant of the sort no longer being issued, signed a contract with their own construction company, and floated a bond issue guaranteed by the Manitoba government. Despite the fact that the Canadian Pacific Railway practically controlled the region, there were many inactive or derelict little railway companies and the growth of the partnership followed this pattern of acquiring such companies for several years. They became more ambitious, buying out the Manitoba branch of the Northern Pacific of St. Paul, Minnesota, which had built a few hundred miles of track in Manitoba.

Mackenzie and Mann were on their way, building a 123-mile railway northwestward across the farming country between Dauphin and Gladstone at the foot of Lake Manitoba where they could connect with existing lines into Winnipeg. The farmers were so happy to get their own railway that they contributed free labour as if it were a community project, as indeed it was. The company in return helped them to get good-quality, low-cost seed wheat. Even before the Dauphin line was finished Mackenzie and Mann started building a second railway in the opposite direction, southeast from Winnipeg towards the Ontario border. By 1898 they were operating this rough-and-ready, thrice-weekly service, called The Muskeg Special. As David B. Hanna, their Scottish-born superintendent who was to become the first president of the Canadian National Railway system in 1918, was to recall: "We began with two engines, fifty new freight cars . . . two second-hand passenger cars . . . and an uncertain number of flat cars which had been used on construction. We had to buy more second hand equipment but as to flat cars our conductor, Percival, had a habit of borrowing such as he could collect in the CPR yards without asking anybody's leave."

Step-by-step Mackenzie and Mann expanded — aided by provincial grants — shrewdly pushing into areas where they could expect profitable traffic more or less immediately. There was nothing fancy about the Canadian Northern Railway, for its roadbed was bumpy and its box cars were wooden-framed long after steel ones had come into use. Its owners built as cheaply as they could; improvements could be made later. It was supported by the Canadian Bank of Commerce, built largely by other people's money, and by 1902 this "farmer's railroad" controlled 1200 miles of profitable track.

It ran westward from their Lake Superior grain terminal at Port Arthur, dubbed "The Silver Gateway of the Golden West," and then through the timberlands of northwest Ontario to Winnipeg where it curved up to Erwood, Saskatchewan, on the margin of the prairies and the northern forest. "From a series of disconnected and apparently unconnectable projections of steel, hanging in suspense, a continuous track was formed," recalled Hanna. They adopted a motto, "Energy, Enterprise, Ability."

There was no indication at the time that the partners had plans for anything more than a regional prairie system. They were doing well, with gross receipts of $1.4 million and a profit of $80,000 after their bills had been paid. Their biggest ambition apparently was to push their steel as far west as Edmonton, though the premiers of British Columbia and Ontario were seductively suggesting that Mackenzie and Mann extend west to the Pacific and east to the St. Lawrence Valley. Then in 1902 the realization that the Grand Trunk planned to invade the West caused them to revise their aims. Mackenzie went to London early that year for fresh financing, and called upon Rivers Wilson to suggest that the Grand Trunk exchange traffic with the Canadian Northern, thus guaranteeing access to the West for the Grand Trunk, and to the East for Canadian Northern. Rivers Wilson was intrigued, as he

Sir William Mackenzie, president of Canadian Northern Railway, parlayed an 84-mile "farmer's railway" into a 9000-mile empire. *Courtesy CN*

Mackenzie and Mann built their Canadian Northern bit by bit across the prairies using local labour and teams of Mexican mules to carve out the right-of-way. *Courtesy CN*

wrote to Hays: "I believe they may be valuable allies, and I shall be glad to know whether you share this opinion, and if so, whether you think that we can allow it to make some practical development."

Hays had his own ideas, however, and urged the Grand Trunk Board in London to follow a policy of "aggression and extension." "My own preference would be the acquisition of a controlling interest in the Canadian Northern line either by purchase of a majority of stock by the Grand Trunk Railway, or by the formation of a syndicate which should do so in the interests of this company." He said the Canadian Northern was "ramshackle," though it had been improving.

During the next two years Hays's aggressive policy was to take various forms. At one stage he hoped to build a line from the Grand Trunk terminus near North Bay around the top of Lake Superior to Port Arthur, taking over the upstart Canadian Northern, much as the Grand Trunk had taken over the Great Western in Ontario in 1882. The Canadian Northern showed no desire to sell, and thus began a long struggle for the honour of becoming Canada's second transcontinental railway. Nobody — the Grand Trunk, the Canadian Northern, or the Canadian taxpayer, was to win — though perhaps the CPR, sitting on the sidelines, benefitted from its two rivals fighting each other. (According to Mann the CPR also tried to buy out the Canadian Northern.)

When rebuffed by Mackenzie and Mann, Hays took a firm line. The way to protect the Grand Trunk's future, he told Rivers Wilson, was to go ahead and plan its own link to the west coast. If, in the process, the Canadian Northern took fright at the thought of the Grand Trunk invading its prairie territory and decided to sell at a reasonable price, so much the better. To buttress his argument, Hays recalled the cautionary tale of the Chicago and Altona Railroad in the United States which, being too timid to expand west of the Missouri River, had lost its gilt-edged status and was boxed in by rivals, whereas the venturesome Atchison, Topeka and Santa Fe had pushed on to the Pacific to become prosperous.

There was no question as to which approach appealed to the vigorous "Little American." He wanted a Grand Trunk subsidiary, to be named the Grand Trunk Pacific, built through the northern prairies to Edmonton, and then to the west coast. The subsidiary would be in a position to apply for substantial federal aid, as the CPR had done, because it would be a major trunk line to the coast rather than a patchwork of feeder lines like the Canadian Northern. "The moment we do this the importance of Messrs. Mackenzie and Mann as a factor in the situation would at once cease and the subsidiaries, concessions, etc., that they would otherwise obtain would be given to the new company." If necessary Hays would starve the Canadian Northern into selling.

Rivers Wilson, as was his custom, went along with Hays, though cautiously. "You know, and I think you share, my aversion to ill-considered extensions of our system," he told Hays. "But I have never concealed my belief that circumstances might arise when vital interests of the Grand Trunk might necessitate a departure from that general principle." Nevertheless, he urged Hays to keep in touch with Mackenzie and Mann for he preferred amalgamation rather than going it alone. In hindsight it would indeed have been more sensible for the Grand Trunk and the Canadian Northern to pool resources and unite.

Certainly the construction of a second trunk line across the prairies to rival the CPR seemed an excellent idea at the turn of the century. Even the CPR president William Van Horne said: "We would hail with delight a parallel route from Atlantic to Pacific to help us develop the country. There is enough of it up there for us all." It was a time when railways were being built, or at least planned, all over the world.

Canada was booming. About the time Sir Wilfrid Laurier became prime minister in 1896 the depression ended and Canadians were beginning to feel confidence in themselves. Laurier, more as a challenge than a promise, said the new era would be "Canada's century" and since no one could foresee the First World War, which set back immigration, foreign investment and western

The Canadian Northern and the Grand Trunk Pacific arrived on the northern prairies at a time when the new Marquis variety of wheat was pushing the growing area ever northward and turning the West into the world's greatest granery. *Courtesy CN*

growth, or the Depression of the 1930s, there seemed no reason to doubt a rosy future. Laurier was receiving support for another western railroad from businessmen across the West, from Winnipeg to Victoria. "The time is now ripe for another transcontinental railway," said the Calgary Board of Trade.

In five years Canada's trade with the world had increased almost 100 per cent. A new industry, pulp and paper, was overtaking lumber as the country's major money-maker. Minerals had been discovered, as had been foretold, north of Lake Superior. In the East industry was growing so quickly that no less than 115 new manufacturing plants — steel mills, lumber mills, canneries, cement works, pulp mills — mushroomed along the Grand Trunk route.

In the West gold had been discovered in the Klondike. The immigration policy was attracting Europeans and Americans to the prairies, and the number of homesteads had soared from 2000 to 32,000 in five years. Plans were afoot to create two new provinces, Saskatchewan and Alberta, to join Manitoba in the Canadian confederation. The grain crop had doubled and the development of hardier, faster-growing Marquis wheat extended the northern range of the prairie breadbox by 200 miles and added 100 million acres to the grain belt. Farmers needed more box cars to move their wheat, which was piling up for lack of transport, and after many years of heavy-handed western monopoly by the CPR, they were finding much to criticize in the operations of that company. The *Manitoba Free Press* of Winnipeg said: "We want all the railways we can get, for Manitoba's proper policy is free trade and we have got to have more railways if the crop of this country is to be moved out in any reasonable time." That a transcontinental road should be built was agreed, but not all believed it should be built immediately, causing Laurier, in the House of Commons, to wax impatient:

To those who urge upon us the policy of tomorrow and tomorrow and tomorrow, to those who tell us, wait, wait, wait; to those who advise us to pause, to consider, to reflect, to calculate and to inquire, our answer is: No, this is not a time for deliberation, this is a time for action. The flood-tide is upon us that leads on to fortune; if we let it pass it may never recur again. If we let it pass, the voyage of our national life, bright as it is today, will be bound in shallows. We cannot wait because time does not wait; we cannot wait, because in these days of wonderful development, time lost is doubly lost; we cannot wait because the prairies of the North-West, which for countless ages have been roamed over by wild herds of bison or by scarcely less wild tribes of red men, are now invaded from all sides by the white race.

Sir Wilfrid Laurier, jaunty in a "dutch-boy" cap during a visit to the West, believed more railways were needed to open the prairies and provide a trade route to the Orient. *Courtesy Public Archives of Canada /C 15568*

Laurier believed that new lines were needed to serve the prairies north of the CPR, and at all events the CPR, which had almost doubled its trackage and increased its annual net earnings to $15 million since it began operations, had been a Conservative venture which should not be allowed to monopolize rail transportation in half of Canada. The Canadian Northern was making money, and in the United States the former Canadian James J. Hill, who had contributed to the birth of the CPR, had built his Great Northern to the U.S. west coast, pushing branch lines into western Canada that threatened to drain off Canadian commerce.

The Grand Trunk itself was in better shape than usual, with freight tonnage and gross receipts up 75 per cent from 1895. The system had benefitted from 1000 miles of double tracking, there had been only a modest increase in fixed charges, passenger traffic had doubled, and the deficit had been eliminated. On the other hand, the railway was facing new competition. The Canadian Northern now had a charter to build a railway from the prairies to the Pacific and eastwards from Lake Superior to Quebec. It was obviously set on invading eastern Canada as the CPR had done in the 1880s. When that occurred the Grand Trunk would lose the grain traffic it was now receiving from the Canadian Northern at the Lakehead, from whence it was carried by boat to the Grand Trunk rail system.

Moreover, if the Grand Trunk failed again to build a transcontinental line there would be others ready and willing, such as the Canadian Northern or the Trans-Canada Railway in Quebec. A newcomer, the Trans-Canada had been born, on paper at least, a few years earlier when Quebec City businessmen led by the Saguenay lumber king William Price had prevailed on the govern-

The daily masthead of the *Quebec Morning Chronicle* in 1903 reflected the determination of businessmen to build the ill-fated Trans-Canada Railway.

ment of the Quebec-born Laurier to issue a charter for a railway from Quebec to the west coast. They were tired of seeing Canadian shipments to Europe, including wheat, bypassing St. Lawrence ports in favour of the Grand Trunk terminal in Maine. They wanted a railway built far north of the usual routes, thus removing any temptation to give traffic to American ports.

The idea had actually come from an American living in England, Col. George Church, who told the Royal Geographical Society that the best "all-red route" lay through the high latitudes 500 miles north of the border. This would cut several hundred miles off the distance covered by American railways, or for that matter 200 miles off the CPR route. The Trans-Canada Railway was to run from Chicoutimi westward to James Bay, then along the northern prairies and through the mountains to the coast. It had been promised a government subsidy in 1901 and had the support of the Roman Catholic Church and the provincial government, which wanted to open northern Quebec for settlement. However, there was reason to believe Laurier would be grateful for an excuse to drop an expensive scheme that could never make money in the empty north. Hays was ready to oblige.

During the summer of 1902 Hays worked on his plans for a western line, in the knowledge that Mackenzie and Mann had applied for a charter to build from the Quebec border to the Skeena River and were showing an interest in taking over the Canada Atlantic in Ontario and also the Intercolonial in order to gain access to the east coast. He knew that Laurier was under pressure to save the Trans-Canada, which had already started work on sixty miles of track west from Roberval, Quebec. By autumn Hays felt it was time for him to make a move, and on 23 October he met with Laurier privately to solicit his support. Writing to Rivers Wilson, Hays reported: "Sir Wilfrid Laurier talked diplomatically as he always does but said he did not hesitate to express the great satisfaction it gave him personally and which he felt would be shared by his colleagues when they knew we were contemplating such a move. He considered the time most opportune and felt his government would doubtless be disposed to deal with us very liberally after ascertaining what our views were as to the assistance we should require."

On 2 November 1902 Hays sent Laurier a confidential document petitioning a charter to build a railway from the Grand Trunk's North Bay terminal to the west coast. The general idea was to cut north for 100 miles and strike west through the Clay Belt, which was expected to attract settlers because of its good

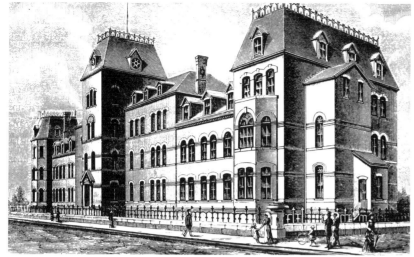

soil. It was easier terrain than that the CPR contended with just north of Lake Superior. The line would cross the prairies on the northern route Fleming had surveyed but the CPR never used. Just where it would cross the Rockies and hit the coast was undecided, though the Peace River, Pine and Yellowhead passes favoured by Fleming were all possibilities, as were terminals at Bute Inlet and Port Simpson, the Hudson's Bay trading post and Indian village near the Alaska border.

In the East, traffic would run over the Grand Trunk line, and the objection that the Grand Trunk favoured Portland, Maine, was to be overcome by a deal with the government-owned Intercolonial Railway in the Maritimes for an "all-red route." Laurier was not enthusiastic, fearing that the Grand Trunk would gobble up the Intercolonial, and there began a series of negotiations which were to stretch over eighteen months. From the Grand Trunk's handsome new building at 360 McGill Street in Montreal, Hays announced to the press on 24 November that he was ready to go ahead with a $100-million western railway to be completed in five years. For trade with the Orient the Grand Trunk would also build a shipping line.

Hays's announcement caused Vancouver's *Daily Province* to comment the next day that it was "regarded with some little surprise by the average resident of the Dominion. With one transcontinental system already in operation and another line [the Canadian Northern] partly constructed and its surveys practically finished for the building of the balance of the road, the question may present itself, what need the country has for a third system or what traffic for some years to come will be furnished for a third transcontinental line." The CPR, despite Van Horne's initial enthu-

siasm, opposed the plan. Mackenzie and Mann called it "unnecessary and wasteful." The backers of the Trans-Canada, realizing it would mean the end of their own project, deplored it. Interior Minister Clifford Sifton was quoted as saying the Grand Trunk Pacific was "premature, ill-conceived, immature of design and of dubious national advantage," but as everyone knew, Sifton was a Manitoba lawyer who had backed the Canadian Northern in his successful campaign to promote the prairie provinces and attract settlers. James Hill of the Great Northern said there was just not enough traffic for a third railway. "The United States has 85 million population and six transcontinental railroads," he said. "At this rate the Republic has one transcontinental line for each 14 million of its inhabitants and the Dominion has one for each two and a half million."

All of this was making Rivers Wilson uneasy, causing him to complain to Hays, "You appear to be mapping out a scheme on much broader lines than was originally contemplated." Since the government had no inclination to provide the subsidies and land grants Hays wanted, Rivers Wilson was anxious lest the Grand Trunk become saddled with debt. Once again he urged Hays to talk to Mackenzie and Mann with a view to collaboration, using the Prime Minister as an "honest broker," a role Laurier was glad to assume since he was beginning to see pitfalls himself in the Hays plan.

One evening in early March 1903 Laurier summoned the two sides to his Ottawa home. The Canadian Northern men showed no interest in selling and Hays showed no inclination to collaborate with Canadian Northern. At this crucial moment in Canada's railway history probably only the prime minister could have broken the stalemate, through pressure on one or other of the companies, or even by threatening to withdraw government support. This he did not do, nor did the strong personalities of Hays and Mackenzie help the negotiations. A second effort was no more successful, Mann suggesting an impossibly high price of $30,000 a mile. Since this was twice as much as it had cost, Hays complained that the Canadian Northern had a "ridiculous idea of the value of their property." Said Mann later, "We offered to build a joint section from North Bay to Port Arthur to be owned jointly by the two companies and we would develop the west and they would develop the east. They refused and would not do anything but try to buy us out. We were too young and ambitious to sell at that time."

Undoubtedly Hays had made a miscalculation in believing he could take over the Canadian Northern, but his error was understandable. It was commonly believed that Mackenzie and Mann were more interested in construction and entrepreneurial wheeling and dealing than running a railway, and that once they had built the Canadian Northern they would be willing to sell. But whatever their original intention, it was now becoming clear that they had grander plans. With 1706 miles of track in operation, mostly in Manitoba and Saskatchewan but also in the East, they were beginning to dream of a transcontinental, integrated transportation system, including ships, to rival the CPR.

His takeover attempt again rebuffed by Mackenzie and Mann, Hays decided to go ahead on his own. On 16 March 1903 he informed Rivers Wilson that at the request of the government he was now proposing to establish the eastern terminal at Quebec City rather than at North Bay. Since there was no business to be had in the backwoods between those two cities, this was obviously to accommodate Laurier by placating eastern businessmen who wanted a share of the grain traffic. By the end of March the Grand Trunk Pacific Railway proposal for a line from Quebec City to the west coast, to be absolutely separate from the old Grand Trunk, was in the hands of the parliamentary Railway Committee in Ottawa.

The whole thing had taken on its own momentum, and Rivers Wilson in London went along with Hays, whatever his misgivings. On 16 April he put the matter to the shareholders at the annual meeting. He reminded them he had been careful in the past to avoid "all adventurous enterprise" where liability would be large and profits uncertain, but he had always reserved the right to recommend expansion. "Such an opportunity presents itself in regard to the railway requirements of the northwest provinces and the necessity almost imposes itself upon the company for its own protection to take steps in securing a share in the advantages offered by the rapid development of those provinces."

Whereas in the past such a statement would have been greeted in silence, it now drew cheers and applause, such was the magic Hays had wrought in the Grand Trunk. In the course of his address, however, Rivers Wilson said something he was later to regret. This would be no speculative enterprise, he declared, for the project would not involve the parent company, the Grand Trunk, in any considerable liabilities.

Travelling to Ottawa, Rivers Wilson found that Laurier had

come up with a new and more extravagant plan. With a general election coming, it was heavily political, setting out to satisfy both the desires of Quebec and those of the Maritimes. On 29 May Laurier proposed "the construction of a National Transcontinental Railway to be operated as a common railway highway within the Dominion of Canada from ocean to ocean and wholly within Canadian territory."

The National Transcontinental would be in two sections; the Grand Trunk would be responsible for the western section and the government would build the 1875-mile portion from Moncton, New Brunswick, to Winnipeg. Since the eastern section would run northwest from Quebec City into the forests where no business could be expected, the Grand Trunk, having always feared such a route, was relieved of the burden of building it. On the other hand, its subsidiary, the Grand Trunk Pacific, was expected eventually to lease and operate this commercially unpromising eastern section, which the *Montreal Star* called: "That mad route, unknown, unsurveyed and uninhabited, through the North country, over granite ranges, from Winnipeg to Quebec." The lease would run fifty years, with an option to renew. No rent need be paid for the first seven years while the line got established, but thereafter the Grand Trunk would pay three per cent annually of the cost of construction, whatever that might be. The Grand Trunk would be expected to supply $20 million of rolling stock for both the eastern and western segments of the National Transcontinental and would purchase or lease enough shipping in the Atlantic and the Pacific to take care of its overseas traffic. The government would not after all shoulder the whole financial responsibility as the board in London had been led to believe. The Grand Trunk was to be held financially responsible. Writing to Hays on 10 July, Rivers Wilson made no bones about his misgivings.

> I am greatly vexed at the turn that events have taken. The idea that the Grand Trunk should enter upon such a vast liability was never entertained for a moment when I was in Canada, and I felt sure could never be in your thoughts. No doubt you have, and with good reason, great faith in the earning powers of the new line. If the government share that view, why should they hesitate to give their credit to the undertaking unreservedly? To throw upon the Grand Trunk the ultimate guarantee for the whole cost of the enterprise, amounting perhaps to some $125 million, is most unreasonable.

The western leg, the Grand Trunk's responsibility, would run 1700 miles from Winnipeg to the coast, probably to Port Simpson, though the final destination had not been decided. One third of that distance would be through mountain country where no business could be expected and where cost of construction would be two or three times the cost on the prairies. The company was to build "to standards not inferior to those on the main line between Montreal and Toronto," which was asking a lot more than the requirements imposed on the Canadian Northern.

As late as 15 July it seemed quite possible the Grand Trunk Board would decide the project was too risky. "Pray believe me," Rivers Wilson told Hays, "that neither directors nor shareholders would be willing to embark on any such liability as seems to have been contemplated from your side." But once more Rivers Wilson did get the directors to agree, and on 24 July cabled their acceptance of the government terms. Five days later, a contract having been signed between the Grand Trunk and the government, the National Railway Bill was introduced, touching off a long parliamentary debate.

The leader of the Conservative opposition, Robert Borden, suggested that the best solution would be to nationalize the uneconomical stretch of CPR track through northern Ontario so that the Grand Trunk and Canadian Northern could also use it. He was coming to the conclusion that the whole of any second Canadian transcontinental railway should be nationalized. Since, in the end, the government would be paying for much of it anyway, why not own the whole thing? (Almost fifteen years later, under a Borden administration, this was in fact exactly what was to happen — with a vengeance.) In his memoirs thirty years later Borden said: "It seems clear that the national transcontinental railway from Quebec to Winnipeg should have been commenced as a colonization road and should have been gradually extended as settlement demanded to the Pacific Coast."

Defending the National Transcontinental Railway in the House of Commons, Laurier said: "I am well aware that this plan may scare the timid and frighten the irresolute. But I may claim that every man who has in his bosom a stout Canadian heart will welcome it as worthy of this young nation." More comfortable with patriotism than economics, Laurier painted a picture of how the National Transcontinental, including the Grand Trunk Pacific, would roll back the map of Canada and add depth to a country which was merely a thin ribbon of population along the American border.

Conservative opposition leader Robert Laird Borden warned that Canada was building too many railways. *Courtesy CN*

THE ONLY ALL CANADIAN

GRAND TRUNK PACIFIC

TRANSCONTINENTAL ROUTE

At 2 A.M. on 2 September 1903 Laurier's railway bill was passed in parliament by the slim majority of six votes, and on 24 October the Grand Trunk Pacific Railway was incorporated with capital stock of $45 million in shares of $100. Along with powers to build 3000 miles of main line and branch lines, it would be empowered, and expected, to own and lease ships, docks, hotels, telegraph lines, and to develop lands. On the same date the government provided for a National Transcontinental Railway from Moncton to Winnipeg, where it would join the Grand Trunk Pacific.

It was not a happy birth. The Grand Trunk directors had begun to realize how deeply responsible they had become for the National Transcontinental, which they had assumed could be kept separate from the Grand Trunk. Rivers Wilson reminded a semi-annual shareholders meeting in October of how Laurier had changed the original plan: "The idea which the Grand Trunk had when it undertook the promotion of what is called 'the Grand Trunk Pacific road' was to acquire a connecting interest with some corporation — a separate corporation, which would construct the road through the prairie districts."

One of the senior directors, George Allan, felt so strongly that the commitment would be the death of the Grand Trunk that he resigned from the board. Rivers Wilson, believing there was no way the board would recommend that the shareholders endorse the agreement when they met in the spring of 1904, asked the government for modifications. Laurier, who would soon face an election fought partially on the railway issue, declined to budge; if the Grand Trunk refused to abide by the agreement, the government would look for a partner elsewhere. Mackenzie and Mann would have been happy for the opportunity.

Only a tremendous sales effort could bring the rebellious directors back into line, and Hays sailed early in February to do as much convincing as he could in advance of the shareholders meeting of 18 March in London. Much like his predecessor Edward Watkin at a crucial meeting of the shareholders twenty-five years earlier, Hays was prepared to stake his reputation on the outcome. With Rivers Wilson and other directors he created a boardroom steamroller to get his western railway approved.

Rivers Wilson led off. Canada's trade with the Orient totalled little more than $3 million a year, but the prospects were enticing and the recent Anglo-Japanese commercial treaty had awakened interest in what could become a market of forty million people. Rivers Wilson admitted he had inadvertently misled the shareholders as to the amount of risk the Grand Trunk was taking on, but assured them the risk was worthwhile. If they took no action at all they would be certain to lose increasing amounts of business. This way they could be sure of securing "valuable new traffic." Said Rivers Wilson: "We consider it alike as a measure of necessity and as affording an opportunity which, if neglected, will never again occur of assuring and improving the fortunes of our company. . . . Surrounded on all sides by elements of progress it is absolutely impossible for our company to stand still."

Enjoying a degree of confidence no other Grand Trunk manager had been able to claim, Hays stood up to assure the shareholders there was really no choice. "[The West] is the only direction in which we can look for increasing traffic," he reminded them. "That traffic will be lost to us if we do not bottle it up." Like the salesman he was, Hays warmed to his theme. "This enterprise which we are advocating today, ladies and gentlemen, combines points and advantages that no other transcontinental line in the United States or Canada can have." What were they? Unlike most new railways the Grand Trunk Pacific, the offspring of the mature Grand Trunk, the first major railway in Canada, would start with the lion's share of existing eastern traffic already under its control, including westbound traffic which now was being lost to the Grand Trunk once it was handed over to the rival CPR at North Bay. The Grand Trunk Pacific would stretch for 1000 miles through the richest wheat belt in the world. The prairie population was growing rapidly, that very year some 50,000 Americans having migrated north to Canada as the frontier in Montana and the Dakotas became populated. Going into British Columbia it would cross the Rockies at two-thirds the elevation the CPR had to climb at Kicking Horse Pass, since the Grand Trunk Pacific was considering breaching the Rockies west of the Peace River country where the mountains are not so high.

Once established on Canada's Pacific shore, the Grand Trunk would be in a better position than any other railway to take advantage of Asian trade, for this would be the shortest route to China and Japan. "There are many of you here today who will live to see the Grand Trunk Pacific hauling as much of its grain towards the Pacific for consumption in China, Japan, and that territory, as will be hauled in this eastern direction," said Hays. Before he sat down, to cheering and applause, Hays said: "To my mind it is difficult to conceive that there can be any objections to this scheme, which promises so much to the Grand Trunk Railway, and which links its fortunes with those of the Government of

Sir Alfred W. Smithers succeeded Charles Rivers Wilson as chairman of the Grand Trunk in 1910. *Courtesy CN*

Canada in a way that the two must work together, not only for the benefit of the country at large, but for the benefit of the country and the Grand Trunk Railway. . . . The question is not what is going to happen to you if you adopt this enterprise, but what is going to happen to you if you do not adopt it."

The rest was anticlimax. Alfred W. Smithers, who had opposed the scheme — and as chairman was to disown it later when it had clearly failed — stood up now to endorse it. He warned the shareholders that failure to support the Grand Trunk Pacific would be failure to take a part in the development of Canada. Canadians would say: "There is that old fogy of a Board in England that cannot settle upon anything; we must rely upon the Canadian Pacific or some other line." Such was the enthusiasm generated that one of the shareholders stated that if the Grand Trunk had only done as much twenty-five years earlier it would have eliminated the CPR syndicate and cornered the West and the Orient all to itself.

After a year and a half of controversy, the construction of the Grand Trunk Pacific was to get underway. Charles Hays was its president while holding the position of vice-president and general manager of the Grand Trunk. He made policy, arranged financing with the Rothschilds of London, and involved himself in such things as deciding on the rail grades the Grand Trunk Pacific was to have, since easy grades lead to easier operations and better profits.

In the building of railways there are many steps. The first, an exploration of the general route, had begun the previous year and since it followed the line surveyed a generation earlier by Sandford Fleming, the government had already paid out $3 million for the purpose. The second step was a detailed survey, carried out at great expense by men with aneroids, compasses and chains tramping out the miles, uphill and down, through forests, swamps and mountains, fording rivers, and exploring wilderness. The third step was construction — cutting out the right-of-way and carving a level road bed. The fourth step was the laying of steel and ballast, a foot of crushed rock or gravel between the rail and ties. Not until 1905, however, did construction begin, and it started a railway boom surpassing those of the 1850s and 1880s.

By that time the Canadian Northern was making a race of it and had its tracks into Edmonton. Even though the Grand Trunk Pacific had won Laurier's support, Mackenzie and Mann had no intention of giving up. "You know, we expected at one time to be the favourite people to build this continental road," Mann told the

Toronto Globe. "Now we must get along as best we can and it may take a little longer than it otherwise would."

The Grand Trunk Pacific was to be built, like the CPR, in segments. The first of these, "station 2475," had been awarded to the Winnipeg contracting firm of Macdonald, Macmillan and Company, and early one August morning in 1905, without any fanfare, foreman James Howard turned the first sod at a place called Sand Hill, a dozen miles from Carberry, Manitoba, 110 miles west of Winnipeg. More than 600 men, 550 horses, 260 earth scrapers and 10 plows began work on the rolling grasslands and gullies of the open prairie.

By the spring of 1906, 5000 men were building the Grand Trunk Pacific main line from Winnipeg to Edmonton. In the East, on the half of the National Transcontinental being built by the government, 2000 men were battling blackflies, muskeg and rock to cut a wide swath through the spruce forests of northern Quebec. "Perhaps no more comprehensive plan of railway construction was ever conceived," said the *Canadian Magazine* of April 1906. "It rivals the great Trans-Siberian Railway, undertaken by the Russian government, and the famous Cape to Cairo Railway which is to connect the two ends of the continent of Africa."

If anything in railway building can be called easy, the prairies were the easiest part of the whole transcontinental route, though

A Canadian Northern grading machine near Cereal, eastern Alberta, plows up the soft prairie turf and conveys it by chute into wagons ranged alongside. *Courtesy Glenbow Museum/NA-2116-1*

there were eleven rivers and gullies to be bridged, the largest being the Pembina, the South Saskatchewan and the Battle rivers. Spanning the Battle River required a bridge 2700 feet long and 180 feet high. It was unnecessary, however, to spend months surveying through forests and mountains, or to hire axemen to cut the trees, or dynamiters to rip a path through rock. Once the surveyors had staked out the way with a row of sticks, horses and mules appeared, dragging scrapers and graders, like sharp-edged snowplows, to peel off the prairie grass and gouge the right-of-way on which wooden ties and steel rails would rest. A dozen horses were hitched to one grader, four abreast, and as the machines cut through a slope or obliterated a mound, a conveyor belt with buckets scooped the loose soil and dumped it into hopper wagons from which it was used to fill hollows or build embankments. In spring the sodden gumbo soil stuck to everything.

When all was going well, which became less frequent as the line advanced and delivery of rails was delayed, a grading team might be disappearing over the western horizon as a crew of track layers was looming into sight on the eastern horizon. Those were the times when the prairie landscape came alive, the centre of activity being a Pioneer tracklayer called a "praying mantis" because from a distance it resembled that insect. A wooden frame on a flat car pushed along by a locomotive, the Pioneer incorporated a system of rollers which conveyed rails and ties to a point where the awkward wooden arms of the A-frame could swing them out into the right-of-way. After they were manhandled into place and

A Pioneer tracklayer was ungainly but capable in 1912 of laying three miles of track a day. A gang of 100 men worked alongside as the "praying mantis" swung rails and ties onto the right-of-way on a system of jibs and rollers. *Courtesy CN*

secured, the machine would lurch ahead a few feet and the process would start again. On a good day a track-laying crew could put down two miles of rail.

Hays came out from Montreal that summer, driving hundreds of miles by horse and buggy over the Grand Trunk Pacific route, which lay between the CPR in the south and the Canadian Northern to the north. The GTP paralleled the CPR for 135 miles out of Winnipeg until it swung northwest to follow the old ox cart trail to Fort Carlton, the Hudson's Bay Company post west of Duck Lake on the North Saskatchewan River, 500 miles from Winnipeg. Rutted by wheels, pocked with the hooves of horses and oxen for almost a century, the Carlton Trail showed plain and twenty-feet wide through the lush buffalo grass which was already giving way to wheat.

Noting that fences were becoming so common that a free-ranging buggy ride like his would soon become difficult, Hays decided it was time the company formed its own immigration department to take advantage of the inflow of settlers that had increased since Saskatchewan had become a province the previous year. Writing to Rivers Wilson, he predicted that by the following summer the GTP could start carrying wheat to Winnipeg. By then GTP rails would stretch 500 miles. "I think that it is very generally admitted that we are going to have the best trans-continental road on this side of the Atlantic," Hays added. "Certainly nothing heretofore done in Canada will approach it."

To achieve a line equal to eastern standards, he spent an extra million dollars to lay down rails that weighed eighty pounds to the yard, rather than the more common sixty-five pound rails, which meant an extra twenty-three tons per mile. "The interest on the cost of such a line will be returned to us ten times and over in the economy of operations and the increased safety of our passengers," Hays said. (Nowadays rails are often 136 pounds to the yard.) Bridges were of steel and concrete rather than wood. Hays, in short, followed a very different policy from Mackenzie and Mann, who with 2500 miles of railway now in operation liked to build cheap and improve later. "Everywhere we went throughout the west we were received with open arms and there is a general clamour for additional railway facilities and a belief that with these facilities would come immediate and great development," reported Hays. The Grand Trunk Pacific had received government financial support but no land grants such as the twenty-five million acres the CPR had acquired, or the five million Mackenzie and Mann had gained from buying up unused charters. The federal government policy of awarding such grants having lapsed in the late 1890s, Hays bought land and formed the Grand Trunk Pacific Town and Development Company which surveyed nearly ninety townships, over a total of 45,000 acres. He sent engineers to lay out "towns made to order" with eighty-foot-wide main streets leading from the tracks where the station would be, and plots for homes, churches and grain elevators, which would be built with lumber brought east from the forests of British Columbia over GTP rails. Of the more than 120 towns that sprang up beside the GTP line, Melville, named after Charles Melville Hays, was typical. It grew in two years from a bald spot on the prairie to a town with a population of 1500, its own phone system, and an assessment value of $1.5 million.

The Grand Trunk Pacific Branch Line Company was formed, chartered to lay 8000 miles of rail, though it actually built less than 1000. The Grand Trunk Pacific organized a commercial telegraph company and strung wires along its right-of-way. Little by

Towns like Wainwright, Alberta, were created by the Grand Trunk Pacific Town and Development Company. *Courtesy British Columbia Provincial Museum*

In 1911, when Canada won its first international grain championship, Canadian wheat was considered the best in the world. *Courtesy CN*

Canadian Northern specialized in hauling grain from hundreds of elevators such as this one at Zealandia, Saskatchewan, photographed in 1909. *Courtesy CN*

The Canadian Northern, known as the "farmer's friend," linked hundreds of northern prairie communities. *Courtesy CN*

Survey party for the Grand Trunk Pacific in the Grand Forks Valley with Mount Robson in the background, 1913. *Courtesy CN*

little, steel was laid and train service began. "Already our trains are running regularly over the whole section 660 miles west of Winnipeg into Alberta," Hays told the *Victoria Daily Times* on 23 December 1908. "The newly-arrived settlers have harvested a great wheat crop, great both in quantity and quality, greater still for the price it is bringing."

Within a year the Grand Trunk Pacific pushed its steel into Edmonton, the provincial capital, four years after the Canadian Northern. It bettered its rival's running time from Winnipeg by four hours, due to heavier rails, better grades and superior rolling stock. "Railroads are not now built as the earlier roads were built, uphill, down dale, on an unballasted road bed of mud," said Hays, taking a swipe at Mackenzie and Mann. "Such economic methods were permissible when there was a mere handful of ranchers and trappers to serve and when the promoter's objective was first of all to earn the land grant from which they issued their bonds."

Hays now was president of both the Grand Trunk Pacific and the Grand Trunk, Rivers Wilson having retired at the end of 1909. "Words fail me," Rivers Wilson said after a visit to the prairies, "to express the magnificence of the country through which our road passes. For hundreds of miles, hundreds of thousands of acres were under harvest. The whole landscape is clothed already with farms and homesteads. All along our road are growing up little towns, some of which will turn into important cities."

By the summer of 1910 the prairie section was complete, nearly 920 miles from Winnipeg to Wolf Creek, a 200-foot-wide stream emptying into the MacLeod River 130 miles west of Edmonton, halfway between that city and the Rocky Mountains. Wolf Creek marked the beginning of the 832-mile mountain section which ran through two mountain ranges to the mouth of the Skeena River.

For three years GTP surveyors like R. W. Jones and Pierre Belcour had been carrying out "flying reconnaissances" in forty passes, valleys, canyons and ravines, looking for the best route through the Rockies. Airplanes nowadays make such work relatively easy, but in those days men went on foot or horseback over thousands of square miles of tangled, unmapped mountains. They learned to fear avalanches, avoid grizzly bears, cross torrential mountain streams, and improvise when they ran out of food. They encountered dead ends and routes that would be impossibly costly. Finally they narrowed their choices to three: the Peace River and Pine River passes, some 250 miles northwest of Edmonton, or the Yellowhead Pass, southwest of Edmonton, the favoured route of Sandford Fleming and Edward Watkin.

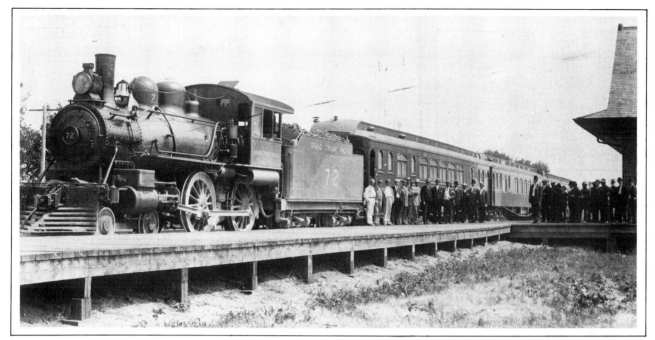

Grand Trunk Pacific Railway passenger train operating from Winnipeg to Portage Laprairie, Manitoba, in 1908. *Courtesy CN*

Lying in the tall shadow of Mount Robson, the highest peak in the Rockies, the Yellowhead Pass, though 1000 feet higher than its northern rivals, was easy when compared with the steep grades the CPR had to climb on the way from Calgary to Kamloops, 200 miles farther south. Whereas the Yellowhead Pass was little more than 3700 feet, the CPR had to contend with 5300 feet on a route bedeviled by avalanches. For generations the Yellowhead had been the pass favoured by Hudson's Bay Company traders bringing sea otter pelts from the Pacific coast to Fort Garry for shipment to England. At one time it was, for that reason, called Leather Pass, but had been renamed Tete Jaune, or Yellowhead, in the 1820s in honour of a blond Métis fur trader, identified as either Pierre Hatsination or François Decoigne.

Hays told Laurier that Yellowhead was "the shortest, most direct and most economical route" to the 8000-foot-high Coast Range that sprawls for 200 miles across the route to the Pacific. Moreover, there was only one summit to cross, rather than the two west of the Peace River, and easier grades were important since they would give the Grand Trunk Pacific a long-term advantage over the CPR, which had to contend with slopes of 116 feet or more to the mile. Hays was insisting on 21 feet, or a grade no more than four tenths of one per cent — in short almost a "prairie grade," even in the mountains. A locomotive could haul twice as much (1058 tons) up a four-tenths grade than up a one per cent grade.

"Four Tenths Van": C. C. Van Arsdol, chief engineer of the Grand Trunk Pacific from the prairies to Prince Rupert. *Courtesy Ted Van Arsdol*

If achieving these grades increased construction cost, Hays felt it was well worth it for the future. Division Engineer C. C. Van Arsdol, a gaunt, taciturn American who had learned his business in the mountains of California, became so adept at finding such grades he was nicknamed "Four Tenths Van." Hays hired Van Arsdol in August 1903 and called him "the foremost railway pathfinder on the North American continent." Van Arsdol was to work steadily for eleven years, supervising all exploration and half the construction between Edmonton and the Pacific. When he wasn't poring over his maps and blueprints in the railway's third floor Edmonton office he was out with the survey gangs "buried in the heart of the great mountain ranges," as Hays put it.

By 1906 he had found that he could get through the Yellowhead at the required four-tenths grade except for several miles where he had to settle for one per cent, which up to that time had been the lowest grade known on the Pacific coast, at Panama. "To grasp its significance," commented the American journal *World's Work*, "it is necessary to recall that no other railway north of the equator can get through the mountains without rising to at least 5000 feet above sea level and to do which no easier rise than 106 feet to the mile is possible. With a grade of only one-fifth this amount and only rising to a maximum altitude of 3712 feet, no wonder there is general belief that the greater part of the traffic across North America will flow over the steel highway between Moncton and the Pacific."

At Wolf Creek, the jumping-off point for the Yellowhead Pass, the hardest construction work the railway had faced began in the summer of 1910. The crew had gone hardly a mile when they had to build two large bridges of six and eight spans; after sixteen miles another bridge had to be built, at Sundance Creek. Whereas on the prairies they had naked land to work on, now they had to hire armies of axemen to clear a path. They worked their way up the broad, beautiful valley of the Athabaska and their first view of the snow-tipped Rockies beyond the green foothills. This was heavily forested country of spruce and lodgepole pine, and one of the richest sources of fur when this had been Hudson's Bay Company territory.

A 184-mile wagon road was built across the mountain slopes to Tete Jaune Cache on the banks of the upper Fraser at a cost of $1,000 a mile so that clumsy freight wagons could haul 30,000 tons of food, lumber and equipment to fifty camps. At Brule Lake the west wind from the mountains filled their excavations with loose soil. Near Jasper Park they got into a tussle with beavers who

At Wolf Creek, in a landscape of low hills and meandering rivers, Grand Trunk Pacific contractors built a bridge and began their push into the Rocky Mountains. *Courtesy British Columbia Provincial Museum*

resented having their dams breached and kept repairing them each night until the railwaymen diplomatically found a way around their pond. Twenty-four steam shovels and 600 horse teams were needed to make the grades in Yellowhead Pass.

The work was being done by one of North America's best railway construction firms, Foley, Welch and Stewart, who had built large stretches of the CPR. The Foley brothers and Patrick Welch were Americans and J. W. (Jack) Stewart, who served as a major general during World War I and built railways to the trenches, came from Vancouver. "It is merely a question of organization," he used to say. "The technical difficulties of construction are of minor importance."

By now Mackenzie and Mann were also pushing their line through the Yellowhead Pass, the British Columbia branch of their empire having been incorporated in March 1910 as the Canadian Northern Pacific Railway. They had been considering British Columbia since 1902 when Premier James Dunsmuir, who owned the Esquimalt and Nanaimo Railway on Vancouver Island, urged them to build via the Yellowhead to Bute Inlet and bridge the islands to Nanaimo. When Laurier put his money on the Grand Trunk Pacific this plan had fallen through, since federal money would have been needed.

As the Grand Trunk Pacific rails crept over Yellowhead Pass to the western slopes of the Rockies, scows ferried supplies from the railhead at Tete Jaune Cache to camps on the upper Fraser River. *Courtesy CN*

Their next plan resembled that of the Grand Trunk Pacific: to push in a northwesterly arc from Edmonton through the mountains of the Peace River country and come out on the coast 500 miles north of Vancouver. When it seemed that the GTP was taking that route, and that there would be little point in having two railway terminals at the mouth of the Skeena, they heeded British Columbia government urgings to run farther south. Having believed they had first rights to Yellowhead Pass they were dismayed to discover that, after much indecision and secrecy, the GTP was taking that route. Their protest to the government, apart from delaying construction for a time, had no effect, and the two railway companies, still competing when common sense suggested co-operation, crammed their lines into the same pass. (The Canadian Northern had the minor satisfaction of achieving a maximum grade through the pass of 0.7 per cent which was a bit lower than the GTP maximum.)

By 1911 the Canadian Northern, in one guise or another, controlled 3000 miles of track, built up in the short span of fifteen years in their own unique system of railway promotion. They had failed to take over the Intercolonial in the Maritimes, but were firmly positioned in Montreal where they were preparing to dig a railway tunnel under Mount Royal. The federal government had just offered financial backing for a 1000-mile line between Montreal and the Lakehead which would let them link their eastern holdings with their prairie network. Now British Columbia was

backing what Premier Richard McBride called "a thoroughly Canadian system, controlled by Canadians." To top it all Mackenzie and Mann had just been knighted.

Work on the Canadian Northern Pacific was well under way from Yellowhead down the centre of the province, the route Fleming had wanted the CPR to take before it decided to cut west from Calgary to Vancouver. The first 250 miles through the North Thompson river valley was not difficult, but the second half of the route, paralleling the CPR tracks between Kamloops and the coast, was hard and costly through Hell's Gate and the Lillooet range. In some areas, because of blasting and rockwork, costs mounted to $300,000 a mile, cheap these days but staggering half a century ago.

When Mackenzie and Mann were first invited into British Columbia, the idea was that they would build on Vancouver Island to make up for CPR's failure to do so. They had agreed to build 120 miles of branch line, but not to attempt to bridge the islands west of Bute Inlet. They were more intent now on getting their line to Vancouver, though at first they had to be content with a terminal at Port Mann, fifteen miles away.

Once over the Yellowhead Pass, the Canadian Northern and the Grand Trunk Pacific ran close together for many miles before the former forked south at Red Pass Junction on a 500-odd-mile journey to the outskirts of Vancouver. As it happened, Hays would have liked to run a GTP line to Vancouver, in addition to the route

Building the Canadian Northern through British Columbia proved costly as the railway set much higher standards there than on the prairies. William Mackenzie, David Hanna and their chief engineer Malcolm H. Mcleod (left to right) check the route near Kamloops, B.C., in 1910. *Courtesy CN*

already planned to the northwest and the mouth of the Skeena, but by 1911 it was too late, though the plan was not completely forgotten. Laurier's Liberals had lost the election and Robert Borden's Conservatives, patrons of the CPR and friendly to the Canadian Northern, were in power. The new railway minister, George Graham, made it clear that he thought a GTP service to Vancouver would be nothing less than "a wanton waste of money." When he suggested that the railways consider a co-operative effort, double tracking between Kamloops and the coast, he got a cool reception.

In any case, the Grand Trunk Pacific would have its hands full building a railway through the maze of mountains in the northwest. From Tete Jaune Cache the line would follow the upper Fraser as it winds north to Prince George, where it makes a U-turn before pouring back down the province to its mouth at Vancouver. For five years survey parties of 15 to 20 men each — at times there were 150 in the field — had been exploring deep into the country as far as the Bulkley and Nechako valleys. As engineer in charge, Van Arsdol had taken to making several trips a year by thirty-horse pack train right down to the mouth of the Skeena.

For more than 100 years, since the explorer Simon Fraser had come over the Peace River pass in 1805 to the river which bears his name, the region had attracted no more than an occasional miner or homesteader. To supply the railway camps, a system of steamboats and barges would have to be organized. Beyond Bulkley Valley would begin the hardest work of all, laying a railway along the Skeena, a river which drops 1000 feet in its 120 miles, making it one of the fastest flowing on the coast as it cuts its way through almost 60 miles of rock walls. From now on "Four Tenths Van" would be hard pressed to maintain the grades Hays insisted on as he pushed across the wild, unpopulated countryside.

4 THE LAST FRONTIER

FOR A PROVINCE whose treasury was almost as empty as its vast terrain, the government of British Columbia was remarkably cool to the ambitious plans of Charles Hays to open up a north rich in timber, fish, minerals and potential farm land. Early in 1903 when vague accounts of the Hays proposal to run the Grand Trunk Pacific Railway through the mountains to one of the Indian villages on the "Rain Coast" 500 miles north of Vancouver reached Premier E. G. Prior, he showed no interest in it. A former mining engineer who had been in office for only a few months, Prior, in a brief flash of prescience, foresaw that it would be a long time before British Columbia had the resources to support another port. Hays came from the United States where population and wealth might be expected to support such a visionary project, but Vancouver, still in its infancy, was no San Francisco. "I do not approve of giving assistance to the scheme to run a railway to Port Simpson, thus building up a rival city to Vancouver, Victoria and other coast cities," said Prior. There was much in what he said even if, in the end, it was the new northern port, rather than Vancouver, that would suffer from such rivalry.

There were other reasons for the lack of hospitality. Like its federal counterpart, the Conservative government of B.C. supported the Canadian Pacific Railway and had no love for the Liberal regime in Ottawa. Moreover, the provincial government had been trying to entice Mackenzie and Mann to build a line south from the Yellowhead Pass to Bute Inlet, where islands permit bridging to Vancouver Island, and thence to Victoria.

Amid growing popular support for a northern port, Prior's opinion was ignored and within three weeks he reversed his posi-

The first train to arrive at Prince Rupert from Winnipeg, on 9 April 1914, brought hope that the closest port to the Orient would soon begin to prosper. *Courtesy British Columbia Provincial Archives /1091*

Paddle-wheelers, which carried everything from live cattle to dynamite up the Skeena to the Grand Trunk Pacific work camps, took a week to get 200 miles upriver against the current. *Courtesy CN*

tion, telling an audience in the inland town of Yale that it might not be a bad idea after all. That summer the fledgling premier was ousted by a more masterful politician, Richard McBride. British Columbia, like the rest of Canada, was caught up in a post-depression boom. Speaking optimistically of the "New British Columbia" in the north, where speculators were buying up land while it was cheap, McBride saw the arrival of the Grand Trunk Pacific as inevitable. He also wanted to get as much as he could out of the new railway, but it was not clear just where it would enter the province, whether through the Peace River Pass, the Pine River Pass, or one of two or three passes farther south. It was not even sure that Port Simpson would, in fact, become the terminus.

A Hudson's Bay fort and trading post founded in 1830 by Capt. Amelius Simpson, Port Simpson had grown from an Indian village to a settlement of frame buildings and became the most important centre in the north, supplying settlers and Hudson's Bay posts far up the Skeena River. In the 1870s Port Simpson had been favoured, particularly by the surveyor Charles Horetzky, as the CPR terminal. More important than Kitimat, which was still an Indian village, it had become the provincial government headquarters in the north, and had an excellent harbour which was a port of call for ships bound for Alaska. But for all its advantages it had the serious drawback of being too close to the Alaska Panhandle whose boundary had been a continuing source of argument between the American and Canadian governments. Prime Minister

While still a place of stumps, rock and muskeg, maps of Prince Rupert in 1907 depicted fine parks, plazas and grand boulevards worthy of a city of 50 000.
Courtesy Public Archives of Canada /C 46484

Laurier had wanted to keep the railway clear of such haggles, since he regarded the National Transcontinental, of which the Grand Trunk Pacific was a part, as an "all-red route" that must remain free of American interference. He suggested that Hays look for a terminus farther south. The search would proceed with secrecy, to discourage speculators.

"We heard very little about the railroad," recalled Walter Wicks, a local resident whose family had settled in "New British Columbia." "It was a rumour, and that's all it was, but occasionally we had seen a little tugboat travelling up and down the coastline. After making enquiries we found out it was a survey boat taking soundings. Over towards Metlakatla we had seen it in what we called Tuck Inlet."

Metlakatla, on the Tsimpsean Peninsula thirty miles south of Port Simpson, was an Indian mission village of 1000 people established in 1862. It was this band which owned the land north of the Skeena estuary, and it was the local Indian agent, George Morrow, who first saw the potential of nearby Kaien Island as a railway terminus and began to stake it out in the summer of 1903. Lying two and a half miles from Metlakatla, Kaien Island was twenty-eight square miles of spruce, cedar, balsam, rock and muskeg. From a range of mountains in the background, it sloped down a mile or two in a northwest direction towards an eight-mile shoreline protected by Digby Island. Best of all was the natural deepwater harbour, a mile wide, stretching fourteen miles into Tuck Inlet. In the autumn of 1903 a Grand Trunk Pacific engineer, J. H.

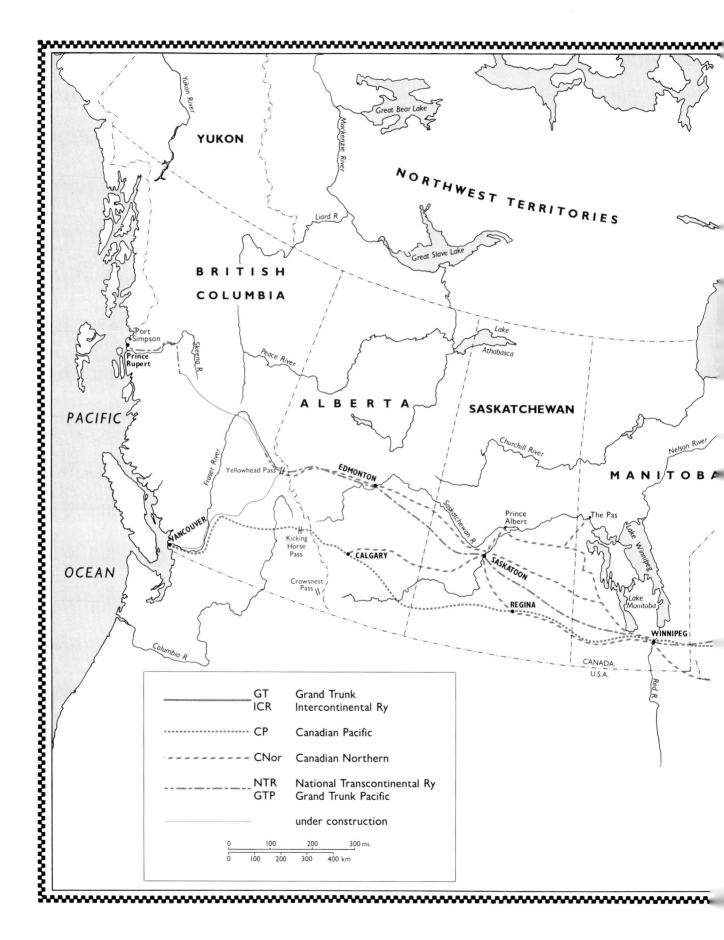

YUKON

Yukon River

NORTHWEST TERRITORIES

Great Bear Lake

Mackenzie River

Liard R

Great Slave Lake

BRITISH COLUMBIA

Port Simpson

Prince Rupert

Skeena R.

Peace River

Lake Athabasca

PACIFIC

ALBERTA

SASKATCHEWAN

Churchill River

Nelson River

MANITOBA

Fraser River

Yellowhead Pass

EDMONTON

Saskatchewan R.

Prince Albert

The Pas

Lake Winnipeg

VANCOUVER

Kicking Horse Pass

CALGARY

SASKATOON

Lake Manitoba

OCEAN

Crowsnest Pass

REGINA

WINNIPEG

Columbia R.

CANADA
U.S.A.

Red R.

	GT	Grand Trunk
	ICR	Intercontinental Ry
	CP	Canadian Pacific
	CNor	Canadian Northern
	NTR	National Transcontinental Ry
	GTP	Grand Trunk Pacific
		under construction

0   100   200   300 mi.
0   100   200   300   400 km

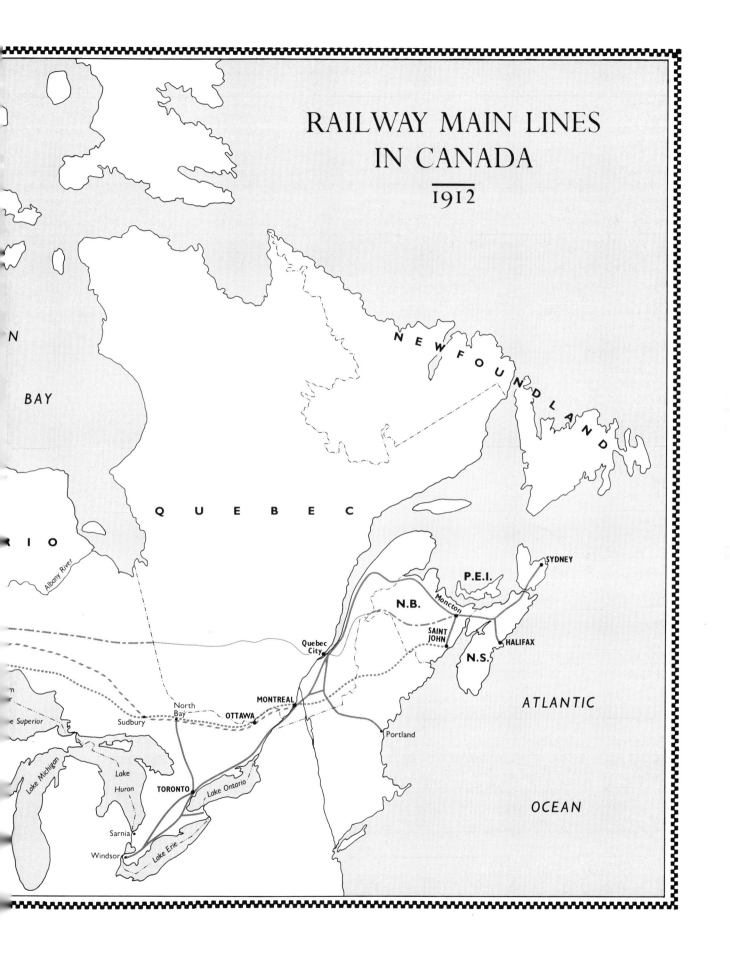

RAILWAY MAIN LINES
IN CANADA
1912

Bacon, surveyed the coast from Port Simpson in the north to Port Neville in the south, but found no location better than Kaien Island, a recommendation seconded by E. G. Russell, who made a second survey six months later. Hays was convinced this was the terminus he wanted but said nothing because he did not want to alert speculators who would drive up land prices as they had done earlier at Port Simpson.

This policy explains the murky transaction in the spring of 1904, involving the provincial government and a group led by Peter Larson, an American railroad builder associated with the Grand Trunk Pacific contractors Foley, Welch and Stewart. The provincial government would normally have been expected to consult the legislature before granting land. Such public action would have meant making the Kaien Island negotiations known to all, however, so the government quietly sold Larson and his friends 10,000 acres of Kaien Island for $1 an acre. To ensure some provincial control over municipal development, one quarter of this was to revert to the province should the place become a town. It is not clear at what stage Larson and his friends began working hand-in-glove with the Grand Trunk Pacific in this matter, but they sold the land fairly soon to the railway for the same amount paid for it. This gave the Grand Trunk Pacific a foothold, though still without commitment to that site. Larson gained no obvious advantage, but admitted later that the sale did improve his position, as a railway contractor, with the Grand Trunk. When a legislative committee dug into the matter two years later, the Grand Trunk Pacific having made public its Kaien Island intentions, it turned up some dubious practices, but the whole affair was soon forgotten.

That autumn Hays himself came west on his first visit, having obtained his board's approval to start building his western railway. With the American-born GTP general manager Frank W. Morse, Hays travelled on the CPR, a journey which made him thankful he had opted for the less precipitous Yellowhead Pass. The CPR had to snake up two summits, one of 5300 feet, the other of 4300 feet. In the CPR stronghold of Vancouver, he found a city, still not twenty years old, increasing at the rate of 1000 people a month and already boasting a population of 60,000. From a sawmill village on the banks of Burrard Inlet, it had grown to a major port, fetching silk, tea and spices from the Orient and exporting lumber from its many mills, as well as sending building material to hundreds of new prairie towns as far east as Winnipeg. Victoria, the old coal mining centre of Nanaimo, and Vancouver Island lumber

Such was the terrain east of Prince Rupert that the Grand Trunk Pacific was obliged to blast a narrow ledge between the hills and the Skeena River for its trains to run on. *Courtesy Public Archives of Canada /C 46338*

towns such as Chemainus and Port Alberni were flourishing.

Heading north aboard the government steamer *Quadra* Hays saw for himself the multitude of inlets, islands, bays and potential harbours which had made choosing a terminus so perplexing. Along a shore vastly different from the bald and uninviting American coastline farther south, he visited Pear Harbour, Cunningham Passage and Port Simpson, where he was "surprised to find flowers, fruit and vegetables grown in great profusion." As a result of the Japan Current, the climate was mild and the bays free of ice in winter. At the mouth of the Skeena, the province's third largest river, he boarded one of the stern-wheelers that had been carrying prospectors and settlers upriver for a decade. As the boat laboured against the fast Skeena current, he entered a wilderness of silent, secluded valleys, rushing waterfalls, gleaming distant mountains, with here and there an Indian village, a prospector's camp, a settler's clearing. At Lorne Creek, which had once been a centre of a gold rush, he found prospectors at work.

At Hazelton, the farthest point of his trip, Hays came upon reminders of two of the great nineteenth-century projects which had petered out in the infinite bush. Near the Indian village of Hegwilget in 1859 Maj. William Downie, exploring the Skeena for a railway route on behalf of Governor Douglas, had put up a sign saying he had located a pass for "the Great Canadian and Pacific railroad." Hazelton itself had been settled by men building a telegraph line from the United States through northern B.C. to Russia and hence into Europe. It had been started in the early 1860s by the American Perry M. Collins but was abandoned because of the successful completion of Cyrus Eaton's more practicable Atlantic cable. Coming back downriver, Hays's impression was of a country rich in timber, gold, copper, silver, lead and coal which would, in time, contribute to the commerce he planned to develop with the Orient. Visiting Tuck Inlet, he ordered a final marine survey to assure himself there were no rocks in the harbour, as an early British Admirality mapmaker had erroneously assumed.

Kaien Island was well situated. Twelve miles from the mouth of the Skeena, alongside which river the railway must run no matter which of the several northern passes it came through, it lay protected from the Pacific storms from the west and from the northeast winds that blow down the Skeena and Nass canyons. It offered one of the best harbours on the coast, not being afflicted by the racing currents which caused difficulties at the entrance to Vancouver's harbour in Burrard Inlet. There was ample land which could be purchased at low cost. Freighters sailing from this northern latitude could cut a day or two off the voyage time between Japan and Vancouver, and even more off the route from San Francisco to Japan.

The next step was to start negotiations with the Tsimpsean Indians, who agreed to sell 13,519 acres at $7.50 an acre. Added to the 10,000-acre government grant, the Grand Trunk Pacific soon held 12,579 acres on Kaien Island, 6700 acres on Digby Island just opposite, more than 4000 acres on the Tsimpsean Peninsula, and the rest on several small islands nearby.

On 17 May 1906, nine months after Grand Trunk Pacific construction had commenced west of Winnipeg, the first working party struggled ashore on Kaien Island in heavy rain, "and in muskeg up to our thighs." Under J. H. Pillsbury were engineers, carpenters, a Chinese cook and labourers, seventeen in all. They cleared a site in the sodden forest for their tents and a tool shed and by July first had built a wharf with a defective pile driver hired from George Cunningham, who lived at Port Essington on the south bank of the Skeena. By August they had put up the first frame building and surveyed the first street, leading up the hill

from the wharf. By Christmas fifteen tents and small buildings had been erected.

People believed the townsite would become a city of 50,000, and there seemed little reason to doubt them. In an impressive public relations campaign launched by the Grand Trunk, a contest was opened. Whoever came up with a suitable name for the little clearing in the woods that was to become Canada's westernmost port city would win $250. It should have no more than three syllables or ten letters, and should not conflict with the name of any other town in the Dominion. Some 12,000 entries were received, the winner being Miss Eleanor MacDonald of Winnipeg, who suggested Prince Rupert, after the first governor of the Hudson's Bay Company. Since her entry was more than ten letters long, two others received consolation prizes for suggesting Port Rupert, which was thought too similar to old Fort Rupert down on Vancouver Island.

There was still no railway construction from the western end, though British Columbia had been led to believe that construction would commence at both ends at the same time. Victoria's *Daily Colonist* complained that too little had been done at Prince Rupert and called for a declaration of intent from the company since "hundreds of people scattered from Montreal in the east to San Francisco in the south . . . are anxiously awaiting the opening of the new town to embark in business." People were not sure that Prince Rupert would really be the terminus, and this uncertainty was "killing investment." Hays came out again that autumn to ginger things up and to announce that Prince Rupert would be the terminus. "Prince Rupert is sure to be on the all-red route around the world, and the all-red route is sure to come, sooner or later," declared *Canadian Magazine*.

By early 1907 large-scale land clearance had begun. Muddy,

The first locomotive seen in Prince Rupert came not by rail but was transported by sea two years before the railway was completed. *Courtesy Glenbow Museum /NA-1864-4*

littered with fallen logs, Prince Rupert was a tent city with 150 inhabitants, mostly workmen, which included 123 Europeans, 15 Japanese, 9 Chinese and 3 local Indians. There was a policeman, W. H. Vickers, from Plymouth, England, who was also notary public, justice of the peace, health inspector, game warden and mining recorder. The railway and the government tried to discourage settlers, but some managed to come in on coastal steamers, such as the *Princess May*, which were calling regularly. John Knox, a Scottish prospector, staked a mining claim, put down roots, and established a little community called Knoxville. The first newspaper, the *Prince Rupert Empire*, a nuisance both to the company and the government, complained in an editorial on 20 July 1907: "None of the land has been divided into lots and blocks. No person has been allowed to locate on it, and there is neither a hotel nor lodging house. Traders are discouraged by the Grand Trunk Pacific. There are, however, located the Canadian Bank of Commerce, two hardwares, one druggist, two doctors, one barber, one butcher, and two construction companies. The customs and post office are in tents. The Church of England is under Bishop Verney, but the Presbyterian Church has not been permitted to locate."

A three-storey hotel and a school building appeared. Brett and Hall, the firm of Boston landscape architects responsible for Montreal's Mount Royal park, was brought in to turn the raw, ugly little settlement into a model town, the first in Canada planned on paper before any substantial buildings went up. The townsite resembled a battlefield, with men using dynamite to clear roads through the granite outcrops behind the shoreline. Sidewalks of lumber had to be raised high above streets full of potholes, hollows, muskeg, boulders and stumps.

Surveying having been completed and 2000 acres cleared of trees, 2400 lots were put up for sale by the railway and the government at a five-day auction in Vancouver in May 1909. Some 2000 people, many of whom had been waiting two years for this day, were in attendance and included bidders from the United States and Europe. "The opening of Prince Rupert, the last great city of the last great West, is without doubt the most spectacular event of the kind in many decades and the interest evidenced in all parts of the globe gives promise of the sale being one of the most picturesque and important events in the history of the whole Pacific coast," said the *Vancouver World*.

Most of the bidders were from the province, including many already squatting on the Prince Rupert site in tents and huts. The

One of the few communities mapped out by town planners before houses were built, Prince Rupert saw its population rise dramatically in the year following the property auctions of 1909. *Courtesy CN*

Western Haver Lumber Company bought the first lot, for $10,600, and more than $1.25 million worth of property was sold at the Vancouver auction and at a subsequent one in Victoria, the record price being $16,500 for a 50-by-100-foot corner lot. Within a year, with a population of 1500, Prince Rupert was incorporated and held its first municipal election, choosing Fred Stork as mayor, a name people felt was appropriate for such an infant community. Prince Rupert was no longer a company town, nor did the Grand Trunk Pacific from then on have the sort of hold on the community the CPR had had on Vancouver in the early days. The Grand Trunk Pacific was building eastward from Prince Rupert now, having commenced on 7 May 1908, three years after construction had started from the other end in Manitoba. As the provincial government had anticipated, this meant jobs and a boost in the economy of the coast as far south as Vancouver.

The railway was now engaged in the most arduous and costly work of the whole transcontinental route. In order to lay 300 miles of track, 12,000 miles of territory had to be surveyed, or at least explored. The Zenardi Rapids leading from Prince Rupert to the mainland had to be bridged, and running the roadbed up the north shore of the Skeena meant having to hack out a ledge for it, so close did the mountains come to the water. For part of the 180 miles up to Hazelton the river runs between cliffs, and to secure a narrow shelf for the railway required ten million pounds of dynamite and black powder, much of it manufactured in Prince Rupert. At Kitselas Canyon, which is half a mile long and 150 feet wide, with cliffs on both sides, 6000 feet of tunneling was required, and the railhead was held up for a year. Dynamite men found themselves hanging on a sheer cliff face to insert their charges and it was here one spring morning that eight men lost

Russian Doukhobor "stationmen" at Mile 312 on the Grand Trunk Pacific line east of Prince Rupert in 1912. A stationman was a subcontractor who prepared a small stretch of roadbed for a fee per yard. *Courtesy Public Archives of Canada /C 46178*

their lives when a charge misfired. In the first 211 miles there were thirteen tunnels, a mile and a half of rockwork.

The workmen included Scots, Scandinavians, and Russian Doukhobors, and 6000 men worked on the British Columbia section at one time. Their camps were crude, temporary affairs, usually housing seventy-five men. Describing one of the smaller camps, E. H. L. Johnson, who had worked on the roadbed, said in *British Columbia Magazine:* "One could hardly imagine a more picturesque spot than that on which the camp was situated. It consisted of three or four log shacks and two or three tents in a small clearing perched on the bank of the river; behind the camp was dense forest with a grade running east and west about 50 yards back from the river. Opposite the camp across the river was spread out before us, when the clouds parted for a moment, a wonderful panorama of mighty, snow-clad mountain peaks with great deep valleys wrapped in dark green."

Every day except Sunday work started at 7 A.M. and ended at 6 P.M. with an hour for lunch. The meals were huge, and the contractors believed that a man could not work steadily for five hours at such heavy labour on a diet of anything but meat. To ward off scurvy there were great barrels of lime juice. A fleet of five paddlewheelers hauled everything needed, from dynamite to thousands of tons of food including live cattle. Such was the force of the river and the difficulties of such stretches as the Whirly-Gig or the Devil's Elbow that the boats had to be wound upriver with a capstan, along the bank. It might take a week to get up the 180 miles to Hazelton; the return trip took only half a day.

At the height of construction on the prairies and in the mountains 10,000 men were at work at one time, but labour was often

The "first cut" to start building the Grand Trunk Pacific eastward from Prince Rupert was made in May 1908, three years after work had begun westward from the prairies. *Courtesy British Columbia Provincial Archives /42146*

To achieve the grades demanded, two million separate blasts of dynamite were required to cut through the rock over the first 200 miles east of Prince Rupert. Construction costs of the 832-mile mountain section totalled $65 million. *Courtesy Glenbow Museum /NA-3658-41*

Expert tunnel men, many of them Italians, were brought in to carve a path through the Cascade Mountains. *Courtesy British Columbia Provincial Archives /292525*

in short supply. With a shortage of 3000 men in the autumn of 1909, the Grand Trunk Pacific tried again — as it had before — to import Oriental labourers as the CPR had done a generation earlier when it employed 15,000 Chinese. "The temporary employment of three or four thousand Asiatics would save us two or three years," Rivers Wilson told the *Winnipeg Free Press*, "and at the end they could be taken back to the Orient." He was supported by Laurier, but the British Columbia government, reflecting a racism that had developed in the province during the previous two decades, opposed all pleas for Oriental labour. In the end the railway had to send agents to Europe, and especially to Scotland, to recruit 5000 men.

With the roadbed stretching from Prince Rupert halfway to Hazelton, Prime Minister Laurier came out in 1910 to view the first stretch of steel. He rode the railway for twenty miles and paid a ceremonial visit to Prince Rupert, where a civic welcome written on tanned moosehide was presented to him and he said it was the dream of his life to ride the National Transcontinental railway from the Atlantic to the Pacific. He found a Prince Rupert racked by growing pains, waking each morning to a new token of progress. The population had reached 5000. Twenty-five real estate offices, one of them established by Charles Hays's brother, David, had sprung up. There were three lawyers and four grocery stores, two banks and a Board of Trade.

The provincial government loaned the municipality $200,000 to improve the hilly townsite with a view to accommodating 10,000 people. The city council tried to exact what the Grand Trunk Pacific considered to be an exorbitant amount in corporate taxes, giving rise to early friction between town and railway; still, the Grand Trunk Pacific had great pride in this new town it had created. "What were Vancouver, Seattle, Tacoma, Portland and Los Angeles 15 years ago?" asked one of its promotional pamphlets. "Some of them were hardly on the map. Look at them today, each a splendid example of what energy, brains and money can and will do in the Golden West, and who can predict what Prince Rupert will be in the next 15 or 20 years, or even in 5 or 10 years?"

There was already much progress. At Seal Cove, on the outskirts of town, a British company was building the Canadian Fish and Cold Storage plant, one of the largest in the world. The annual salmon pack in the little settlements at the mouth of the Skeena, such as Port Essington, ran to 200,000 cases, valued at $1 million. To develop the industry the Grand Trunk Pacific ordered

As sole agent of the Grand Trunk Pacific real estate branch, David H. Hays, brother of Charles Melville Hays, set up a false-front office. *Courtesy Prince Rupert City Archives*

100 special refrigerator cars. (In Montreal the Canada Car Company was working on an order of 12,000 freight cars and 250 passenger cars for the Grand Trunk Pacific.)

The railway company secured a $2 million subsidy from the federal government to build a drydock and shipyard capable of handling ships of 20,000 tons. (Unfortunately, there was rarely much business for it and until World War II there were usually only local vessels to repair.) It was plowing profits from its sale of lots back into harbour installations, not only at Prince Rupert but at Seattle, Victoria and Vancouver where it leased or purchased docks. Recalling the Grand Trunk Pacific's frequent promises to get into the shipping business to compete with the CPR, Victoria's *Daily Colonist* observed: "A port without adequate steamship service is of little use and it may be taken for granted that the Grand Trunk Pacific directorate is making arrangements to have good steamship services on the Pacific Ocean, as soon as its trains reach the Pacific Coast. It is well known that the Grand Trunk Pacific Company intends to boom this route for all it is worth as the shortest and most convenient obtainable between Great Britain and the Orient for eclipsing the Suez Canal route and also every other known line across the Continent."

For the moment the railway was content with a coastal shipping service. The Grand Trunk Pacific Coast Steamship Company,

In 1913, a year before the Grand Trunk Pacific was completed, the Prince Rupert docks were already busy with ships bringing supplies and construction gangs from Vancouver. (Below) The *Prince Rupert* began coastal service between Seattle, Vancouver, Victoria and Prince Rupert in 1910. Sold to a Japanese company in 1956, she was scrapped a few years later. *Courtesy CN*

headed by Capt. C. H. Nicholson, purchased two new twin screw steamers, the *Prince Rupert* and the *Prince George*, for a bi-weekly service between Seattle, Victoria, Vancouver and Prince Rupert. Since one of the Grand Trunk Pacific's purposes was to develop trade, there were high hopes that coastal shipping would mature into a trans-Pacific line. "We have first of all a magnificent harbour," said Hays. "When Prince Rupert has been connected with Sydney across the Pacific by a good line of steamships — and that will come soon — the connection will have been completed of the two very finest harbours in the British Empire. So at least a friend of mine assures me who has recently seen both, and let me dare to add, gives the palm to Prince Rupert. Recall, also, that our route cuts down the distance to the Far East and in these days, where mankind is forever in a hurry, the saving of two or three days will often decide the choice of route."

Hays had a well-developed sense of public relations, and the Grand Trunk Pacific brought out a brochure extolling Prince Rupert in tones almost poetic:

> To this new port will come the ships of the Seven Seas. Ships of the East, laden with silk and rice, will soon be riding at anchor in this splendid harbour, to sail away laden with lumber; ships from the shores of far-off continents trading through the new and picturesque port of Prince Rupert.
>
> The distance from Liverpool to Yokohama by this route is 10,031 miles, as against 10,829 via New York and San Francisco. . . . Ships sailing from Prince Rupert begin their journey across the Pacific 500 miles nearer the East than a ship would be when sailing at the same time from another Pacific port.

Grand Trunk Pacific Coast Steamship Company docks at Vancouver in 1912. Plans to expand into a trans-Pacific service never materialized; (below) docks at Seattle, which burned in 1914. *Courtesy CN*

Translated into practical terms, this meant a freighter might make three more voyages a year from Prince Rupert than from Vancouver and five more than from San Francisco.

The Canadian Northern also had plans for a trans-Pacific shipping service. Mackenzie and Mann had been building their transcontinental railway from Quebec City to Vancouver, and late in 1911 Mann said it would be completed "within 18 months." There were persistent reports that the Canadian Northern was negotiating a contract with the B.C. government to establish steamship routes to Japan, China, New Zealand and Australia. Mann himself gave flesh to the rumours when he told the press that "before the Canadian Northern Railway line to the Pacific coast is completed the Canadian Northern Steamship Company will have a steamship line in operation on the Pacific Ocean." (In fact the Canadian Northern did purchase and run two steamships, but on the Atlantic rather than the Pacific.)

It suddenly dawned on Canadians that, with a population of barely six million, Canada was to have not two transcontinental railways but three, giving the Dominion a mile of railway per 185 people, as compared with 400 people per mile in the United States and 2000 in the British Isles. Most of the new track would run through areas virtually unpopulated. Concern was mounting, for GTP construction was two years behind schedule and Hays announced that the railway would not be completed until 1913. Delays in getting steel rails by ship around Cape Horn had been compounded by labour shortages and strikes for higher wages. Construction costs doubled, particularly in the mountain region where they had been budgeted at $60,000 per mile; even before steel had been laid the cost had reached $80,000 and was expected

Sir Alfred Smithers, Grand Trunk chairman, with Charles M. Hays at Swanson, British Columbia, in 1910, during Hays's last visit West before his death two years later. *Courtesy Public Archives of Canada /PA 21910*

to come out at about $105,000. Clinging to his promise to build a line to last, Hays had ordered that all twenty-six bridges in the mountain section be built of expensive steel and concrete rather than wood. The land sales the railway had been depending on to help defray costs were drying up, and the real estate boom was ending with three quarters of the land still unsold. The company had to get a loan of $10 million, guaranteed by the Grand Trunk, from the federal government.

The Grand Trunk Pacific began to pull back from many projects, including a "branch line" to Vancouver. Instead, it decided to join forces with the Pacific Great Eastern, which had a charter to open the interior by building a north-south railway from Vancouver to Prince George where it was to link up with the east-west GTP. The plan was to use this route to run GTP trains into Vancouver, but it was to be decades before the Pacific Great Eastern was completed and the plan never matured.

Amid mounting concern came tragedy. In February 1912 Charles Hays, accompanied by his wife and a daughter, had sailed for London. For weeks he remained closeted with the directors of the Grand Trunk, who found themselves tied, despite their wishes, to the fate of the Grand Trunk Pacific. There were rumours that Hays was trying to fashion a master stroke to save the railway. Some said he wanted to divorce the Grand Trunk Pacific from the National Transcontinental's government-run eastern wing (Winnipeg to Moncton), which would obviously lose money because it lay mostly through unpopulated territory. Others said he wanted to connect the Grand Trunk Pacific to the Grand Trunk terminal in Chicago and run lucrative silk trains from Prince Rupert to New York thirty-six hours faster than the CPR could deliver silk from Vancouver. He had tried to interest one of the major British shipping companies, the Blue Funnel Line, which ran freighters in the Orient and also between the United Kingdom and Vancouver via the Suez Canal, in developing Prince Rupert as a major port. There was a report Hays was negotiating a contract with a syndicate of Pittsburg businessmen for a $10-million deal to export coal from a mine in Belmont County, Ohio, through Canadian ports. Apart from indications that he was seeking a reorganization of the parent company that would have given the railway more money to spend at the expense of the shareholders, we shall never know what he was planning.

At approximatly 2:20 A.M. on 15 April, on his way back to New York, Charles Hays was one of the 1503 people who lost their lives in the sinking of the *Titanic*. His wife and daughter, whom he had wrapped in a blanket and placed in a lifeboat before going back up to the deck with the other men, were rescued. His railway business car, the *Canada*, which had been sent to New York to fetch him home, returned to Montreal empty, and on 25 April there was five minutes of silence throughout the whole Grand Trunk system to mourn his death.

According to a report in the *Montreal Gazette* on 7 May his body was recovered by a search ship and brought to Halifax along with papers said to pertain to "the construction of the Grand Trunk Pacific." What those documents might have contained has been lost to history, and it is difficult to imagine what, at that date, might have been done to save the Grand Trunk Pacific, though if anyone could have done it that man would have been Charles Hays, or so it was believed. Just one month short of his fifty-sixth birthday when he died, Hays was at the height of his powers. His efforts to improve trade with Pacific Asia had prompted the Emperor of Japan to award him the Order of the Rising Sun, and the British had planned to offer him a knighthood. At Prince Rupert, Mount Hays had been named after him. Laurier, to whom he was obviously a kindred spirit, called him "beyond question the greatest railway genius in Canada," though there would be those, including Sir Joseph Flavelle, the Toronto financier who became chairman of the Grand Trunk during its last years, who would question Hays's judgement in building the Grand Trunk Pacific.

Hays's successor, Edson J. Chamberlin, one of his vice-presidents and a man of considerably lesser talent, clung as long as he could to the dream of making Prince Rupert "a trade centre" for the Orient. The pre-war boom was still at its height, the Grand Trunk Pacific was hauling large quantities of grain, and there seemed every likelihood that Prince Rupert would become a terminal to match that at the Lakehead. On his first tour in June 1912 Chamberlin told the *Vancouver News Advertiser* that a Grand Trunk Pacific steamship service to the Orient would be established. He said that the railway would have been completed by now if the company had been able to recruit all the men it needed. "There would be flourishing towns where there are none now, and Prince Rupert would be a busy port with a largely increased population." The track was now into the Bulkley valley where the Grand Trunk Pacific acquired 17,000 acres and began to mine coal. By the end of 1913 it was at Burns Lake, 316 miles east of Prince Rupert.

In the spring of 1914 the Grand Trunk Pacific Railway was completed. On 6 April, with the construction crews from east and west only a mile apart, arrangements were made for each gang to

Edson J. Chamberlin succeeded Charles M. Hays as president of the Grand Trunk in 1912. *Courtesy CN*

Laying the last rail, a "praying mantis" Pioneer tracklayer lurches forward and a Grand Trunk Pacific official prepares to raise the Union Jack. *Courtesy British Columbia Provincial Archives /79487*

(Below) Chief Engineer B. B. Kelliher drives the last spike into the Grand Trunk Pacific line to Prince Rupert, 7 April 1914, B.C. *Courtesy CN*

lay half a mile of track, racing the other to the finish line. Early the next day — a sunny spring morning — trains brought in officials and guests, including President Chamberlin, Chairman Smithers and C. C. Van Arsdol. The race to the finish was won by the margin of a few minutes by the crew laying track from the east. A standard rail was cut to smaller size to fill the last gap, the final spike was driven by chief engineer B. B. Kelliher, and Chamberlin presented the foremen with gold watches. On the last rail to be placed were painted the words, "Point of Completion April 7, 1914." The place was Finmoore, a mile east of Fort Fraser and 416 miles east of Prince Rupert. From the time the first sod was turned on the prairie, the job had taken nine years less four months.

The government's section of the National Transcontinental had been completed five months earlier from Moncton to Winnipeg at a cost so high that the Grand Trunk Pacific decided it could not afford to run it at a three per cent rental based on construction costs as originally agreed. The government reluctantly found itself having to operate the eastern National Transcontinental as it operated the Intercolonial.

In January 1915 Mackenzie and Mann completed their transcontinental railway, with Mackenzie, now Sir William, driving the last spike at Basque, 189 miles east of the Pacific coast. Canada now had 30,000 miles of railway and ranked fifth in the world in total mileage and first as to mileage in proportion to population. There was a minimum of ceremony, not only because there was a war going on but also because, like the Grand Trunk Pacific, the Canadian Northern was facing serious financial difficulties.

Although the railway would soon run into Vancouver, there was no hope now of honouring such promises as building a trans-Pacific steamship service.

Depression had set in across the country. Exports dwindled, immigration all but disappeared, prices increased, rail traffic fell and with it revenue. The railway boom that had begun in an atmosphere of hopeful prosperity had ended in depression and pessimism. In 1915 the chairman of the Grand Trunk in London, Alfred W. Smithers, expressed regret to the shareholders that he had ever been persuaded to support the Grand Trunk Pacific project. Confessing to "inexpressibly bitter disappointment," Smithers asked the Canadian government to take over the Grand Trunk Pacific because the parent company could no longer support it.

As for the projects that had looked so promising for the northwest coast of British Columbia, the company was dropping them one by one. There would be no trans-Pacific steamship service. The plans to build a $2-million hotel at Prince Rupert, designed by the famous architect Francis M. Rattenbury, with 450 bedrooms and a dining room for 265 people, were abandoned in the excavation stage. Few ships appeared at the port, and what traffic there was over the railway from Yellowhead Pass was mainly local. The town that Charles Hays built became a backwater. Of the two reasons the Grand Trunk Pacific was built, trade with the Orient and development of the northern prairies, only the second was realized.

The year the Grand Trunk Pacific was completed, 1914, saw introduction of the big "tank engine" locomotives in eastern Canada. *Courtesy CN*

5 THE ASIAN DREAM

"Up to the present moment we have markets chiefly in Europe, but the time has come when we must seek markets in the Orient, in Japan and China. . . . We are in a position to profit more from this than any other portion of the civilized globe."

Prime Minister Wilfrid Laurier, 1906

BY LAURIER'S TIME, belief in the fabulous rewards to be found in trade with the Orient had been shaping history for at least 600 years. Inspired by Marco Polo's thirteenth-century travels to the court of Kublai Khan in China, medieval merchants grew wealthy importing spices, silk, gems and perfumes over the complex and dangerous overland route to Europe. The Chinese tried to simplify the trade when, in 1405, Admiral Cheng Ho sailed as far as East Africa with ships laden with silk, spices and porcelain. After Vasco da Gama found the sea route around the Cape of Good Hope in 1497, Portugal, England and Holland achieved power out of all proportion to their own resources by exploiting the wealth of enfeebled Asian empires.

With a Latin edition of Marco Polo's *Travels* in his luggage, Columbus had already brought the search to the Americas in 1492, apparently believing to his dying day that his "Indians" in the Caribbean were natives of some outlying islands of Asia. In a way he was right since their remote ancestors arguably came from there to North America over a prehistoric land bridge. The quest moved north five years later when John Cabot sailed to Nova Scotia and Newfoundland, finding no spices on what he believed to be the coast of the Great Khan.

As a Pacific Rim port, Vancouver enjoyed contact with the Orient from its early days as a lumber mill community in the 1860s. The imperial Chinese emissary Li Hung Chang visited the city in 1896, greeted by the growing Chinese community. *Courtesy Vancouver City Archives*

During the sixteenth century the search led ever westward. The rapids near Montreal, discovered by Jacques Cartier, were named La Chine. Some believed that the Saguenay River, which flows into the St. Lawrence from Lac St-Jean, was a northwest passage to Cathay. Sir Martin Frobisher, supported by Queen Elizabeth, got a little closer to the answer in 1576 when he sailed as far as Frobisher Bay at the entrance to Hudson Strait but was prevented from "sailing to China" by orders to come home. John Davis, sent out a decade later, did little better, and Henry Hudson, commissioned to sail the *Hopewell* to China by way of the North Pole, discovered Hudson Bay in 1610 and there lost his life. Never quite giving up hope, for another 250 years men tried to find a northwest passage, until they were finally convinced the way was impassable to commerce.

In the meantime, the French, who had settled on the St. Lawrence, had quietly started their own export trade to China. Aware of how the Chinese prized ginseng, Jesuit priests had discovered the medicinal root growing wild near Montreal and arranged in the 1730s to have it exported aboard vessels of the Compagnie des Indes which traded to the Orient over more conventional routes. It was neither well prepared nor of good quality, but it sold at immense profit, leading the producers to the mistaken conclusion many others have made since: that China is an inexhaustible market. Within twenty years the demand fell off, and in any case the Quebec supply had been overharvested. After the conquest, the English made no effort to continue the trade.

The East India Company, with its monopoly on British trade in Asia and its preoccupation with the immense profits it received selling tea to Europe and Indian opium to China, showed no interest in eastern Canadian ginseng, though it did take some momentary interest in the astonishing size and amount of standing timber on Canada's west coast. In 1784, six years after Capt. James Cook arrived at Nootka Sound in his exploration of the Pacific, an East India Company agent who stopped there to trade for sea otter furs had occasion to write: "There is no doubt that the timber with which this coast is covered (and which in its size and fine grain is nowhere to be excelled) would compose a valuable addition to our trading, as this article carried a very advanced price in China and is always in demand there."

However it was left to a private English trader who arrived about the same time, Capt. John Meares, to begin the first recorded timber export trade. So as to avoid the long arm of the East India Company, Meares set up a trading firm in the Portuguese enclave of Macao, near Canton, and from there sailed his ship *Felice* to Nootka in search of furs to ornament the robes of mandarins. He began the habit, which was followed by others, of topping up cargoes of fur with a deckload of masts, spars and lumber for the Canton market. He imported seventy Chinese labourers to his little trading post at Nootka and built the first ship on the coast, the forty-ton *North West America*. Meares was forced to leave when the Spaniards seized Nootka and held it for five years, before being driven off by the threat of the British Navy. With Meares gone it would be half a century before timber exports were resumed.

After 1833, the year the East India Company gave up its monopoly, private trading companies flourished on the China coast under Taipans, or "Great Traders," as the Chinese called European businessmen. The British had spread beyond India, their original commercial foothold, and in 1841, under the Treaty of Nanking, the Chinese ports of Foochow, Amoy and Ningpo were opened. Hong Kong became a British colony, a prize won during the "Opium Wars" when the Chinese first tried to get rid of that shameful trade. Shanghai became a free port with enclaves of British, French and other foreigners who made it the centre of international trade. After two centuries of virtual seclusion Japan also began to open to the world.

With the appearance of steamships, which increased carrying capacity and gave a dependability of movement unknown to sailing ships, Britain's position in the Orient was greatly strengthened. The first steamer to arrive on the China coast, on 19 April 1866, was the 2000-ton *Achilles*, operated by Alfred Holt & Company of Liverpool. Within three years the opening of the Suez Canal cut more than 3000 miles off the eastern route to the Orient, and with coaling stations and colonies flying the Union Jack from the mouth of the Mediterranean to China, the "all-red route" had taken on new meaning.

A steamship that could reach the China coast in less than 80 days, compared with the 120 days taken by the clipper ships, brought East and West closer together. British companies, which had arrived in China early in the century to make fortunes in tea and opium, began to invest in other commodities. There were tin mines and rubber plantations in Malaysia, operated from offices in Singapore, strategically placed as it is halfway between India and China. With capital in the rice paddies of Burma, in copra production, in Chinese silk filatures and tea plantations, the British built a commercial empire that would last until it was destroyed by the

The *Canadian Sower,* one of the pioneers of the Canadian Government Merchant Marine which permitted manufacturers to send their goods to foreign markets via direct routes rather than having to transship. *Courtesy CN*

Japanese during World War II. By the early 1900s the British were contributing half of China's total imports and buying a fifth of her exports.

From British Columbia more or less continuous commerce with the Orient started in the late 1860s, though two decades earlier the Hudson's Bay Company at Victoria, on Vancouver Island, had begun to export lumber and salted salmon to the Sandwich Islands (Hawaii) for the booming sugar industry. The colony was still isolated, with little contact with Britain or eastern Canada, and as its lumber industry grew it exported to the only places it could — down the coast to California or across the Pacific to China, Australia, New Zealand, Tahiti and Hawaii. This trade was a minor one until the coming of the Canadian Pacific Railway and the founding of the city of Vancouver in 1886. Exports were mainly timber, as they would be for a long time to come. Imports were tea and silk from China and Japan, shipments which in the past had gone to San Francisco.

In the 1890s the pace of trans-Pacific commerce quickened and the government of Canada subsidized a route from Vancouver, an addition to the British routes via the Suez Canal and the Cape of Good Hope. CPR ships ran mail, passengers and freight to Japan and China, and the Canadian Australian Line sailed between Sydney and Vancouver with calls at Honolulu, Fiji, Brisbane and Victoria, British Columbia. Under the Canada Trade and Commerce Act, the first permanent, full-time trade officers were appointed to remove "one of the principal obstacles [lack of representation] in the way of extended traffic with countries with which we now have regular and frequent steamship communication." The first officer to go to a Pacific Rim country was John Larke, a Toronto businessman and journalist, who arrived in Sydney in 1894.

With Australia buying Canadian timber, furniture, cotton cloth, leather goods and bicycles, Larke's job was to investigate business opportunities, supply Canadians with the names of firms dealing in products made in Canada, and answer correspondence from Australians and Canadians. He was dismayed, as were his colleagues in later years, by the reluctance of Canadian businessmen to cultivate new markets; most were content to stick with the established trade to Britain and the United States, each of which accounted for 45 per cent of Canada's exports. Even those who troubled to come out to Australia, said Larke, failed to make efforts to adjust to the new countries. "Some come over, expect to travel four or five thousand miles, do a large trade, and get back by the next steamer," he said. "When this cannot be done they fret and grumble at things that do not happen to be like those in Canada. They must remember that they and their goods are new and unknown in this country . . . it requires time, some money, and patience and without this equipment I would not advise any man to come."

In Shanghai British traders were promoting the tantalizing prospect — which turned out to be a myth — of half a billion Chinese ready and waiting for western products. They do not appear to have delved into the question of whether the Chinese really wanted Canadian sewing machines or pots and pans, or if they did, whether the Chinese would have the foreign exchange to pay for them. But it was a fact that imports into China were no longer limited to opium and cotton; they had been broadening out to include sugar, tobacco and kerosene. Wheat and flour now made up seven per cent of the country's import total. In 1891 China bought coal from Vancouver Island and a quantity of prairie wheat the following year.

Then there was the Japanese market. Since Japan had shed her anti-foreign policy in the 1870s and begun to industrialize, commerce with Canada had increased. The first export to Japan on the books of the Grand Trunk in Montreal was a shipment of sewing machines which a newspaper called "a new and important epoch in shipping." The general Japanese trading companies — the *sogo hosha* — had begun to emerge, Mitsubishi being established by the

Workhorses of the Canadian Government Merchant Marine fleet: (from top) a Pacific coaster, the *Canadian Volunteer;* the *Canadian Settler;* a collier, the *Canadian Miner. Courtesy CN*

In the 1920s Canada exported automobiles to Pacific Rim countries; by the mid-1960s the trade in automobiles was flowing the other way, from Japan. *Courtesy Vancouver Public Library*

Tosa provincial government in 1873 as a small coastal trading business. It expanded into shipbuilding, steel-making, banking, insurance, mining and international trade. Its competitor, Mitsui, was founded in 1876. In 1889 Japan established its first official presence in Canada, a consular office in Vancouver.

It had been the prospect of trade with the Orient, and particularly the sale of wheat from prairie farms, that helped sustain Laurier in his battles to build the Grand Trunk Pacific, which he believed would "provide immediate means whereby the products of these new settlers may find an exit to the ocean" at the least possible cost. "We would be blind to the times if we failed to realize that there is a market of four or five hundred millions in the Orient," said Laurier. "I want Canadian merchants to bear wheat and flour into that market." Recalling the rate at which tea had been arriving in Canada, Laurier had suggested that wheat would soon be going in equal quantities to the Far East and thus would become "the tea of the Orient."

The Japanese had been showing interest in Canadian wheat and flour since it was introduced at the Yokohama fair in 1896 by Sinkichi Tamura, a Japanese who had settled in Vancouver. Bread had been known in Japan for generations, having been introduced there by the Portuguese. To promote interest in Canadian wheat, Laurier sent his agricultural minister, Stanley Fisher, to attend the Osaka National Industrial Exhibition in 1903, where Canada's prize-winning exhibit was the largest. As Japanese crowded

The *Canadian Importer,* 8360 tons, sailing from Vancouver for Sydney, Melbourne and Auckland, 23 February 1920, opened a new era for Canadian manufacturers trading to Australia and New Zealand. *Courtesy CN*

around the ovens for samples of the hot, brown loaves, Canadians received the erroneous impression that the people were on the verge of trading their rice bowls for bread and butter knives. The exhibit, which included the first shipment of B.C. Douglas-fir, was a success, but Fisher's main commission failed. He tried to interest the Japanese foreign office in a trade treaty, but they pointed out politely that it would be best for Canada, as a British colony, simply to adhere to the existing Anglo-Japanese accord. Canada did so, though it sent its own commercial agent to Yokohama in 1904.

Two years later a friend of Laurier's, W. T. R. Preston, was given the new title of Trade Commissioner and sent to Japan, China and Korea to sell wheat and lumber. In 1908 he set up shop in Shanghai so that Canada now had representatives in Australia, Japan and China. Whatever the lack of enthusiasm among Canadian manufacturers, the federal government was registering modest success in promoting Pacific trade, at least in Australia and New Zealand. Between 1900 and 1910 exports more than doubled and Australasia was Canada's third largest market, though lagging far behind Britain and the United States.

Laurier continued at every opportunity to further his vision of trans-Pacific trade over an all-red route which would link Britain to Pacific Rim countries via Canada. It was on his agenda at the 1907 Colonial Conference and part of his speech repertoire, as when he told an audience of enthusiastic Toronto supporters, "We

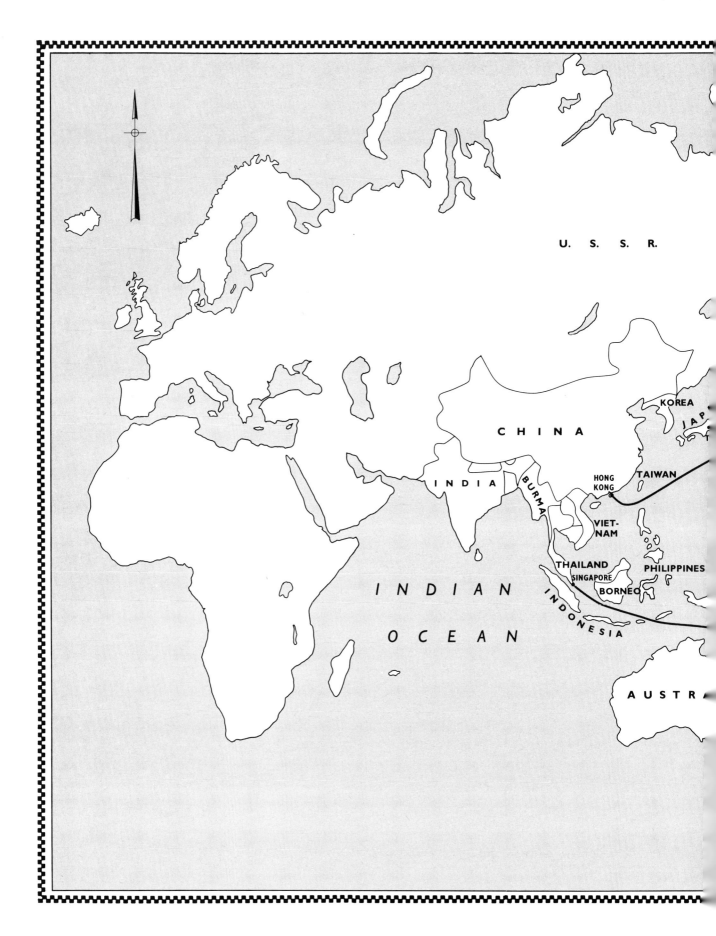

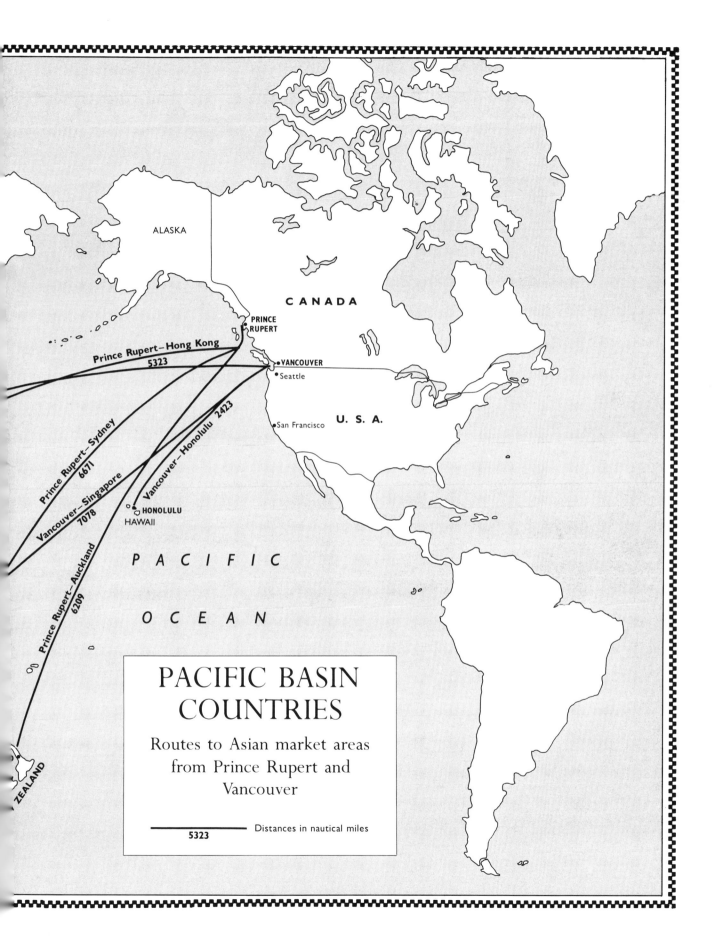

ALASKA

CANADA

PRINCE
RUPERT

VANCOUVER
Seattle

Prince Rupert–Hong Kong
5323

Prince Rupert–Sydney
6671

Vancouver–Singapore
7078

Vancouver–Honolulu 2423

San Francisco

U. S. A.

HONOLULU
HAWAII

Prince Rupert–Auckland
6209

ZEALAND

PACIFIC

OCEAN

PACIFIC BASIN COUNTRIES

Routes to Asian market areas
from Prince Rupert and
Vancouver

―――――――― Distances in nautical miles
5323

The *Canadian Prospector,* first of the Canadian Government Merchant Marine ships to sail on regular service to Japan, Shanghai and Australia, loading wool at Melbourne in 1920. *Courtesy CN*

have a better route over the Pacific. Mark my words, and by and by we shall see train upon train carrying passengers from the Orient to Europe, and from Europe to the Orient."

Canadian trade had been increasing since the recession of the 1890s, and Laurier saw its expansion across the Pacific as a means of lessening dependence on the United States. It would, moreover, help provide the wealth necessary to ensure that the twentieth century would belong to Canada "as the 19th century was that of the United States." In the long view of history Laurier's belief that Pacific Rim nations would inevitably become prime markets made good sense, though it would take much longer than he anticipated. In the short term Laurier's hopes, even if premature and exaggerated, were understandable in the heady optimism of the early years of "Canada's century." During the first years of the twentieth century, shipping tonnage through the ports of Vancouver and Victoria increased 200 per cent.

Shipping lines linking Vancouver to the Orient included Blue Funnel operated by Holt of Liverpool, which carried 60 per cent of the silk and tea from China, and the Nippon Yusen Kaisha, which carried 75 per cent of those commodities from Japan. There was the Osaka Shosen Kaisha, which dubbed one of its ships *Canada Maru,* the British-owned Royal Mail Steam Packet Company, and the CPR's Empress line sailing between British Columbia, Hong Kong, Shanghai and Manila. The Canadian Australian

Line, managed by the Union Steamship Company of New Zealand, maintained a regular schedule between Vancouver and Sydney via Victoria, Honolulu, Suva and Auckland.

Laurier told Hays that his government was prepared to support a Grand Trunk Pacific shipping line, for he believed competition was needed. The Japanese had found that Canadian wheat was costing 10 per cent more than American wheat because of higher shipping costs. Preston, now commercial councillor in Tokyo, had complained to Laurier that this situation was due to unhealthy co-operation among shipping lines, and that the CPR had shown more interest in carrying subsidized mail than in pushing cheap freight. This attitude, he told Laurier in a letter dated 15 January 1908, meant that the CPR "was one of the greatest hindrances that exist to the Canadian trade to the Orient."

In 1911 Canada and Japan signed a reciprocal "most favoured nation" trade agreement, and the *Vancouver Province* said: "The Orient is awakening with a suddenness that even the most brilliant statesmen cannot fathom. It is progressing with a speed that the best and ablest statisticians cannot calculate; it is looking out beyond the walls of its cities to new lands." Then, within a space of two years, the two men most responsible for trying to turn Canada towards the Pacific disappeared dramatically from power. Laurier suffered a defeat at the polls in 1911 and Charles Hays was drowned aboard the Titanic in 1912. Nor is there reason to believe that had they remained in power they could have rescued the Grand Trunk Pacific from bankruptcy and ensured the viability of Prince Rupert as a port to rival Vancouver and Seattle. That time had come and gone when Laurier had declined to force, as he might have done, the amalgamation of the GTP and the Canadian Northern when they were still in a position to co-operate on a united transcontinental rail line.

Laurier's successor, the Nova Scotia Conservative Robert L. Borden who opposed the Grand Trunk Pacific scheme, would have to deal with what became known as "Canada's railway problem." The trouble began with the depression of 1913. Wheat sales fell off, accounting for only a small part of the unsatisfactory $1.4 million in Canadian exports to Japan. Exports to China, equalling those to Japan, were largely confined to silver ore. Lumber sales were sagging, for Canadians had lost control by permitting American traders in San Francisco to corner the market.

In an effort to improve business, the Borden government hired the former head of the British trade service in Canada, Richard Grigg, and sent him to Japan and China. In Shanghai, Grigg found

In 1925 ships like the *Canadian Spinner,* seen here in the Suez Canal, linked eastern Canada with the Asian Pacific in a monthly service. *Courtesy CN*

prospects unpromising because of social unrest, but in Yokohama, Kobe, Nagasaki and Tokyo he was astonished at the speed of industrial development. There was, he concluded, a definite place for Canada in north Pacific trade, and recommended that exporters continue to push wheat, flour and lumber. British Columbia exporters had begun to get the name of being "in and outers," meaning they exported only when there was no domestic market available and forgot about overseas trade when local business was thriving. Grigg's complaint that they were doing too little to secure and maintain overseas business hit a nerve. At the urging of British Columbia lumbermen, the federal government in 1915 appointed the young provincial chief forester, H. R. MacMillan, to journey around the world to check out the market. His itinerary took him to Britain and France, South Africa, India, Ceylon, Burma and Australia, and though he was called home before he got to China and Japan (to be offered Grigg's job, which he refused), MacMillan was able to draw up a blueprint of how Canadians could improve trade. It gathered dust in an Ottawa pigeonhole, but it did give MacMillan the insight to mount his own export drive and expand his small lumber trading company into a multinational corporation.

The opening of the Panama Canal in 1914 gave lumbermen, and the port of Vancouver, a tremendous boost, since it allowed them to ship their product at competitive rates to the North American east coast and Britain. It helped turn Vancouver into a grain port, and the elevator there was to take pressure off the Lakehead and eastern Canada elevators, which had sometimes been unable to handle the prairie crop.

But while Vancouver prospered, the port of Prince Rupert languished. The completion of the Grand Trunk Pacific to Prince Rupert in 1914 failed to attract the boom everyone had been led to expect. People began to drift away from the town, though more than 5000 stayed, living off the salmon and halibut industry. Lumbering had not yet become a major enterprise in the north, and now that the railway had been finished there was no construction work. The drydock was nearing completion, but there were no major orders, nor would there be until 1919 when the keel for a steel freighter was laid.

E. J. Chamberlin, who had succeeded Hays, believed Prince Rupert's plight lay in a dearth of British ships. When the port was planned, British shipping lines still controlled the north Pacific, but the World War I demand for Atlantic shipping, plus losses caused by German submarines, had severely reduced available tonnage. Moreover, even before the war the Japanese had been taking over a major portion of freight carriage in the north Pacific. Now with the British navy occupied in the Atlantic, Japanese predominance was demonstrated when her naval ships made appearances off the British Columbia coast, keeping marauding German raiders away from shipping lanes. While acknowledging that there would not be enough business "for a long time" to support a regular schedule out of Prince Rupert, Chamberlin wrote to Prime Minister Borden asking that the port be assured enough shipping to at least keep it alive. "We have hoped for a long time to be able to arrange with some British line, like the Blue Funnel, for their boats, after leaving Vancouver, to call at Prince Rupert," Chamberlin said. He suggested that ships call at Prince Rupert on their return voyages from Asia, which would give the Grand Trunk Pacific first chance at cargo destined for eastern North America, including silk and tea. Chamberlin said the Japanese were interested, and asked Borden how the government would feel about an alliance with a Japanese line. Borden was not interested, and Chamberlin's attempt to revive Prince Rupert died stillborn.

In 1917 the government forced the Grand Trunk Pacific and Canadian Northern to double up over a long stretch near Yellowhead Pass. Two hundred miles of track were ripped up and shipped off to France to be used in the war effort. *Courtesy CN*

The Grand Trunk Pacific now had more pressing worries. Informing Borden that the Grand Trunk was "at the end of our tether with regard to Grand Trunk Pacific financing," chairman Smithers in London said, "the railway situation in Canada is a serious one, and any default on the part of the Grand Trunk Railway Company might lead to grave consequences to the general financial position in Canada." Borden was not sympathetic to Smithers's request for yet another loan, feeling that more public money had been poured into Canada's 30,000 miles of railways than the country could afford. Moreover, the Canadian Northern was in such serious financial trouble that it threatened the position of its major financial backer, the Bank of Commerce. As a result of the war, British financing was no longer available.

By this time the Grand Trunk Pacific had 2732 miles of track, the Grand Trunk itself had 4000, and the government's National Transcontinental had 2000. More than 3000 miles of the National Transcontinental and Grand Trunk Pacific were really not essential to the business of the country nor were the 1000 miles of the Canadian Northern east of Port Arthur.

Faced with the choice of letting the Grand Trunk Pacific and the Canadian Northern go into receivership, or taking them over and running them as a nationalized entity, Borden bought time and advice in the usual way of Canadian governments faced with

trouble. He appointed a royal commission. Meeting in 1916, in the midst of the upheaval of the war, the commission consisted of Sir Henry Drayton, Chairman of the Canadian Railway Commission, A. H. Smith, a vice-president of the New York Central Railroad, and W. H. Acworth, a British railway expert.

In 1917 the commissioners brought in their recommendations. Suggestions that all the Canadian railways be nationalized, including the CPR, were rejected on the grounds that this would create an intolerable monopoly, and besides the CPR was in a position to stand on its own feet. Also rejected was a minority report, submitted by the American railroadman Smith, whose philosophy did not include nationalization. Smith's recommendation was that the Grand Trunk, which was also in financial difficulties, should be permitted to go on operating as before in the East, taking over the Canadian Northern's eastern assets, and that the Canadian Northern take over the Grand Trunk Pacific and go on operating in the West. It was a compromise in which considerable public funding would be needed.

The majority report, signed by Drayton and Acworth, recommended that the three ailing commercial railways, including the Grand Trunk, be nationalized, or as they put it, "be assumed by the people of Canada." To protect the system against political interference they further recommended that the government not run the railways directly but that an expert board of trustees be appointed by parliament. They summed up the "railway problem" and its solution as follows:

> The Canadian Northern is weak in the East. The Grand Trunk, with the inadequate prairie branches of the Grand Trunk Pacific, would be almost powerless to compete in the west with the Canadian Northern and the Canadian Pacific. The natural tendency of the Grand Trunk and the Canadian Northern organizations, if left separate, would be for each to invade the territory of the other. Remaining separate, the Grand Trunk and the Grand Trunk Pacific systems would need to spend many millions of dollars on new branches in the west, in order to hold its own with the Canadian Pacific and the Canadian Northern. And this money would be needed at once, for till it was spent neither organization would possess a complete system. Canada cannot afford all these new railways, and does not need three competitive systems.

Public ownership of the Grand Trunk Pacific and the Canadian Northern had been advocated by Borden for many years and he naturally welcomed the recommendation; given the gravity of the railway situation he moved quickly to implement it. Step-by-step over the next four years, first the Canadian Northern, then the Grand Trunk Pacific and finally the Grand Trunk itself were nationalized to create the Canadian National Railways, making it the biggest system in the country and the largest in the world apart from that of Russia. It operated over 22,110 miles of track including 1300 miles in the United States (the CPR had 13,402 miles of track), had a staff of more than 99,000, which made it the largest industrial employer in the country, and had inherited a debt of $1.3 billion.

Mackenzie and Mann retired, with a token 100 shares each as mementoes of a quarter-century of work. They dropped out of public life, and neither died a rich man. By 1918 the Canadian Northern's David B. Hanna and his management team found themselves running not only the Canadian Northern but also the government railways, including the National Transcontinental and the Intercolonial, which Borden had integrated. The Grand Trunk Pacific joined the system in 1920, but the Grand Trunk was nationalized only in 1922. Sir Joseph Flavelle, the Toronto financier who was Grand Trunk chairman in its last days, thought that without the GTP losses the Grand Trunk itself would have survived. In January 1923 the final act to incorporate the Canadian National Railways Company was passed.

Hanna took over as president in September 1918 and during the next two years, despite post-war disruptions, the industrial recession, the infamous Spanish flu epidemic and one of the worst winters in Canadian history, he built up the system. By the end of 1921 he was able to report, "the Canadian National was the only transcontinental line in North America to increase its gross earnings over those of 1920." A small "margin of net earnings" raised hopes that the new organization was getting on its feet.

In the midst of domestic reorganization, efforts were begun to establish a more integrated transportation system so as to compete more effectively with the CPR. With agents already at work in Europe, Canada's new national railway decided to open offices in Australasia and the Orient. The trans-Pacific potential anticipated a generation earlier by Laurier and Hays had finally begun to materialize, as shown by the fact that United States trade in the area had climbed from $12 million to $770 million in less than forty years. In the past eight years Canada's own exports had increased ten-fold to China, and twelve-fold to Japan.

The Canadian government was intent on improving the Pacific

David B. Hanna, vice-president of the Canadian Northern, became the first president of Canadian National Railways. *Courtesy CN*

market, but for the railway the clinching argument for opening the overseas offices lay in an entirely new development. Canada was creating its own merchant navy which, like CN, was to be a nationalized enterprise. And who better to run it than Canadian National Railways? CN's officers, mostly Canadian Northern men, had operated fast ships on the Atlantic and therefore had experience; the national railway needed a shipping arm of its own to compete with the CPR.

Canadians had always built and sailed ships. The "wooden ships and iron men" of the Maritime provinces had, like those of New England, been known around the world, but the Canadian Government Merchant Marine (CGMM) was to be something new, built and owned by the people of Canada. Its conception was due largely to Borden and to C. C. Ballantyne, the federal minister of Marine and Fisheries. A Montreal businessman who had started his career as a paint salesman, Ballantyne was fancifully described by a member of parliament as "a sort of Christopher Columbus, going over the world finding new places for Canada's export trade."

Noting that Canada had been caught short during the war by a dearth of ships, Ballantyne said it was high time Canada had its own fleet "to carry the products of our fields, mines and forests across the seas to the various countries with which I hope Canada will be doing a large export trade." He pointed out that there were fourteen shipyards around the country, most of them established during the war to build ships for Britain, that would go out of business, with a loss of 40,000 jobs, unless Canada began a building program of her own. He could not know that within four years British and American ships would be laid up because of lack of business, and there would be a glut of shipping.

Born in 1919, the Canadian Government Merchant Marine was to grow to sixty-six ships at a cost of $80 million and provide jobs for 2000 seamen. The first to go into service to the Pacific was the *Canadian Raider*, which left Vancouver on 31 January 1920 for Melbourne with a full cargo of lumber, followed a month later by the *Canadian Importer* bound for New Zealand with newsprint and lumber from British Columbia and a general cargo which included corsets from Quebec, rubber tires and chocolates from Toronto, underwear from Hamilton and bicycles from western Ontario. To handle this new traffic CN and CGMM opened the first of their joint offices in the Pacific, located at Auckland, New Zealand, and headed by George E. Bunting, a former Grand Trunk man.

That autumn a service to the Pacific from eastern Canada was begun when the *Canadian Pioneer* left Montreal for a long voyage which took her tramping to Karachi, Bombay, Calcutta, Rangoon, Singapore, the Straits Settlements and the Dutch East Indies ports of Batavia and Surabaya. "The day is not far distant," said an enthusiastic, if premature, CGMM announcement, "when the ships of our merchant marine will meet in Calcutta from both our Atlantic and Pacific ports . . . a nationally-owned transportation system that belts the world." Canada, it seemed, was to have its own version of the British all-red route, served by the largest government-owned merchant fleet in the Empire. Its house flag was a pennant of red, white and blue with an autumn-tinted maple leaf in its centre.

In 1919 the Canadian Government Merchant Marine completed 47 voyages and in 1920, 144, but these were not enough in themselves to "belt the world." An opposition member of parliament called them, unkindly, "slow tramp steamers." To fill the gaps, an arrangement was made with the British India Steam Navigation Company for a joint service from the Canadian east coast through the Suez Canal to India, and on to the Straits Settlements and Java. For ships out of British Columbia ports a similar agreement was made with Holt's Blue Funnel Line. Each company was to provide four ships to serve Japan, China, Hong Kong and the Philippines and special attention was to be paid to developing business with China through Holt's agents, Butterfield & Swires in Shanghai.

By 1921 the CGMM had fifty-four ships at sea — a feat in itself since all were built in Canadian yards in incredibly short time — sailing to Britain, Europe, the West Indies, South America, Africa and Asia. The *Canadian Prospector* had begun regular service to Kobe and Shanghai from Vancouver, there were monthly schedules direct to Australasia, and monthly sailings from the Canadian east coast to Shanghai, Java, India and Australasia.

The depression had cut freight rates by as much as 25 per cent in 1921, but the Canadian Government Merchant Marine manager, R. B. Teakle, reported that $50 million worth of goods had been shipped on his vessels. Handling only a small portion of all the Canadian foreign trade shipped that year, Teakle said, the CGMM nevertheless brought in "money that previously went into the pockets of outside carriers [and] now finds its way into the Treasury of Canada." CN's railway earnings due to Canadian Government Merchant Marine traffic were $1.5 million.

A prime reason for commencing Canadian Government Merchant Marine operations had been the promotion of British Columbia's lumber trade. Lumber shipments to Australia had

Sir Joseph Flavelle, chairman of the Grand Trunk in its final year of existence, 1921–22, blamed Charles M. Hays for the Grand Trunk's demise. *Courtesy CN*

The Canadian Government Merchant Marine operated for nearly eighteen years before it was sold off in 1936. *Courtesy CN*

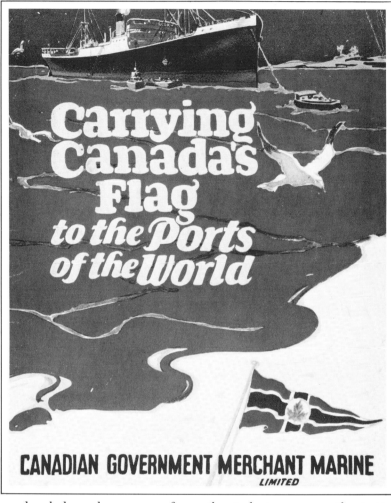

quadrupled, and response from the industry was enthusiastic. H. R. MacMillan, for one, writing to say his firm had earned a million dollars, which would otherwise have gone to American companies, in sales of rough lumber to China and Douglas-fir railway ties to India.

The CGMM was now carrying most of the Canadian exports, worth $10.5 million annually, to Australia. CN opened offices in Sydney and Melbourne and to compete with the long-established CPR, whose White Empresses were famous in Australia, it launched a drive to make itself known by advertising in the local daily newspapers as well as the *Farmers & Graziers Magazine* and the *Pastoralists Review*. Gordon F. Johnston, the manager in Sydney and a former passenger agent in Prince Rupert, devoted much time to mailing out pamphlets about Canada to doctors, lawyers, wool shippers and other potential travellers, aiming at a different group every month.

By this time Canadians had lost the romantic notion that China and Japan would become fantastically rich markets, but with Canada-China trade increasing modestly, the CN opened its first office in the Orient. In January 1922, on the eve of the Chinese New Year when the city was loud with fireworks and even the poorest coolie had taken time off to celebrate, August Brostedt arrived in Shanghai and rented space in the Glen Line building.

Born in Sweden, a Canadian since he was five years old, CN's new man in the Orient had worked his way up from telegrapher. He became a freight agent for the Canadian Northern in Calgary and for seven years was general traffic and passenger agent in Vancouver, which had given him experience in Pacific trade. At the age of forty-one, assisted by Gary M. Hemsworth and Donald E. Ross, the stocky, politely formal Brostedt began to collect the information needed so that the CN and the Canadian Government Merchant Marine could sell their prime product, which was transportation whether by sea or rail. "We tried very hard," Brostedt said, "to open the door to China and the rest of the Orient for Canadian produce and manufacturers."

Concern for CGMM traffic was only a part of his job. A constant task of a CN representative was to cultivate the contacts that would permit him to see the manifests of the various ships in harbour, and then obtain approval to stamp "Via Canadian National" in the column marked "On Carriage." This ensured that CN would get the business when the cargo, whoever carried it, arrived in North America. A commission was paid to the shipping firm involved.

Like most of the foreign population in Shanghai, which according to his reports then numbered upward of 20,000, Brostedt did much of his business on the Bund, the pleasant, wide avenue of banks and foreign firms. Jardine, Matheson & Company, Butterfield & Swires, the American Trading Company, the China Merchants Steam Shipping Company, the China Mutual Navigation Company, the Bank of Hong Kong and Shanghai, the Yokohama Specie Bank, and the Mercantile Bank of India, China and Japan were there, as well as the Shanghai Club, which did its biggest business at twelve noon and at 5 P.M. Foreigners lived in one of the self-contained international settlements, which had their own banks, clubs, churches, hotels, homes and law courts, and which contained on their forbidding gates the sign "no dogs or Chinese allowed."

Outside the international concession gates, Shanghai was a city of a million people. British, French and German warships lay down

The *Iwatesan Maru* and the *Indien* at Japan Dock, Vancouver, built in the 1920s because of the increase in trade with the Orient. *Courtesy Vancouver Public Library*

August Brostedt was sent by CN to Shanghai in 1922 to build up a network of agents throughout the Orient. *Courtesy CN*

in the Huangpu River among the deep-sea cargo vessels and the fish-shaped wooden junks, their prows painted with eyes to guide the helmsman. Along the river the storage sheds, or godowns, and the works where rag paper was made by hand and silk unwound in filatures, were being shouldered aside by new bicycle, chemical and sugar factories. There were docks and shipyards and railway shops, from whence young Chinese technicians would soon depart for CN shops in Montreal to learn new skills.

But after two generations of supremacy as the centre of trade, Shanghai was giving pride of place to the British colony down the coast. "Hong Kong is considered the centre of the Orient," Brostedt wrote to CN headquarters in Montreal, "and is a stopover and transfer point for practically all travellers. . . . Our prestige in the Far East is steadily increasing to such an extent, in fact, that we now consider we should entrench ourselves further by locating our headquarters in Hong Kong." In 1923 Brostedt moved the Asian headquarters to Hong Kong where he occupied offices in the Asiatic Petroleum Company on Queen's Road.

As Asiatic traffic manager, Brostedt's territory was huge, encompassing Japan, Malaya, Burma, Ceylon, India, the Dutch East Indies and Thailand, and within the next few years CN opened offices in Yokohama and Singapore. From Japan, Brostedt's prime interest was silk; from China, tea; rubber and pig tin from Malaysia; and jute, hemp and cotton from India. Freight from countries west of Singapore travelled to eastern Canadian ports; freight obtained east of Singapore went to Vancouver. He noted in a letter to head office:

> It will be realized that the task of securing business against the very effective competition of the CPR with their splendid ships on the Pacific, has been a difficult one. But I think substantial progress has been made; and when world conditions improve I believe our progress will be more marked than in the past. We have established cordial working arrangements with all the steamship companies serving Pacific and Atlantic ports, and I feel that these connections will be of increasing value to us in our canvass for cargo destined for Canadian and U.S.A. points reached by lines of our system.

There was an increase in Canada-China trade in 1922 but exports to Japan increased even faster, standing at $14 million compared with half a million twelve years earlier. A buyer of wood products, lead, zinc, wheat and flour, Japan was becoming one of

Canada's best customers. Its sales to Canada were poor, however, and to improve them Japan sent its first silk commission to Canada, having taken over from China the lion's share of the silk trade as a result of more modern production methods.

Vancouver, now the third largest city in Canada, had a population of 230,000, half the population of the province, and had become the major centre for all western Canada as far as eastern Saskatchewan. Import traffic had doubled in two decades. Rubber, tin, copra, eucalyptus, herbs, spices, silk and tea, ivory and ebony came to Vancouver, but it was the outbound traffic which increased most dramatically. Wheat exports sometimes were bigger than those of Montreal. Lumber sales had soared 600 per cent in ten years, though the increase to Japan was due less to sales efforts than to a natural catastrophe.

On 1 September 1923 an earthquake devastated Tokyo and Yokohama, killing thousands of people and wrecking thousands of homes. Canada sent $200,000 in relief aid, but over the long term its biggest contribution was to be lumber for reconstruction. The H. R. MacMillan Export Company found itself with so much business it was forced to open offices in Yokohama and Kobe. With his company dispatching two lumber cargoes every week on hired vessels, MacMillan decided to go into the shipping business on his own, organizing the Canadian Transport Company. In co-operation with his agents, Jardine Matheson in China and the Mitsui and Mitsubishi companies in Japan, MacMillan built up a thriving business, his thirty ships plying to Australia, Japan, China and India with wheat as well as lumber.

The industrialization of the British Columbia forest industry through the use of steam logging machines and the growth of the prairie wheat bowl were assuring Canada's place as one of the great exporting nations. The year 1923 produced the largest grain crop ever. The number of grain cars dispatched by CN increased by 70 per cent to the new Vancouver elevator, most of the wheat going to Britain by way of the Panama Canal, but increasing amounts moving to China, Japan and India. Manufactured goods were joining the flow and were to become a quarter of the value of Canada's exports to Japan before World War II. (It is interesting to note that they included many of the items — automobiles and electrical equipment — Canada currently imports from Japan.) With pulp and paper now being exported from new British Columbia mills at Powell River and Ocean Falls, the *Commercial Intelligence Journal* in Vancouver suggested that demand for manufactured goods by Asian nations would lead to establishment "on a

CN's Shanghai office on The Bund, 1922.
Courtesy CN

127

Sir Henry W. Thornton, president and chairman of the CN Board, 1922–32.

Courtesy CN

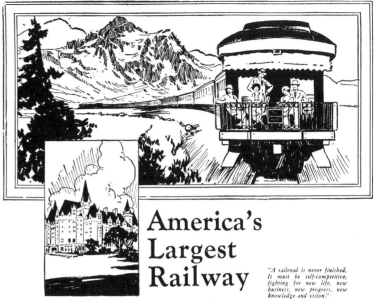

America's
Largest
Railway

"A railroad is never finished. It must be self-competitive, fighting for new life, new business, new progress, new knowledge and vision."
Sir Henry W. Thornton
Chairman and President
Canadian National Railways

~ is ever expanding

The largest railway system on this continent is Canadian National Railways. It is the very nerve and blood and sinew of a great Dominion. It is never finished because it is always growing. It is alive with enterprise and purpose, pushing forward always to new achievement, like the country of which it is a part.

Its 23,000 miles of track extend from great cities of the United States to everywhere in Canada, join Atlantic to Pacific and reach to the shores of Hudson Bay.

Canadian National is not only the largest railway in America — it serves every phase of travel and communication. It operates magnificent hotels, vacation resorts, hunting and fishing camps, steamships on two oceans, a telegraph system, radio

stations, and express service. It has more than 100,000 employees.

Radio is an attractive feature on Canadian National de luxe trains. Canadian National was the first railway in the world to provide this facility. To-day they have telephone connection on moving trains with home and office.

To-morrow the shining steel of the Canadian National network will give new life and find new wealth across far country which to-day seems only a wilderness.

Maxima in luxury and efficiency are the standards throughout the Canadian National system. To-morrow these maxima will be superseded by new achievements—finer, better, greater.

Truly it is said — America's largest railway system is ever expanding.

HONG KONG: Asiatic Bldg., Queen's Rd., C.
SHANGHAI: 608 Robert Dollar Bldg., 3 Canton Rd.

SINGAPORE: Hong Kong Bank Chambers.
YOKOHAMA: No. 7 Yamashita-Cho.

CANADIAN·NATIONAL
The Largest Railway System in America

large scale of manufacturing industries on the Pacific coast of Canada, as is becoming the case in the U.S."

Unfortunately CN's shipping organization, CGMM, was not doing well in the Asian Pacific trade. Many of its ships were unsuitable, either because of size or for other reasons, and many were better equipped for tramp service than for set schedules. The CGMM had carried little, if any, of the important wheat and silk trade, but it was not a service that CN's new president, Sir Henry Thornton, was prepared to close down. "I should say we ought to continue our Oriental service," Thornton told a parliamentary committee. "The more we study it, the more we find that it can be developed. . . . I should not feel disposed at this stage of the game to throw up the sponge and retire from the ring."

On the retirement of David Hanna eighteen months earlier, Thornton had been hired, at the urging of Prime Minister Mackenzie King, and his instinct was towards making things work rather than dismantling them. An American from Indiana who had first made his reputation with the Pennsylvania Railroad, at the age of fifty-three he was known for pulling railway operations out of trouble. Hired by the ailing Great Eastern in England, he had renovated that railway and during the war had been Inspector General of Transportation for the British Army, with the honorary rank of Major General, a service which won him a knighthood.

By the end of his first year at CN, building on what the *Ottawa Journal* called "the foundations which [Hanna] laid, wisely and courageously," Thornton reduced operating expenses and increased net earnings and his first annual report said that in an underdeveloped country like Canada the traditional methods of railway progress, such as improving its physical condition and operating methods, would not be enough. It would be necessary, he said, to go into the "matter of building up the country to support the railways." Since this was a challenge not only for the railways but also for the country as a whole, CN for its part would get on with building its freight and passenger services into an integrated transportation system that neither the Grand Trunk nor the Canadian Northern had been able to achieve. At home and abroad it would seek out new commerce and compete for existing trade with the CPR, and in the Pacific this meant going after that most prestigious of commodities, silk.

6 SILK TRAINS & SCRAP IRON

For half a century silk was the aristocrat of Canadian freight traffic, guarded by armed railway police and coddled in paper-lined express cars. Produced by worms, and prized in the 1920s and thirties for the making of ladies' stockings, its rarity, fragility and cost made it prestige cargo, and pound for pound it brought more money to the railways than passengers did.

The silk trains followed no regular schedule but appeared out of the distance like ghosts rushing past while all other traffic waited on sidings. Myths grew up about them. Nor did they always, in fact, carry silk. In eight months between July 1917 and April 1918, sixty-seven "silk trains" were cleared through from Vancouver to Halifax. Only after the war was it learned that those sealed trains actually carried 48,708 Indo-Chinese sent overseas to work as labourers behind the allied trenches in France.

Since the arrival in Vancouver on 14 July 1887 of the S.S. *Abyssinia* with sixty-five bales of silk, along with mail and eighty Chinese steerage passengers, silk had been carried by the CPR, which built special cars the better to compete with the U.S.'s Union Pacific. Charles Melville Hays had been after this trade for the Grand Trunk Pacific and the port of Prince Rupert, but up to the mid-1920s the CPR maintained its monopoly. Such was that company's grip on the trade that when CN established its first offices in the Orient it found itself obliged to take what it could get. Because of better technology, Japan had replaced China as producer of most of the world's silk, which is obtained by unravelling the cocoons made by worms fed on mulberry or oak leaves. Yokohama was the greatest silk port, and silk accounted for 40 per cent of the country's exports.

CN's largest-ever silk train, twenty-seven cars in two sections, being made up in Vancouver in October 1927. Between 1925 and 1932 CN operated more than 100 special silk trains. *Courtesy Vancouver Public Library*

Over the years Japanese merchants had arranged with the CPR to carry all the silk it possibly could even though its Empress boats had to compete with the Dollar Line which plied to San Francisco or the Nippon Yessen Kaisha ships to Portland and Seattle. Having discovered in bumper years that there was always more silk to be handled than ships to carry it, August Brostedt, CN's chief agent in the Orient, made arrangements with the Blue Funnel Line or with Japanese ships to carry silk consigned to the CN at Vancouver. Thus the CN began to get some of the trade, though in the beginning it consisted of only a car or two of baled silk attached to a regular passenger train. For the CN's aggressive president, Sir Henry Thornton, such a small share of such an important commodity was simply not enough.

With CN's revenue climbing, expenses dropping, and net earnings increasing year by year, Thornton was out to compete in any way he could with the CPR, building hotels, adding steamship routes, improving passenger services. The company was expanding its rail freight traffic and nothing could better show that CN meant business than capturing a good share of the high-status silk traffic.

In the fifteenth century, merchants considered themselves fortunate if they received their orders of silk two years after it left Canton, but since the 1880s a tradition had grown up of moving it across North America by rail at the greatest possible speed. Silk was perishable as well as valuable, and the insurance rates were as high as six per cent per hour from the time the cargo came off the boat until, under the responsibility of the carrier, it reached its destination. Most of it was sent to New York, where the National Silk Exchange was located; little inventory was kept on hand there, and brokers ordered it as needed. The Japanese merchants who controlled the shipments all the way to New York wanted it delivered to schedule since commodity prices were erratic and on a good day a pound of silk might fetch $7, but a delay might mean considerable loss of money.

To break into this market, CN had arranged that on 1 July 1925 it would start its first silk special from Vancouver to New York. If it could move silk a few hours faster via the suspension bridge at Niagara Falls than the CPR could move it through the border crossing point at Prescott, Ontario, CN could be assured of new business. Almost as if a royal train were coming through, the men responsible for the shipment were alerted well in advance. On 20 June division points from Vancouver to the U.S.-Ontario border were told to expect a cargo so valuable "it was important that

every minute possible be saved." Like the pony express of the Old West the special was to be handled like a relay race. Every 150 miles or so train crews and engines were to be changed and running gear lubricated. Dockside loading would be just as fast. Freight agents often boarded a silk boat at Victoria in order to complete their paper work before the vessel tied up at the Vancouver dock. (Later, to save a few precious hours, CN experimented with unloading at Victoria and forwarding the silk to the mainland aboard a CN ferry.) Once a silk boat had docked and the "all fast" signal was given, and long before passengers started streaming off, longshoremen were unloading baled silk in cargo slings or on conveyor belts. A bale usually weighed 133 pounds and was 36 inches tall, 24 inches wide and 12 inches deep, and some 1000 bales an hour could be unloaded. The precious commodity was encased in dingy burlap sacking and stencilled with black hieroglypics giving origin and destination. As well as raw silk there might be silk cloth in the cargo, or wild silk, which is a lower grade by-product of the unravelled cocoon.

An intriguing myth was perpetuated over the years that within each bale were living silk worms, spinning their hearts out while silk trains roared through the night on the way to New York. It makes a pretty picture but was not true; there was nothing in the bales but raw silk. It could hardly have been otherwise, since the secret of making silk, developed in north-central China 4000 years ago, lies in knowing just exactly when to kill the caterpillar while it is still in the chrysalis stage. If left too late the emerging chrysalis could wreck a cocoon; if done too early the silk would not be ready for market. Only a sericulturist highly trained and working in controlled conditions could perform this act, and certainly not in a New York warehouse.

Longshoremen in Vancouver prided themselves on loading a thirty-ton box car in fifteen minutes. From the time a ship docked to the time the train headed east, only three hours might elapse. An average time can be seen in the log of the S.S. *Achilles* of the Blue Funnel Line, which landed silk for CN at Vancouver on 19 October 1927, a year when silk imports represented 62 per cent of all Canada's inbound traffic from Japan.

Silk was packed in bales weighing 130-odd pounds and wrapped in burlap. *Courtesy CN*

Docked	7:25 A.M.
Unloading started	7:47
Loading into rail cars started	7:50
Unloading from ship finished	9:52
Loading into cars finished	10:20
Train left dock	10:26

The first CN silk train that pulled away from the Vancouver waterfront on 1 July 1925 contained a typical "silker consist" of eight sealed express (or baggage) cars, lined with protective paper against dirt and damp and guarded by two CN police with sidearms. The cargo was worth $2 million.

Veterans of the 1930s sometimes argue about the reliability of reports of how long it took each relay crew to clear the first CN silk train through on that July day more than sixty years ago. Some find the recorded times unlikely. The crew at Boston Bar, on the lower Fraser, claimed to have taken only four minutes to check all eight cars, couple on a new locomotive, and send it on its way into the mountains. At Kamloops, and again at Jasper, a minute was

A silk train changing crews and being checked over in seven minutes flat at Jasper, near Yellowhead Pass. These trains sometimes reached speeds of ninety miles an hour but few accidents were recorded. *Courtesy CN*

clipped off that time. As the train hustled down out of Yellowhead Pass towards division headquarters at Edmonton, the superintendent received a laconic message: "Nothing was left undone to help the movement of this train." Out into the wheat fields of the prairies, registering a mile a minute, the special stopped four minutes at Wainwright, Biggar and Watrous. Winnipeg, with its sprawling, busy yards, required a sluggish seven minutes. In little more than fifty hours the special was at Armstrong in the forests of northern Ontario, 1963 miles from Vancouver. Twenty hours later it was in Toronto, and three hours after that it was crossing the suspension bridge at Niagara Falls.

Up to that point the 2749-mile trip had cost CN $5,000, apart from the cost of delaying regular traffic. For the pampered silker, green lights had been glowing all the way across the country. Freight trains had been warned to get out of the way forty-five minutes before the silker came through, and even crack passenger trains were switched onto sidings. At the American border there was a rapid customs inspection in which cars were partially unloaded, the bales counted, and samples taken to verify that it was in fact duty free raw silk. The New York Central Railroad took over now for the final dash from Buffalo to New York City, or more precisely to the silk warehouses at Manufacturers Terminal in Hoboken, across the Hudson River.

Jean G. Coté recalled one of those early CN specials and marvelled at its speed:

I was working as a stenographer in the dispatcher's office in Edmonton and I learned a silk train was to leave Calder Yard at 1800 hours. I took my bicycle up the old Canadian Northern line to North Edmonton and, by pedalling hard, I got there in time to hear the 5100-class steam engine whistling off for its departure, two miles to the west.

As I stood near the signal tower the towerman cleared the main line signals for the special. In two minutes the headlight of the locomotive had expanded from pin-point size to a solar dimension, and the engine blew up a cloud of steam in the wintry twilight as it roared by. The train raised a considerable cloud of cinders, clattering away over the diamond into the twilight; soon only the twin red eyes of its last car-marker lights were visible.

The log of one train of fourteen express cars, neither the slowest nor the fastest of trips, gives some idea of a silk special's speed across the continent:

Leave Vancouver	August 15	18:21
Leave Winnipeg	August 16	15:03
Leave Hornepayne	August 18	7:45
Arrive Toronto	August 19	4:35
Leave Toronto	August 19	4:47
Arrive New York	August 19	19:50

For all their speed and prestige, the silkers were not operated by specially picked men, as might be imagined, but by whichever train crew happened to be "next up" at a terminal point. The only staff out of the ordinary consisted of two policemen who shared the tail-end combination baggage-passenger car with two brakemen and the conductor in charge of the train. Up front with the engineer, the fireman shovelled coal, except in the mountains where oil burners were used. The engines were passenger locomotives, for speed.

L. E. Scott of White Rock, British Columbia, who did his prairie railroading in the 1920s and 1930s, remembered one trip he made over a 129-mile lap from Watrous to Melville. "We had five express cars and the combination express-passenger car for the crew. The engine was 5155, a passenger type. The engineman was 'Boomer' Cardwell, one of the best." Since there was always danger the journal boxes would overheat, causing a fire and a costly delay, one of the brakemen would go out periodically onto the rear platform to sniff the air for the peculiar and unmistakable smell of an overheated hotbox. Scott recollected:

There is a rise of about 400 feet from Watrous to Kelliher, Saskatchewan, so the engine had to work hard to keep a good speed, but from there to Melville there is a drop with straight tracks for the final 30 miles. I believe we were doing well over 90 miles an hour, because small stones were sucked up onto the rear platform. On arrival at Melville the yardmaster had a switch already lined up for our engine to go to the shops where its first stop was the water tank because the tender was dry. I believe it was the first time a train had travelled non-stop over that stretch. The outgoing engine was backed onto the train and a car man checked each journal box, gave it a shot of oil from his spout can, slammed back the lid and hurried on to the next. The other fellow, making the braking test, would signal to the engineman with his lantern to apply the brakes as he walked past each car, to ensure the piston was in braking position. On arrival up at the engine he reported "six cars, all working," meaning the brakes on all cars were okay. With that done the train departed. The average time at each terminal was less than ten minutes, so I wonder when I hear reports that they were ever done in three minutes.

There were remarkably few accidents. Coté recalled one:

In December 1928, or 1929, the Canadian National lost several cars of silk in the Fraser Valley . . . the bales were picked up at the derailment site, loaded into boxcars, and moved by the first freight available to Edmonton. As the accident occurred just before Christmas, the Edmonton freight handlers were called to work overtime on December twenty-fifth hauling the bales of silk from freight cars to passenger-service cars. Jim Low, who loved a challenge, told chief dispatcher Arthur McRae that he would have the freight shed crew fired if they did not transfer that cargo pronto, even on Christmas Day. But he did not have to carry out his threat. The bales were transshipped and the silk special departed promptly from Edmonton without further incident.

The most serious accident occurred between Haig and Yale in the Fraser canyon of British Columbia on 21 September 1927, the CPR's first silk special accident though it had been running silk trains for three decades. While rounding a curve, one of the cars

Even crack passenger trains, like the Confederation Limited seen crossing Cisco Bridge in B.C.'s Fraser Canyon, had to give priority to silk trains. *Courtesy CN*

of a ten-car train fell into the river and sank. Two or three others followed it to the water's edge, one of them spilling silk into the Fraser. Most of the bales were soaked with mud and water and weighed three times more than their normal 130-odd pounds by the time they were recovered. The salvage experts kept them wet, pouring water on them all the way to Hoboken, where they were to be reconditioned. C. C. LaFrenay, of U.S. customs at Ogdensburg, New York, was on duty when the salvaged silk came through: "At the time I was the acting appraiser and together with other officers was called to the New York Central freight terminal to inspect and appraise the silk. Upon the opening of the cars we found the bales to be water soaked and much of it appeared to us to be worthless on account of mud and the fact that moisture had caused a portion to heat."

During the next decade, from 1925 to about 1936, CN competed neck and neck with the CPR and the Great Northern which started from Seattle. In 1930 the freight rate on silk from Vancouver to New York was $9 per 100 pounds, and the portion of this earned by CN was $7.85, the balance going to the American railroad handling shipments beyond the Ontario–New York border. The largest CN special ran in October 1927, consisting of twenty-one cars in two sections and containing 7200 bales worth $7 million. Someone estimated that it had taken two billion worms to produce that much silk.

R. H. Davis of *Railroad Magazine* recalled his encounter with that particular train while heading west on CN's Confederation Limited and being sidetracked at Armstrong, Ontario, to let it roar through:

Two miles westward an aura of light burst against the black night. A whistle screamed as out of the dark, the headlight shining along the glistening rails, thundered Section One with its precious cargo. The brakes groaned, the engine whistled, and the silk special brought up with tremendous clanking. A new engine replaced the hot monster that had come through the last 147 miles; the train crew gave way to a fresh detachment; the cars were watered, the brakes inspected, the locks in each car examined by special officers; and in exactly four minutes Section One was on its way. . . .

The peak year for silk traffic was 1929 when Vancouver and the American west coast ports between them sent half a million bales valued at $325 million by rail to New York. Because silk was shuttled across the country from coast to coast under lock and key, its movement was on the "land bridge" principle, which means that a commodity is brought by ship to a west coast port, carried by rail to the east coast, and then by ship again to Europe. Since silk usually stopped at New York, this term might more aptly be applied to the large movement of Asian lily bulbs to Europe. The lily bulbs were carried by Japanese ships to Vancouver, by CN rail to the east coast, and by Cunard ships to Europe and took about twenty-one days against forty-five via southeast Asia and the Suez. So many problems were encountered that this traffic was abandoned, though it would be tried again in the 1960s for the transport of mandarin oranges from Japan to Europe.

Canada's trade with the Asian Pacific Rim countries in 1929 consisted of $87 million in exports and $33 million worth of imports. The *Port of Vancouver News* boasted that "taken all in all, this is Canada's era in the Pacific. . . . Vancouver, rather than San Francisco is now considered the leading Pacific port." In a decade the number of piers — one of them named the Japan Wharf — had doubled to twenty-four and could handle sixty-three vessels at one time. No less than thirty steamship lines were serving the port. Where there had been one oil refinery in 1920 there now were four. Two drydocks had been built. Vancouver's lumber shipments had increased five-fold, and it had replaced the Lakehead as the grain export terminal for Alberta and much of Saskatchewan. From one elevator in 1920 the port now had seven and there were elevators in Victoria, New Westminster and Prince Rupert, where the first Japanese-owned grain ship had arrived in 1926.

The export of flour, only a small business in 1920, had increased ten-fold with Japan becoming the principal market. The "Flour King" of Japan, Tuechiro Shoda, who owned twelve mills, said during a visit to Vancouver in 1929 that fifteen years earlier Vancouver had been unknown as a grain exporter and he had been dependent on the United States. In 1921 he had begun to receive small quantities from Vancouver and now most of Japan's needs were being supplied via that port.

Canada was sending Japan more than one third of its wood pulp requirements, a million and a half cases of salmon, and large quantities of lead and zinc. Imports from Japan were, as usual, considerably smaller, a quarter the size of Canada's exports, though Canada was Japan's best customer for rice and its second best market for tea. In two years trade had increased 30 per cent and Japan now was Canada's third best customer, after the United States and the United Kingdom. The Japanese government chose Vancouver as headquarters for its first North American trade commissioner, whose territory was to include Washington and Oregon as well as western Canada. That same year, 1929, diplomatic relations were established, with Prince Iemasa Tokygawa heading the mission to Ottawa. Herbert Marler, a Montreal lawyer, businessman and former Liberal cabinet minister, headed the legation in Tokyo, which was the third Canada had opened in the world, the others being in Washington and Paris.

Exports to China, smaller than those to Japan, had increased by 1929 to the point where Canada was China's fifth largest trading partner after Japan, the United States, Britain and Germany. Exports were wheat, timber and silver bullion. As with Japan, Canada had a favourable, even top-heavy, trade balance, imports from China being a fifth the size of exports and consisting largely of nuts. Hong Kong's importance as an entrepôt for China, Siam, Java and the Straits Settlements, had grown, prompting the Canadian government to open a trade commissioner's office six years after CN's Hong Kong office was established.

August Brostedt was keen to capture some of the CPR's long-established passenger business in the same manner he had gone after silk, for in addition to selling freight services to Canada, CN was in the passenger business both to Canada and to Europe, and

By the late 1920s Vancouver rivalled San Francisco as North America's leading Pacific port. *Courtesy CN*

served as booking agents for the great shipping lines. "Practically all the travellers to and from the East stop over at Hong Kong for at least one or two days, inasmuch as they have to transfer from one steamer to another," Brostedt informed C. W. Johnston, the general passenger traffic agent in Montreal. To solicit their business he needed offices more accessible than those on the second floor of the Asiatic Petroleum Company Building and his choice was the ground floor of the new Gloucester Building on Peddar Street, one of Hong Kong's main thoroughfares on the way from the passenger docks to the Hong Kong Hotel. When these quarters were opened, complete with Canadian scenes on the walls and a reception area that looked more like a private sitting room than a railway office, Brostedt declared, "I feel that we now have an office worthy of our standing in the transportation world and one that will greatly enhance our prestige throughout the Orient."

Brostedt was responsible for agents in Yokohama, Shanghai and Singapore, the latter beginning to secure valuable traffic in crude rubber, canned pineapples, tin from the Straits Settlements, rice from Burma, and jute, burlap and tea from India and Ceylon. In that era before fast airliners it was impossible to provide much supervision from Hong Kong. "As you are aware," Brostedt informed Montreal head office, "to all intents and purposes these offices are at present operating as separate entities, financing expenditures by letters of credit on Montreal, signing and receiving advice direct on cargo movements, solicitation requests, etc."

The increasing business handled by CN's Asian offices in the late 1920s was a distant echo of the growth of CN in Canada. The prosperity of the second half of the decade coupled with Sir Henry Thornton's exuberance had built one of the world's finest railway passenger services. More to the point, since in Canada the carriage of freight rather than passengers is what makes or breaks a railway, Thornton and his staff increased freight revenue. Taking advantage of traffic from the new industrial plants springing up across the country, the CN doubled revenue year after year and began to pay off the heavy debt inherited from its predecessor companies.

Not all the news was good. While CN's shipping company, the CGMM, was doing well enough to Australasia, it was losing money heavily on its other Pacific services. The Japanese merchant marine had increased dramatically in size until it ranked third, after Britain and the United States, and too many ships were competing for traffic. Canadian operating costs were too high, freight rates too low. CN decided to pull the CGMM out of the Orient and turn to a more promising route, the West Indies.

As the Great Depression began to spread, few Canadian politicians or business leaders seemed to understand that trade with the Orient was entering a long period of decline rather than growth. "The greatest event in trade in the next few years will be the growth and swing of Asian trade away from Europe across the Pacific to North America," asserted the *Vancouver Sun* on 3 October 1930. Not long before his defeat by the Conservatives, Prime Minister Mackenzie King had written with similar optimism to the Canadian minister in Tokyo, Marler: "The whole country is beginning to realize the possibilities of trade with the Orient."

With the election of the Conservatives under Richard B. Bennett, the new minister of trade and commerce, Henry H. Stevens, declared: "The greatest expansion will be achieved in the northern Pacific in development of trade with the Orient." Stevens gave his blessing to an Asian trade delegation organized by the Canadian Chamber of Commerce, which included a representative of CN. On that occasion John M. Imrie, managing director of the *Edmonton Journal* and the delegation leader, anticipated the Canadian export trade that was to develop only a generation later:

Many have expressed regret that Canada's great area of agricultural land is in the West and therefore far removed from Europe. But changing world conditions may make this a matter for congratulation rather than regret. It has become trite but nonetheless true to say that the centre of world trade is being shifted from the

Atlantic to the Pacific. British Columbia is Canada's front door on the Pacific seaboard. Most important of all, Canada's chief exports are in large measure a complement to domestic production in Japan and China. To those two countries Canada is closer geographically than any other Occidental nation.

Chinese labourers unloading grain on the Shanghai docks. Canadian efforts to compete with the United States and Australia in wheat sales went largely unrewarded until the early 1960s. *Courtesy China Morning Post, Hong Kong*

Soon after the Canadian Chamber of Commerce visit, trade with the Orient declined and Australia supplanted Canada as Japan's principal grain supplier. After an effort to increase grain sales, Marler returned from a trip to China "a very disappointed man." While there were possibilities, he said, they were neither very great nor could they be expected in the near future. "For two years I have been trying to persuade grain growers and millers to investigate conditions in the Oriental market, but so far entirely without success."

In Ottawa Stevens, too, blamed Canadian businessmen. Many of the ships in Canada's own merchant marine were equipped with a passenger cabin or two so businessmen could sail out to the Orient themselves, and Canada had set up an extensive network of trade commissioners. Neither the ships nor the commissioners had been made proper use of. "It is abundantly clear to all thoughtful persons that there is an existing market, of which Canada is not securing her reasonable share due to lack of enterprise on the part of her people," Stevens contended. There were commissioners in Tokyo, Kobe, Shanghai, Hong Kong, Singapore/Batavia, and in the North China cities of Tientsin and Darian. "It is hopeless for the government to provide these facilities if the merchants and manufacturers of Canada do not themselves make direct personal contact in these foreign countries and develop their own trade connections," he said. To combat what he saw as Canada's commercial lethargy, Stevens called in his world-wide trade commissioners to tour Canada and whip up enthusiasm for foreign trade, but because of the Depression his efforts proved largely irrelevant.

As an indicator of the times, CN's earnings had fallen 40 per cent below its peak year of 1928. CN was carrying only half the traffic of two years earlier, the effects of the economic downturn having been exacerbated by a smaller grain crop than normal and the increasing tendency of the Japanese to ship their silk to the east coast via the Panama Canal.

From 1926 to 1930 Thornton's policy of spending money to make money had been supported by the Liberal government, but the Conservatives had come to power and the onset of the Depression called for grim retrenchment. There was talk of amalgamating CN with the CPR, for a saving of some $60 million. A royal commission under Justice L. P. Duff, established to look into the whole railway setup, was highly critical, asserting that "the serious and continuing deficits of the Canadian National Railways system, and the diminishing revenues of the CPR . . . have been brought about in part by duplication of tracks, facilities and services of every kind."

Sir Henry, while agreeing that his predecessors had "in an outburst of enthusiasm and perhaps undue optimism" overbuilt, felt the commission findings unfair. Since the days of David B. Hanna a heterogeneous, nearly bankrupt collection of railways, some 22,000 miles of track, had been moulded into an efficient system. In the optimistic years of growth in the mid-twenties, Sir Henry, a larger-than-life figure in more ways than merely his imposing physical size, had seemed the ideal man to run the railway. He had an instinct for attracting loyal support for himself and CN by such actions as his midnight visits to the rail yards to chat with train crews. This did wonders for the morale of a company still struggling to unite various predecessor organizations, some of whom had competed in the past, spread over

thousands of miles. But what had seemed good, progressive management in more prosperous times was now, with the onslaught of the Depression, looked upon as extravagance. He had done what he had been expected to do, even if the cost was too great and expansion too fast. Like Tyler of the Grand Trunk during the troubled economy of the 1890s, Thornton was a victim of a depressed era. In 1932, the last year of Thornton's presidency, CN's operating revenues decreased 20 per cent from the previous year. Tired and ailing, Thornton handed in his resignation. Less than a year after he left, on 14 March, he died at the age of sixty-two at the home of a relative in New York City, hours before a testimonial dinner was to have been given for him. His successor, Samuel J. Hungerford, who had been vice-president in charge of operations, was more in the traditional mould, a former master mechanic for Canadian Northern whose work had taken him into every division across the country.

Within a year business began to improve through Canada's efforts to increase trade with other members of the Empire. With Canada's exports falling 30 per cent as the Depression gripped the world, Prime Minister Bennett had invoked the solidarity of the British Empire to revive trade. In Ottawa during four weeks of the summer of 1932 the first Imperial Economic Conference ever held outside England devised quotas and increased customs duties on non-Empire trade, and as a result exports doubled to countries like India, which took to buying Canadian rather than American automobiles. Trade improved to the Straits Settlements, Ceylon and, to a lesser extent, Hong Kong. There was a notable increase in trade with Australasia since Canada was able to recapture the lumber market from the Americans and increase shipments of

The Japanese freighters *Yeiufuku Maru* and *Aden Maru* taking aboard the first grain shipments from Prince Rupert, 22 October 1926. Despite the new elevator, the port saw only moderate traffic, and within four years even that was eliminated by the Great Depression. *Courtesy Public Archives of Canada /PA 95649* newsprint, canned salmon and automobiles. The effects were felt throughout the CN organization, including the CGMM, which chalked up increases in ocean freight revenues hauling newsprint and automobiles to Sydney and Melbourne.

Business was picking up generally by 1936 and CN had ten agents in the Pacific. The Australian staff under Gordon F. Johnston consisted of three. In Yokohama were general agent Donald E. Ross, Jack M. Middlecoat and T. Nishimura, a local man who covered Kobe and Osaka. The Japanese office was responsible for Japan's colonies, Korea and Taiwan. Southeast Asia was covered from Singapore by Lawrence L. Lawler and Harold G. S. Barlow, whose territory also included Burma, India, Ceylon and Siam. With Brostedt in Hong Kong were Charles T. Barr and Wilfred J. Dyment, and the agent in Shanghai was Gary M. Hemsworth. The ending of the Depression, however, was bringing some unwelcome changes in trade patterns. Since the Japanese invasion of Manchuria in 1932, trade with China had been decreasing. Ninety per cent of Japan's silk trade was reaching New York via the Panama Canal, robbing Canada's railways of valuable freight. In 1936 the CN-operated Canadian Government Merchant Marine went out of business, the Depression being only one of many reasons for its demise. In the end the only run the CGMM had been able to make money on was the service to Australia and New Zealand. Wheat exports to Japan were a third of what they had been four years earlier, due to competition from Australia, which now dominated the market. To complicate matters, Canada and Japan got into a brief trade war when Canada raised protectionist tariffs against Japanese imports, as it did against other non-Empire goods, and the Japanese retaliated by levying heavy duty on Canadian wheat and forest products. Commercial co-operation between the two nations was resumed when the Liberal government of Mackenzie King came to power in 1935 and exports to Japan reached a new high of $26 million.

But then the Japanese began to restrict imports not vital to their preparations for a war and, except for one notable commodity, strategic metal, exports to Japan started to decline. Unable to produce sufficient iron and steel themselves for the ships and guns they were turning out, the Japanese removed customs duties and offered dealers high prices for steel, aluminum, lead, nickel and zinc. Once Britain and the United States, Japan's main suppliers of metals and scrap iron, cut off sales of these commodities, the Japanese turned to Canada. By 1938 Canadian scrap metal exports to Japan had increased to $1 million a year, and many Canadians

In the years before World War II, scrap iron for the Japanese war effort was one of Canada's major exports to that country.
Courtesy Vancouver Public Library

realizing the implication of such sales, became alarmed. Demonstrators appeared on the docks of Vancouver to protest, and there were sharp debates in parliament. "During the past four years, despite all our protestations of peace, this country has continued to be a source of supply for the aggressive nations who are rearming," said Tommy Douglas, leader of the CCF party in the House of Commons. But the government decided against sanctions, on grounds they would prove counter-productive; only in 1939 were Canada's steel and scrap iron exports suspended, and it was early 1940 before embargoes were applied to other strategic metals.

As Japan's anti-western "Greater East Asia Co-prosperity Sphere" policy spread through the Orient, travel disruptions and restrictions made normal business difficult. When the Japanese began a full-scale war in China and seized Shanghai in 1937, CN, in common with other western firms, closed its office. The outbreak of war with Europe in September 1939, followed by Japan's hostile attitude towards Britain and the United States, and her 1940 treaty of alliance with Germany and Italy, raised the question of whether Canadians should try to maintain business as usual. Brostedt recommended that the three remaining offices, in Hong Kong, Yokohama and Singapore, remain open, each staffed with

R. C. Vaughan, president of CN during the war years. *Courtesy CN*

two men. Brostedt himself, after almost twenty years in the Far East, was about to retire in Canada, and occupied himself with recommendations as to how the CN offices should be organized once the crisis, which he saw largely limited to China, began to abate. So successful had the Japanese war planners been in concealing their intentions that there was little realization in the Canadian business community that Japan was preparing to fight Britain and the United States.

By the spring of 1941, however, it was clear that Japan was seeking a pretext to break off diplomatic relations, and in July Canadian businessmen, including the CN staff in Yokohama, found themselves in trouble. Britain denounced all her trade treaties with Japan and then, on 26 July, Britain, Canada and the United States froze Japanese assets. Japan at once took similar measures against the two western powers, effectively shutting down all trade. With Canadian firms automatically falling onto Japan's "black list," CN had no alternative but to close its Yokohama office. Before the end of that hectic day, CN president Robert C. Vaughan in Montreal tried to contact the two Canadians in Yokohama, Donald Ross and his assistant, Stanley Healey. With normal communications disrupted, Vaughan's instructions had to be sent through the Department of External Affairs in Ottawa to the Canadian Chargé d'Affaires in Tokyo, D'arcy McGreer, whose message to Ross read: "I have received word that you and Healey are to leave Japan at once. You should confer with CPR suggesting common action regarding offices. You are authorized to use your discretion in the matter of office closing."

Ross, a twenty-five year veteran of CN service, was in poor health and under doctor's care. He was instructed to return to Canada by ship with his wife. Healey, a bachelor from San Francisco, who had been employed by CN in Yokohama for four years, would stay behind to close the office. He was then to proceed to Hong Kong to assist Jack Middlecoat, an Australian. Those preparations were to drag on two months and for Healey would turn into a nightmare.

Complications and hostility mounted. In August a group of Canadian missionaries was arrested for taking photographs in a military zone. The newspapers reported that under a new law foreigners must seek permission to leave Japan, first from the Ministry of Finance in Tokyo and then from the local police. Further inquiry revealed that though there was no law to that effect on the books, it was common practice for a foreign firm closing down to pay Japanese staff the equivalent of one month's salary for every year worked. "To put it bluntly," Healey reported, "the police intimated that 'no allowances for the Japanese staff, no permit to leave Japan will be granted.' " The local staff consisted of a secretary, Miss Y. Kasai, a freight solicitor, T. Nishimura, both of whom had more than twelve years' service, and an office boy. Although CN was not adverse to severance pay, there was not sufficient money in the company's local account, even if Healey could get it unfrozen, and Montreal's efforts to get the money to Japan were blocked by harsh new restrictions. Eventually, however, Middlecoat at Hong Kong was able to get the money through and the employees received their severance pay.

Ross's health made it advisable that he and his wife sail as soon as possible, but the rush of foreigners out of the country limited the possibility of getting ship accommodations. Ross received permission to sail from Kobe on a Japanese ship, only to find there was no room. Finally, armed with documents from the Kagacho district police station in Yokohama, he booked passage aboard a Japanese ship sailing from Kobe to Shanghai; the Rosses were at last able to start their journey back to Canada.

"After Mr. and Mrs. Ross sailed," recalled Healey, "the situation in Japan became most unpleasant and for a time it looked as though I would have to remain in Japan for an indefinite period. We were informed that a British evacuation vessel was to call at Yokohama. Immediately on hearing this I applied to the British consulate to secure passage to Hong Kong. The British Consul General was quite prepared to accept me, but being an American, the Japanese authorities refused me permission to sail, claiming the vessel was for British only."

At the CN office in the Butterfield & Swires Building at 7 Yamashita-cho, Healey, having destroyed the company's confidential documents, found himself frequently visited by the police. "They stated that before any permission to leave would be granted they wished to satisfy themselves that we were leaving no unpaid bills behind and that they wished to inspect every transaction from the time of the 'freeze-up.' They found nothing to complain about." Healey's personal funds were running out and because of the freeze he could bring in no money. He sold off office furniture, carefully accounting to Montreal for every dollar.

Finally in late September Healey was informed by the police that he could depart. The only stipulation was that he was to be accompanied by a Japanese citizen, Nishimura of CN, who would

Jack Middlecoat: his knowledge of Far East trade helped build the CN network.
Courtesy CN

149

Stanley Healey returned to the Far East after World War II in an effort to renew CN's contacts. *Courtesy CN*

be responsible for his "conduct in passing through the fortified areas of Shininosaki, Moji, Satsebo and while in Nagasaki." Healey left by train the same day. As he recalled:

> Boarding the *Shanghai Maru* at Nagasaki will remain forever in my mind as a nightmare. The arrogance of the customs officials was at its best. Being a designated foreigner, they made me personally transfer my baggage from the pier to the customs house and back again, a distance of one good city block. No Japanese transfer men or red caps were allowed to touch my baggage nor was Mr. Nishimura allowed to come anywhere near the pier or customs house to help me. My wardrobe trunk, weighing over two hundred pounds, proved a difficulty. The customs inspection was terribly severe, going so far as having me remove my shoes, looking into the lining of my neckties. . . . The parting words of our Mr. Nishimura were 'Mr. Healey, as a Japanese gentleman I am ashamed of the way you have been treated today.' It was, I must say, just an out-and-out case of humiliation.

As unpleasant as the experience was for Healey and hundreds of westerners like him, it had its sequel and more on the other side of the Pacific when 20,000 Japanese Canadians lost their homes and businesses and the government consigned them to internment camps far from the west coast.

Joining Middlecoat in Hong Kong, where he found a newly arrived Canadian force of two battalions sent out to help the British army contingent, Healey wrote that "for the first time in months I have a feeling of security." He did not have long to enjoy it, for with the opening of war, heralded by the raid on Pearl Harbor early in December, the Japanese attacked Hong Kong, which fell on Christmas Day 1941. It was the first time Canadian troops were engaged in combat in World War II; 290 soldiers lost their lives while another 260 died in internment camps. Four days later CN vice-president Alistair Fraser in Montreal wrote to Vaughan, "I am sorry to have to report that since the occupation of the island of Hong Kong by the Japanese, we have heard no more of our representatives at that point, and it is presumed they were still on the island at the time of the Japanese occupation." Not until June 1942 did CN receive word of the fate of Middlecoat, his wife and Healey. Seized with only the clothes they had on, they had spent six months in an internment camp and were now being transported on a Japanese ship to Lourenço Marques, Mozambique, the neutral Portuguese colony in East Africa, for

During the war the Prince Rupert shipyard built a dozen 10 000-ton ships and several naval vessels. Up to then its largest projects had been two Canadian Government Merchant Marine vessels in the 1920s.
Courtesy CN

transfer to the Swedish prisoner exchange ship *Gripsholm*. They arrived in New York 25 August with 1450 others, including sixty Canadians and the American Ambassador to Tokyo, Joseph C. Grew. Middlecoat would spend the rest of the war years working at CN head office in Montreal; Healey joined the American navy as a transport officer.

Twenty years of CN effort to promote Asian Pacific trade had come to a violent end. There is no doubt the effort had been useful, contributing to the prosperity of the country, the national railway, and the growth of the port of Vancouver. Unfortunately the port specifically built for Asian trade, Prince Rupert, had hardly benefitted at all. For all the talk of its relative proximity to Japan, its isolation and the lack of population in northern British Columbia had worked against it. Since the amalgamation in the early 1920s of the Grand Trunk Pacific and the Canadian North-

Canada's only armoured train was built by CN to patrol its line east of Prince Rupert when a Japanese invasion seemed possible early in World War II. Pulled by one of the first diesel engines, it consisted of half a dozen armoured cars. *Courtesy CN*

ern, most of the trains of Canadian National Railways took the southern route from Red Pass Junction, west of the Yellowhead Pass, to Vancouver. Few ships called at Prince Rupert except to pick up an occasional load of grain. The only activity to prosper in the community of 6000 people was the halibut industry.

But early in 1942 the war in the Pacific achieved what years of peacetime efforts had failed to do. With the Japanese army over-running Attu and Kiska in the foggy Aleutians and edging dangerously close to mainland North America, the United States Army was building up defence forces in Alaska. The Joint Chiefs of Staff in Washington had discovered that the CN northern line connected with the transportation network of the United States and ended only eighty miles from Alaska's port of Ketchikan. From Seattle, ships travelled more than 1000 miles to reach Alaska, but a railhead at Prince Rupert would eliminate one third of that haul and permit a faster buildup of troops and supplies.

With Canadian assent, the American army turned Prince Rupert into a major supply base in a matter of months. Docks, warehouses and administrative buildings sprang up, and on Acropolis Hill above the town, barracks housed 3500 soldiers. Watson Island was turned into a munitions dump to contain 200,000 tons of high explosives, part of the millions of tons of war matériel hauled in over the northern line. The passenger service, which had run three trains to Prince Rupert a week, now had to organize four or five troop trains every day as 75,000 soldiers bound for Alaska arrived in a steady stream. In one month more tonnage came down the single-tracked railway than arrived in a year before the war.

A highway to Prince Rupert was built beside the tracks from Hazelton. Soldiers guarded bridges like the 195-foot span at Skeena Crossing, and CN mounted Canada's first armoured train, to patrol from Prince Rupert deep into the interior. At Prince Rupert two forts and an airbase were built and the shipyard had the task of repairing 400 ships in the course of the war and building a dozen 10,000-ton merchant ships as well as four minesweepers. The population rose to more than 20,000, a size it had never known before.

7 THE NEW PACIFIC

"This is the beginning of the new Pacific Age, an age which will open the doors of the twenty-first century."

Prime Minister Zenko Suzuki of Japan, June 1982

IN 1947, THE YEAR ZENKO SUZUKI left his work in the fishing industry and entered politics, the idea that Japan would lead the world into a new age would have seemed wildly improbable to all but the omniscient. Japan's economy had been shattered by a war that had ended in the terror of the atom bomb. National production had been reduced by two thirds. A nation which must import its raw material had been stripped of the colonies that provided resources and accounted for half of Japan's pre-war territory, including Korea and Taiwan. The *zaibatus*, the great combines that had activated and dominated economic life, had been disbanded. Trade, such as it was, was controlled by a foreign power in the form of the American army of occupation. On a Canadian mission to Tokyo that year, Gen. H. D. Crerar, representing one of the few nations still capable of healthy foreign trade, predicted it would be a long time indeed before Japan would be able to engage in normal commerce.

Prospects were little better across the Yellow Sea, where China was caught up in the civil war that would result in its turning to Communism. And in the great sweep of Southeast Asia a militant nationalism portended the end of the colonial empires of the Netherlands, Britain, France and Portugal. Canadian business, traditionally reluctant to penetrate the mysteries of the Orient, had little reason to do so now. The future, it seemed, lay in North America and a reborn Europe.

The New Pacific. In little over a century Hong Kong has grown from a fishing village into a city of five and a half million people, with a market economy based on light industry and international trade. *Courtesy CN (Hong Kong)*

155

But few wars have stifled trade for long, and barely four months after the end of World War II the first signs that the Orient was reopening for business began to reach CN headquarters through the mails. A travel agent who had done business with CN in the 1930s wrote in to ask about the railway's plans; a former employee in Hong Kong enquired about a job; there were queries from firms in Calcutta and Singapore. Alistair Fraser, vice-president of the freight traffic (marketing) department, pulled out Brostedt's plans for post-war deployment and asked his passenger and freight managers where to begin. "The present is not an opportune time to open any offices in the Orient," they said. About all anyone could tell with certainty was that the Far East was undergoing terrific change.

Shipping, released from military duty, became available again. Two new lines established service between Vancouver, Shanghai, the Philippines and Singapore and expressed a desire to work closely with the CN, whose own shipping arm in the Pacific, the CGMM, had been sold off in the 1930s. The silk trade, which had all but died before the war, revived briefly when the S.S. *Windermere Park* docked at Vancouver with 244 bales, which were loaded into one of CN's new steel box cars for New York.

In 1946 prospects looked a little brighter, at least in the British colonies, and both CN and CPR decided to reopen offices in Hong Kong, less because of the trade potential in the colony itself than for its reputation as an entrepôt. Many of the people who had served in the East were retired or dead, but Jack Middlecoat was available, and in October he was back in the city he had last seen as a prisoner of war. Whereas the CPR opened a second office in Shanghai, CN broke new ground by sending Stan Healey, now demobilized from the U.S. armed forces, to Calcutta. CN had never had an agent in India before, but business looked promising in the 1930s and there was a big post-war demand for jute, rubber and tea, all of which India produced. Within months of reaching his new post in March 1947, Healey wrote that he was in a position to report on "every pound of cargo leaving India destined to Canadian ports."

Being at the source of the traffic, rather than at the final destination, Middlecoat and Healey were able to improve on what had been more or less random efforts by CN freight solicitors in Canada to ascertain what cargoes were en route so they could be picked up at dockside and moved inland by rail. Unfortunately, the Far East economy was too confused to yield the volume of business they had hoped for. Commerce with China, which had been promising while the Nationalists maintained a purchasing mission in Ottawa during the war, dwindled as the Communists assumed control of the country. Diplomatic relations with the Communists were strained and would soon be broken off, and an effort to establish a shipping link between Shanghai and Prince Rupert came to nothing. The cost of maintaining an agent in India, even working out of his own home, was proving more than anticipated. As for Japan, it was in no position to export goods, and its imports from Canada were valued at an insignificant half million dollars a year. In August 1948 Middlecoat and Healey were ordered back home because of "unsettled conditions." Almost fifteen years would pass before a permanent CN office was re-established in the Far East, and while there can be no doubt that some business was lost during this long hiatus there was not, in the early years, a great deal of traffic of the sort that would have brought much profit. At all events, CN had pressing priorities elsewhere.

Like other North American railways it had been drained by fifteen years of economic depression and war. It was struggling with the vast debt inherited from its predecessor companies at the time of amalgamation, and concerned with replacing worn equipment. It had grown into one of Canada's largest companies, with more than 110,000 employees, but was in danger of becoming more of a national institution than a vibrant, multi-faceted transportation service. To rejuvenate the crown corporation the government hired Donald Gordon, a large, ebullient Scot who had left the Bank of Canada to run the Wartime Prices and Trade Board. He took over as president in 1950 and began the costly task of converting the railway from steam to diesel. Its trans-Atlantic sales organization, started by the Grand Trunk in 1908, was beefed up to 125 people in anticipation of a renewal of trade with Britain and Europe. The Pacific would have to wait, as Gordon intimated to an audience in Prince Rupert during his first trip to the West in 1950: "It may be that the recent political developments in the Far East have robbed you, for the time being at least, of an important trade potential."

Although it brought no benefits to Prince Rupert, the trade prospect in the Pacific began to change that very year. The outbreak of the Korean war caused a surge of westbound traffic through Vancouver. American military spending in Japan restored a measure of economic health to that country, and by the time the Japanese peace treaty was signed in 1951, giving Japan the freedom to conduct its own trade, the economy had grown considerably from its post-war low. An urgent need for food and raw materials pushed imports from Canada to $100 million a year, and the arrival of the first Japanese freighters at Vancouver was a harbinger of prosperity to come. The port of Vancouver, having grown steadily in importance since the opening of the Panama Canal in 1914 and the subsequent construction of grain terminals, entered a new era.

Patterns now began to emerge — including Canada's adherence to the Colombo Plan for Co-operative Economic Development in South and Southeast Asia — which drew Canada into the Asian Pacific to a degree unheard of before the war. Canada befriended Japan when it needed all the friends it could get, supporting it at international meetings on trade and tariffs and supplying it with the cereals, wood products and minerals its own colonies had supplied before the war. Prime Minister Sigeru Yoshida visited Ottawa, and Prime Minister Louis St. Laurent became the first Canadian head of government to visit Japan. In 1954 the two nations signed a commercial agreement which, due largely to exports of wheat, restored Japan to the rank of Canada's third largest customer, after the United States and Britain.

Not that this did the railways much good, because wheat was a commodity on which they lost money. This had been the case for over half a century, since the signing of the Crow's Nest Pass Agreement in 1897, wherein grain shippers were required to pay only a fifth of the rail freight cost while the railways absorbed the balance. So at a time when wheat began to account for a quarter of all freight traffic, CN was getting only 10 per cent of its revenue from it. Lumber, the other major western export, was potentially more lucrative, but since it was produced near the coast, exports to the Pacific required short rail hauls at best.

Rail business with Australia, on the other hand, was profitable because that country was buying Canadian manufactured goods, including automobiles, which turn a profit. The Australians being great travellers, Australia also promised a lucrative passenger business as people resumed their pilgrimages to "the Old Country." To prevent the CPR from getting all that business, the Cunard Line in England, which had worked closely with CN since it tied in with the Canadian Northern many years earlier, suggested the two companies team up. Cunard would carry passengers by ship from Australia to Vancouver, CN would rail them across the country and the shipping company would pick them up again at an east coast port and transport them to England. Gordon, who was keen to transform the national railway into what he called "a complete

transportation service," approved the idea and hosted a dinner for the two CN passenger agents picked to go to Australasia to establish the service. While he was at it he approved a proposal to send Middlecoat, the company's ranking expert on the Far East, to look over prospects in Japan.

CN revenue from Pacific trade was hardly a fifth of its income from trans-Atlantic business, though there had been impressive growth in exports, not only of wheat but also of scrap iron for Japan's new steel mills and lumber for a country that had depleted its own forests. Japan in turn was exporting textiles, household goods and steel products for Alberta's new oil industry. "The general impression I have gained is that business is picking up month by month and that Canada is in the market very strongly," reported Middlecoat, after visiting seventy business concerns in Tokyo, Yokohama, Kobe, Osaka and Nagoya in 1956. He also found time in a busy five weeks to solicit 4000 tons of rail freight business. "I feel confident that with direct representation we should be able to build up our business and goodwill," he said.

In Montreal his recommendation was welcomed by William A. Watson, manager of the foreign freight department and a veteran of pre-war service in Singapore, and endorsed by the passenger and general freight departments and senior vice-president Maynard Metcalf. But once more the efforts to re-establish CN in the Pacific bumped to a halt. After a spurt of profitability, domestic freight traffic slumped, and the surplus of 1955 and 1956 turned into a deficit. Given the notable increase in Japanese exports and the relatively modest cost of establishing a person in Yokohama, the reason for delay in doing so was not as convincing as it had been in 1948, but for better or worse it would be another five years before a CN office was opened there. That it happened then reflected the enthusiasm, persistence and patience of a passenger agent named Bill Neale who had, as it happened, once worked in the CN station in Prince Rupert, the fishing town that had never forgotten it was supposed to have become a gateway to the Orient.

William H. Neale had joined CN in Winnipeg in 1942 after trying his hand at journalism; he had worked in the passenger departments in New York, Boston and Seattle, and was one of the most travelled of the young men on staff. He had been one of two selected by Gordon for the CN-Cunard project, but with passenger business shrinking all over the world as airlines developed, Neale decided he would rather be in freight, which now accounted for most of CN's revenue. Like many CN foreign service people, he had been looking forward to a posting in London, but a year or two in Sydney had shown him a potential in the Pacific that CN had hardly touched. During the slack passenger travel season in 1957 he arranged for leave, boarded a cruise ship, and at his own expense took a tour of the Pacific.

"I visited Hong Kong, Manila, Taipeh and Singapore, finding a substantial tonnage moving to Canada through all these ports, but with no CN representation," he recalls. At twenty firms in Yokohama and Tokyo he found that freight to Canada had increased 50 per cent since Middlecoat's visit the previous year and that the reborn Japanese trading companies were establishing offices in Canada, an indication of a stable future. As Neale described his findings:

> I discovered that the CN's Japan-to-Canada tonnage was actually ten times greater than that going from Australia to Canada. In other words, in Australia with a CN staff of six we were producing only one tenth of the business Japan was generating with no representation in that country at all. Moreover in what was obviously to be a new era in the Asian Pacific I found that our competitor, by virtue of its new airline to the Orient, was making Canadian Pacific a familiar name to Asian businessmen. I returned to Sydney with the belief that re-establishment of the Canadian National name was of prime importance.
>
> I recommended that we immediately set up representation through an established agency such as the Everett Steamship Corporation, whose headquarters I had visited in Yokohama and who had branch offices throughout Asia. With a permanent CN supervisor in the region it would be unnecessary to build an elaborate staff of the sort we had in Asia before the war. But I got no reaction to my report, and surmised that because the project was not officially sponsored it had got buried somewhere at headquarters.

Henry Craig, CN foreign freight manager, decided CN needed representation in the Far East in 1961. *Courtesy CN*

Marketing techniques were crude compared with those of today, but by any yardstick European prospects were much better than those of the Pacific, and CN was concentrating on building up its trans-Atlantic business, leaving the Orient largely to the CPR. Neale was promoted to the post of district passenger agent in Toronto, but having what he called a liking "for the romance of world trade" he soon got himself transferred to Montreal as assistant to Henry Craig, manager of the foreign freight department. When he dug out his two-year-old Asian report he found a sympathetic audience in Craig and in Alec H. Hart, a Nova Scotia lawyer who had started his career in the CN legal section and was now vice-president of the newly organized marketing department.

One of the CN executives who had worked their way up from office boy, Craig joined the foreign freight department, his views of the world having been broadened by night courses at McGill University, a recognized centre for Asian studies. He decided that the time had come to get CN back into Asia, and in a seventy-two-day tour of the huge semi-circle between Hawaii and Ceylon in 1960 he found confirmation that the CN was not getting its proper share of Pacific Rim business. His days were full of meetings and his nights full of entertaining or being entertained. "I checked my notes this morning," he wrote when only two thirds of the way through his trip, "and find I have called on over eighty steamship lines, agencies, shippers, trade commissioners and the like since leaving Montreal. It is nice to have a quiet day since all I seem to have is too little time and too little sleep."

In Singapore Craig made contact with the agency Neale had recommended, the Everett Shipping Corporation, where the local agents were Capt. Ronald Todd from Vancouver and Ronald Betall from Alberta. "They strike me to be a lively and aggressive group," he reported to Montreal, deciding to call on the Everett head office in Yokohama before making a final decision about representation. Founded in Shanghai in 1917 by an American shipping agent, Leonard Everett, the corporation had grown into a complete maritime service under its post-war chairman, George P. Bradford, a Californian from San Mateo. It ran a travel service, had a fleet of more than thirty cargo ships and maintained twenty-six offices in eleven Asian countries, seven of them in Japan where a staff of 300 included cargo specialists in wheat, steel and other commodities. Representing Canada's national railway carried considerable commercial cachet, and Bradford was agreeable to a commission arrangement highly favourable to the CN, which could not hope to establish such complete coverage on its own at such a low cost. Everett would be CN's freight representatives in Japan, Korea, Hong Kong, the Philippines, Singapore, Thailand and India. Ceylon would be covered by an agreement signed by the British firm of Aitken, Spence and Company.

Neale was appointed Sales Manager–Orient, a three-pronged job that included providing head office reports on the general economy of the region, publicizing CN, and overseeing the work of the Everett agents. It was no longer the practice to get the "CN" rail routing stamped on a manifest before a ship sailed, since the consignees themselves were controlling the routing. Instead reports of impending shipments and the names of the consignees were telexed to CN freight agents in Canada, enabling them to go after the rail business.

Neale arrived at Yokohama one Saturday afternoon in April 1961 to begin his work, the first permanent CN representative in Japan in almost twenty years. Knowing practically no one in Japan, he booked himself into the Grand Hotel and spent a lonely, if instructive, Sunday strolling along the docks before reporting early Monday to Everett headquarters where he was assigned a desk in a large room occupied by ninety Everett employees. "I encountered

CANADIAN NATIONAL RAILWAYS

Donald Gordon (front centre), the first CN president to visit the Orient, at a 1966 reception in Hong Kong, flanked by CN Asian manager Bill Neale and a Mandarin-gowned official of a Hong Kong shipping company.
Courtesy CN

all the problems that moving to a strange land entails," recalls Neale, a bachelor. "For example I found an apartment and paid a deposit on it, but the day I was to move in I couldn't find it again! There were no street names or house numbers and in fact I never did find it and had to start house hunting all over again."

Although an argument could be made that CN should have moved faster and established its post-war Asian operation five years earlier, Neale found, as Craig had predicted, that 1961 was a good year to begin. Canadian purchases from Japan had doubled in four years, as had Canadian exports to Japan. A joint Canada-Japan ministerial committee had been established to develop trade, and Prime Minister Ikeda Hayto, during a visit to Canada that spring, noted the growing trend of Japanese investment in Canada. Most of the initiative was coming from the reconstituted trading companies, such as Mitsubishi and Mitsui, but more than a dozen Canadian firms now had offices in Japan, and in a visit to Tokyo Prime Minister John Diefenbaker assured his hosts that "Canada attaches major importance to Japan as a large and growing market for Canadian exports."

Trade with Japan was the chief reason Neale had been sent out and he therefore spent his first few months developing contacts and establishing an intelligence network which, as he put it, would allow the CN to compete "pound for pound" with the long-established CPR. Although CN had been securing business before Neale's arrival, on the basis of what the freight sales representative in Canada could learn about cargo movements, Neale increased it by his daily reports from Yokohama. He was soon reporting on cargo movements of 3000 tons a month of which CN could generally count on getting about half in the form of rail business.

That autumn Neale set out on the first of what were to become annual tours of a region that stretched from Japan to Pakistan. The airplane had transformed the scope and staffing needs of companies operating in the Asian Pacific, and during that first trip Neale established a routine he was to follow for the next nineteen years. This consisted of checking into a hotel, calling at the Canadian embassy, where the trade commissioners were invariably helpful, lunching with the Everett employee assigned exclusively to the CN account, and spending the rest of the day visiting contacts, before taking the Everett manager out to dinner. In Hong Kong, where light industry was flourishing, trade had doubled since the war and CN was getting a large part of it. From Singapore, which had regained its place as a major shipping centre for Southeast Asia, he travelled by train into the jungles of Malaya to make contact with that country's largest rubber producers — rubber and tin being the major commodities exported to Canada from Southeast Asia which in turn was buying increasing amounts of Canadian products. Trade out of Manila and Bangkok was slight, but in Bombay, Calcutta and Colombo a large volume of burlap, tea, cotton and rubber was being exported to Canada.

Travelling four months of every year over tens of thousands of miles, Neale was to witness the dramatic changes that led to the emergence of the New Pacific. Except in outports of the archipelagoes, the timeless world of Joseph Conrad was gone forever, and even in the countryside the new transistor radios from Japan brought the world to the villages. If there was any common theme in that huge area of over twenty separate nations and many cultures it was the demise of old-fashioned colonialism; the white man's burden was being assumed by Asians as independence came to country after country and the administrators went home. Those who remained were businessmen who no longer gathered in places like the famous Long Bar at the Raffles Hotel in Singapore to do their daily commerce, but could be found in air-conditioned offices, coaching the young Asians who would eventually take over their jobs.

In 1963 Neale made his first trip to China, which two years earlier, after years of insignificant trade, had begun to order large quantities of Canadian wheat. In a country that revered Dr. Norman Bethune, the Canadian doctor who died in 1939 while serving with the Communist army in China, Canada could count on special status, as it was to discover during the next decade. Neale recalls:

There were virtually no foreign businessmen working in China at the time except those attending the annual Canton Trade Fair each spring, the only place they could display their stock in trade. There was no Canadian embassy as yet, so my contact was the British Ambassador, though when I arrived I was in the hands of the Chinese government and was taken to a western-style hotel where a foreign correspondent and I seemed to be the only occupants. There was a set policy, it seemed, for handling us foreigners, whom they called "Friends of China." I was picked up every morning at 9 A.M. by two guides to tour museums and hear lectures on Mao and the cultural revolution; I was returned to my hotel at 5 P.M. and the whole process began again the next morning. After five days of this I was allowed to meet with some of the large trading companies doing business with the West, and though they did not sign contracts with us themselves they did give their approval for CN to do business with their sole agent on the west coast, a Canadian based in Vancouver.

The trade in wheat did a lot to dispel the Cold War attitudes of the 1950s, though as usual it was not much help to railway business because of the strictures of the Crow's Nest Pass Agreement. Imports from China were only 10 per cent of the total trade. Neale had made some valuable contacts, however, and at a time when there was no official representation in China, as representative of a crown corporation he functioned as something of an unofficial ambassador.

During his first four years, Neale hoed a rather lonely row as one of the few Canadians working the western Pacific Rim. Then, he recalls, things began to change as Canadians "discovered" the Far East. Visitors began to appear from head office, including Dr. Robert Bandeen, later CN president but then a vice-president in charge of research and development. Bandeen came out to represent CN at the first Asian Pacific trade fair, which was held in

Bangkok in 1966, and recalls that diplomatic representation was so thin on the ground he found himself representing Canada as well as CN at diplomatic functions.

If any one year can be called the turning point it was 1965. Japan's world exports had begun to grow at a rapid and sustained rate, exceeding imports for the first time. A joint Canada-Japan governmental committee met to develop Canadian exports of raw materials. An indication of the importance the Japanese attached to this breakthrough in economic and political relations occurred when not only government leaders but also the Crown Prince received British Columbia's premier, W. A. C. Bennett. Later, addressing a Colombo Plan conference in Victoria, Bennett assured his audience that the province which stood most to benefit from trans-Pacific trade was very much a part of the Pacific Rim, while admitting that "in a sense it may be said that our relationships across the Pacific in the past have been ad hoc and sometimes accidental." When Donald Gordon, the first CN president to visit the Orient, came to Tokyo the following year to show the flag, he took back home an agreement to interchange specialists between CN and Japan National Railways. At a time the Canadian government was beginning to express a desire for diplomatic relations with China, Gordon took the opportunity of a visit to Hong Kong to extoll the renewal of trade and cultural relations between the two countries.

During the next two years many organizations were founded to further the economies of the western Pacific Rim. The Association of South East Asian Nations (ASEAN) embraced the undeveloped nations of Indonesia, Malaysia, the Philippines, Thailand and the prosperous city state of Singapore. Canada became the sixth largest shareholder in the Asian Development Bank, as Canadian investment began to swing from its traditional recipient, Latin America, to Pacific Asia. Canadian assistance in the Pacific, which dated from the Colombo Plan in 1951, was augmented by the Canadian Industrial Development Agency (CIDA), established to provide third world countries with aid loans.

So far, most of the contacts between Canada and the Far East had been governmental, adding fuel to the old criticism that the Canadian business establishment took little interest in the area. In 1967 this image changed to some extent when Canadian businesses joined with their counterparts in Japan, Australia, New Zealand and the United States to form the Pacific Basin Economic Council (PBEC). The Canadian committee of PBEC, supported by the Canadian Manufacturers Association and the Canadian Cham-

Dock workers unloading Canadian produce at Calcutta. Canada's adherence to the Colombo Plan to provide aid to Asia in the 1950s increased involvement in the Pacific. *Courtesy Everett Shipping Corp., India*

ber of Commerce, has acted as advisor to the federal government and contributed to an awareness of Canada throughout the Pacific in an organization which now includes South Korea, the Philippines, Indonesia and Fiji.

The volume of cargo through the port of Vancouver had tripled in less than a decade to thirty million tons a year. China was buying an average of $200 million worth of wheat annually, along with large quantities of British Columbia pulp and aluminum. Japan's two-way trade with Canada in 1967 passed the billion dollar mark, four times what it had been when the CN opened its Yokohama office in 1961. A random selection of port statistics listed a tremendous variety of goods: 12,000 Japanese automobiles, 31,000 bicycles, 7 million square feet of mahogany plywood, 170,000 cameras, 957 pianos, 60,000 tons of steel rods, and 23,780 tulip bulbs.

The tulip bulbs represented the latest effort to establish the land bridge concept, wherein three weeks could be saved by shipping goods from Asia to Vancouver, railing it across the country, and shipping it on to Europe, rather than moving it via Southeast Asia and the Suez Canal. Neale describes trying this concept to move mandarin oranges, which the English import in large quantities every year as a Christmas treat:

> Since Japanese oranges were not allowed into the United States, moving them via the land bridge technique would have been a wholly Canadian effort. Unfortunately the same problems were encountered as in the first land bridge efforts before the war. These were caused primarily by the exact timing required by ship-rail-ship schedules, which were not helped by the uncertain weather of a Canadian winter. Also the speed of the container ships which were beginning to appear in 1968 was nearly double that of the older, conventional freighters, and their transit time through the Panama Canal was competitive, without the risk of meeting the tight sea-rail-sea schedules. So again the land bridge was abandoned.

Containers of one kind or another are as old as transportation itself, but the modern system in which everything from racks of silk dresses to consignments of lumber is packed into metal boxes and transported in an "intermodal" system of ships, flatcars and trucks without disturbance to the contents came into use on the London, Midland and Scottish Railway in 1926. It was perfected by the U.S. military during the war and introduced into Canada by CN, which used containers in the Maritimes just after the war. By 1968, when the first of the new breed of big Japanese container ships began to arrive at Vancouver, containers and other new methods of moving bulk commodities had revolutionized the cargo industry.

That most of the container traffic consisted of imports reflected the fact that less than three per cent of Canada's exports to Japan were manufactured goods. (Their volume was relatively smaller than it had been in the 1920s.) Since the early 1960s, a time when the Canadian and Japanese economies were expanding at more or less the same pace, Japan had far outdistanced Canada in manufacturing, but as the world's largest importer of raw material there was one area in which Japanese interest in Canada had not waned: Canada's destiny, it seemed, was to be Japan's source of natural resources, much like Manchuria's had been before the war.

Whereas grain had once been the only major bulk commodity, accounting for a third of Vancouver's tonnage, now there were others. Sulphur, which has a large number of industrial uses, joined the list as a result of the oil explorations that transformed Alberta from a farming and cattle province into a major producer

of oil and gas. Mountains of yellow sulphur pellets, a by-product of sour gas, mushroomed on the docks of Burrard Inlet's north shore. One of the world's largest deposits of natural potash, used in fertilizer, had been discovered in Saskatchewan, the remnants of a prehistoric sea 3000 feet below the wheat fields. Both were in great demand in the western Pacific. And the fastest, most economical way to move such bulk commodities was found to be "unit trains" which consisted of up to 100 gondola or hopper cars, all carrying the same product and shuttling back and forth from mine to port on a rigid schedule. CN had pioneered unit trains for potash and now was using them for other products, including coal.

Since coal had been discovered on northern Vancouver Island in 1835, there had been occasional sales to California and even across the Pacific, but the main customers had been the coal-burning railways. As the industry flourished, mines were opened in the Alberta foothills and southeastern British Columbia, but when the railways switched to diesel oil the mines fell on hard times. The revival that was to make coal the monarch of the export commod-

(Top) Four 3000-horsepower engines are pulling this ninety-eight-car unit train, so-called because it carries only one bulk commodity. *Courtesy CN*
(Below) Roberts Bank (Westshore Terminals) just south of the port of Vancouver, was built in the late 1960s to handle the increase in coal imports to Japan. *Courtesy B.C. Resources Investment Corp.*

ities came in the mid-1960s when labour troubles disrupted supplies from Australia, Japan's closest and most economic source. Wishing to diversify its sources, Japan turned to Canada and by 1968 was importing three million tons a year through Vancouver.

The movement of bulk cargoes such as coal depended on devising cheap methods of transporting them long distances, and along with the unit trains had come their sea-going counterparts — monster ships of up to 200,000 tons. Such large carriers were not designed for a busy port like Vancouver so the Canadian Harbours Board (Ports Canada), which operates major harbours across the country, invested in a massive coal terminal a few miles south of the city. A man-made island was dredged out of the mudflats at Roberts Bank, and facilities were installed to handle four times the capacity loaded at Neptune Terminals in Vancouver's inner harbour.

The tremendous increase in bulk and container traffic considerably altered Bill Neale's work. He became involved in freight rate negotiations with Japanese steel companies and container ship firms, both of which were tied to the trading companies. The rates both railways quoted in the beginning, in competition with the Australians whose mines are much nearer the ports than those in Canada, proved too low and had to be revised upward. Since the shipping companies owned the containers, solicited freight from manufacturers and shippers, and controlled the flow of cargo,

Unloading automobiles in Vancouver and sending them across Canada by rail saves weeks, as compared with shipping them completely by sea to eastern Canada. To handle this traffic CN maintains 2000 two- and three-level carriers. *Courtesy CN*

contracts had to be negotiated to carry the containers inland in Canada. CN pioneered a system of inland container terminals in cities such as Toronto and Montreal which were in effect extensions of the original port of entry and to which containers could be sent by rail for eventual distribution.

In 1968 Neale moved out of his obscure office at Everett Shipping, where visitors had to pick their way through rows of shipping company clerks to get to him, and opened CN's own office in Tokyo's first skyscraper. In keeping with a trend among foreign firms to recruit local people into senior positions he hired Tadashi Kunita, an Everett employee who had worked on the CN account for several years, as his second in command and manager for Japan. "We had been growing slowly during the 1960s," said Neale, "but suddenly there was a dramatic increase in the magnitude of business. We appointed a representative in Kobe to look after our interests in southern Japan and opened our own office in Hong Kong in co-operation with Air Canada. Then as Canada became of greater interest to other Asian countries, CN strengthened its position in Korea, Taiwan, Pakistan, India and Sri Lanka. Australia and New Zealand came under the jurisdiction of the Tokyo office. Canadian National had achieved a firm foothold in the Pacific Rim countries."

CN also achieved a firmer foothold in Vancouver. Despite a legacy of tracks, real estate, a station, and a hotel, all inherited

Container traffic, in which goods are packed into metal boxes, such as these seen on the Hong Kong docks, began to pick up about 1968. In 1984 the port of Vancouver handled 140 000 container units. *Courtesy CN*

from the Canadian Northern, the city had been regarded as a CPR stronghold. Since the mid-1950s, however, CN had been improving its position in Vancouver, securing its track to the growing terminal complex on the north shore of the harbour so it would not have to run over CPR tracks. From then on it began to compete on more or less equal terms with its rival. The nearest CN vice-president maintained his headquarters in Edmonton on the other side of the mountains, but in 1971, CN traffic through the port having doubled in five years, senior corporate vice-president A. H. Hart, the former vice-president of marketing, arrived from Montreal to open a high-level corporate office, improve relations with Premier W. A. C. Bennett, and generally "enhance the CN presence in the Pacific Rim countries." Within two months of his arrival Hart was off on the first of a series of visits to Tokyo where he not only promoted CN traffic through Vancouver but also drew Japanese attention to the under-utilized port of Prince Rupert. He became chairman of the PBEC transportation committee, an excellent vantage point from which to attract business. "We had always had a large CN establishment in the United States and Europe," Hart explained, "but it was clear there was going to be a lot of business available in the Pacific. The Japanese had started to come to Canada in large numbers and PBEC was building a trans-Pacific network of businessmen from many countries."

Canada had established diplomatic relations with the People's Republic of China in 1970, pointing the way for the United States to do the same a few years later, opening a new page in the history of Sino-American relations. In 1972, 500 Canadians, including Neale, journeyed to Beijing when Canada became the first non-Communist country permitted its own trade fair. Canadian exports to China, worth $9 million twelve years earlier, were close to $200 million, and Canada ranked as China's fourth largest supplier. Trade with South Korea, Taiwan and Hong Kong, called "the little dragons" because of their emulation of Japan, had increased substantially.

The prodigious growth of trans-Pacific trade had turned Vancouver into one of the ten busiest ports in the world, ranking second in North America after New York. Every year more than 2000 deep-sea vessels called at one or another of its thirty terminals, which sprawled over an area of fifty square miles. Few ports have seen such rapid growth in such a short time. Exports were five times greater in volume than imports, but inbound automobiles and containers were elbowing for more room. It was the only west coast Canadian port of any magnitude, the half dozen on Vancouver Island being used mainly to export only wood products. Despite the opening of Roberts Bank, Vancouver was feeling the strain, both on the single-line railways that fed it and in the capacity of the terminals to handle grain.

Four railways serve Vancouver. The Burlington Northern Railroad is American and comes north from Washington State. BC Rail, the former Pacific Great Eastern, runs through the interior almost to the border with the Northwest Territories. The two major lines, Canadian National Railways and CP Rail, run in from the east through territory prone to bad weather and snowslides, and issue out of the lower Fraser Valley and into the port area as into the mouth of a funnel. With cargo tonnage expected to increase by a fourth during the next ten years, both these railways had begun a massive improvement program that included double tracking. Meantime, 500 miles to the north, and a day nearer Japan in sailing time, Prince Rupert was a port begging for traffic.

8 THE CITY OF RAINBOWS

"So we were a dream city. A collection of almost unattainable hopes and dreams."

The Daily News, Prince Rupert, 27 September 1977

WHEN THE AMERICAN ARMY left Prince Rupert in 1945, half the population went with it. Instead of half a dozen trains a day, CN cut its service back to three a week to serve a population of less than 10,000. On Acropolis Hill, where the U.S. army had housed thousands of troops, a few rows of concrete foundations overgrown with brush were all that remained, and the hill was renamed Franklin Delano Roosevelt Park. The war had provided a glimpse of what might have been had the port developed to plan, but the post-war years bore witness as to why it had not. While rich in resources, northern British Columbia had failed to draw the population that would have made Prince Rupert an important centre, and few commercial or manufacturing activities had been attracted. Vancouver, with its banks, shipping agencies and modern terminals, naturally monopolized the port business, whether it was grain from the prairies or transistor radios from Taiwan.

With no one to take the place of Charles Melville Hays, the little port that makes a virtue out of rainfall by calling itself "the city of rainbows" was surviving on its own. For one thing it was the closest rail head to one of the most prolific fishing areas in the Pacific. Each evening a long procession of fishing vessels — sometimes as many as 150 — glided out past Hays Cove and Melville Arm for the night's catch of halibut, herring, cod, crab and shrimp. The Skeena River had long been the best salmon stream in the province; now fishermen called the port "the halibut capital of

In the 1960s the grain elevator built at Prince Rupert a generation earlier was underutilized, and few ships called at the port. *Courtesy CN*

175

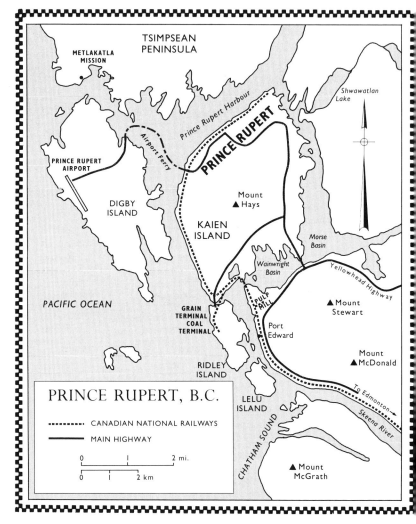

the world," and the local co-operative built a large cannery and shipped their pack off east via CN rail. The population edged back up to 15,000 and a commercial airport was opened on Digby Island across the harbour.

Henry Craig, who had been in charge of CN's grain section before becoming manager of foreign freight, got the federal government to reopen the grain elevator to export barley from the northern prairies to Japan. To secure some of the freight business flowing north to Alaska, the railway started a rail barge service. The most important development, however, was the opening of a pulp mill at nearby Port Edward that did more than anything to provide much-needed employment and stabilize the economy. But during the 1950s there were two particularly severe disappointments. CN closed the money-losing shipyard and sold the drydock, which was towed south to Seattle, and an Aluminum Company of Canada smelter, established to sell ingots to Japan, was built not at Prince Rupert but at Kitimat, eighty-six miles down the coast.

By the early 1960s a small export business in lumber and minerals from the interior was building up, and fifty ships called in the course of a year. "More grain has been brought to this port for export this year than in any year in its history," reported the *Daily News* of 25 September 1961. "There is more traffic along its waterfront roads to the sawmill, to the fish companies, to the grain elevator than at any time previously." The cargoes through Prince Rupert were all for export, since the town suffered then as it does now from being too far from population centres to encourage import business. People have talked occasionally of using Prince Rupert as a "land bridge port," but while it is relatively close to Japan it is relatively far from the Atlantic, and a land bridge between southern California ports and the Gulf of Mexico would be more effective.

Adding to Prince Rupert's frustrations was the fact that it had less dock space than it had thirty years earlier. The Coastal Dock had outlived its usefulness and had been demolished, and Ottawa, which with British Columbia owned half the waterfront, showed little interest in replacing it. The other half of the waterfront was controlled by the CN, which the City Drydock Committee, fighting a losing battle to have the dock kept where it was, accused of having lost interest in the port. "The drydock is a vital portion of the Laurier plan of bridging the Pacific to the markets of the Orient, a vision Donald Gordon appears unable to grasp," said George B. Casey, an American-born union organizer and Prince Rupert alderman for twenty-three years. "If Donald Gordon's wish and will come true, then the words uttered many years ago by Sir George Foster, Borden's trade minister, that the port of Prince Rupert appears to be struggling under a curse will come true beyond doubt."

Since neither the federal nor provincial governments displayed any interest in improving the port, the city took the initiative. After decades of more or less unorganized lobbying, a Port Development Commission was established in 1964 with W. J. (Joe) Scott as its chairman. For Scott, who ran a prosperous family hardware business, campaigning to put Prince Rupert on the map was almost a family affair. His grandfather, Joseph G. Scott, a Manitoba-born carpenter, had arrived in Prince Rupert via the Yukon in 1907 when it was a raw tent town. Those were the days when the Grand Trunk Pacific was promising a city of 50,000 and

In the 1960s CN began a lucrative rail barge service between Prince Rupert and Whittier, Alaska. The barges transport railway cars which travel on from Whittier to their destinations over the Alaska railroad. Produce and pulp are but two of the commodities carried on these "aquatrains." *Courtesy CN*

twenty T-shaped wharfs along the harbour front, and it seemed just the place for a young carpenter. A generation later Scott's father, tired of waiting for the promises to materialize, joined a delegation to Ottawa to lobby the government, with no appreciable result. Since then the government's responses had been sporadic and easily affected by economics and geography. So long as Vancouver could handle the traffic there seemed no reason to spend a lot of money on Prince Rupert. Backed by the city and the Chamber of Commerce, Scott renewed the old battle.

As the most visible presence on the neglected waterfront, CN was singled out for a well-publicized attack by Scott's commission, which recalled how a decade earlier, during a visit to the town, Donald Gordon had assured people that what was good for Prince Rupert was good for CN. The attack brought reaction. Gordon ordered Mountain Region vice-president G. Roger Graham in Edmonton to see what was going on. "CN is too conscious of rail development instead of port development," Scott told him. Within a year CN produced a development plan that called for new docks, a bulk loading terminal on uninhabited Ridley Island three miles south of town, and a local port authority. "Such a project, of course, will develop only if huge quantities of bulk cargo are available from the hinterland," said the *Vancouver Province*, "and with the growing expansion of the mining industry in the Skeena and Stikine Valleys of British Columbia it is hoped that such a project will prove feasible. Among the bulk products that might be shipped out of Prince Rupert, as foreseen in the report, are coal, iron ore, potash, and mineral concentrates."

Scott, Mayor Peter Lester and others were making headway. Dr. William Hick, a China missionary's son with a practice in Prince Rupert and the rather unusual hobby of studying port activities, recruited eight businessmen who contributed $56,000 of their own money to hire an engineering firm to design a waterfront dock. "We wanted to get something going, to embarrass Ottawa into taking action," explained Hick, a lanky, blue-eyed man whose enthusiasm is contagious. "People in the town who had been waiting for decades for something to happen were growing bitter. Every time there was an election the politicians would come and tell us that if they were elected they would do something, but nothing ever happened."

The Cinderella of the northwest coast had become a political issue. The federal transport minister, Jack W. Pickersgill, toured the waterfront and expressed dismay at what he found, but back in Ottawa, the National Harbours Board showed little interest in including Prince Rupert among its national network of ports of "national importance," even though CN offered to transfer its waterfront real estate to the government. The one positive move was to increase capacity of the grain elevator, once owned by the railway and now by the federal government; even then only eight grain ships called in 1969.

The premiers of Saskatchewan and Alberta, Ross Thatcher and Ernest C. Manning, told Prime Minister Lester B. Pearson that their landlocked provinces needed a second west coast port. Said Manning:

> During my recent trip to Japan the major industrialists indicated to me that they were greatly interested in the development of the harbour at Prince Rupert for three particular reasons: the ever-increasing volume of traffic in the busy port of Vancouver; the ability of Prince Rupert to take large vessels; and the savings in sailing time between Japanese ports and Prince Rupert. There are very definite indications that within the next five years the increase in exportable resource materials from Alberta and Saskatchewan will create further congestion at the Port of Vancouver and the question arises as to the ability of the port to handle such a high volume of traffic.

Scott's commission, having completed its own study, failed to convince three different transport ministers to support it. "We were getting pushed around," said Scott. "They said you show us the traffic and we'll develop the port." So little revenue was

In August 1970 Joe Scott's port commission engaged the interest of Prime Minister Pierre Trudeau, who had recently been to Japan and was opening diplomatic relations with China. Prince Rupert needed grain and coal terminals to become a gateway to the Orient. *Courtesy CN*

coming in that it would take years to pay for a new cargo dock. Industry was waiting for government to provide facilities; government was waiting for commitment from industry. Premier W. A. C. Bennett told the legislature that Prince Rupert should become a "superport" like Roberts Bank, but at the same time the government-owned British Columbia Railway was siphoning off northern freight to Vancouver.

This was the state of affairs one hot August day in 1970 when Prince Rupert played host to Prime Minister Pierre Trudeau, still new to office and, like his fellow Quebecker Sir Wilfrid Laurier, interested in Asian commerce as an antidote to the country's overwhelming dependency on trade with the United States. In a visit to the Osaka international fair that year, during which he met with Prime Minister Eisaku Sato, Trudeau said that the area which nineteenth-century Englishmen had called "the Far East" was in reality Canada's "New West." Trudeau had come to power with a promise to extend Canadian interests "westward across the Pacific to Australia, Japan, China and the countries of Asia." With trans-Atlantic trade diminishing, and Britain about to join the Common Market, Canada's future would be tied more closely with the countries of the western Pacific. In Prince Rupert, Trudeau spent much of the day listening to Scott explaining the problems of transforming the town into "a gateway to the Pacific." "The government had already made a decision to develop a northern port," Scott recalled, "and we convinced them it should be Prince Rupert." The other contender was Kitimat down the coast which, with its aluminum smelter and Eurocan pulp mill built in the late

Early one morning in June 1973, a $10-million fire demolished Prince Rupert's only remaining wharf, the Ocean Dock, destroying boxcars, warehouses and a fish cannery and putting 300 people out of work. *Courtesy CN*

sixties, had a larger industrial base though a smaller historical claim.

A federal, provincial and municipal working group was formed to develop the port "in the national interest" with federal and provincial funds. On 23 March 1972, sixty years after Prince Rupert had been proclaimed a public harbour, it became one of the select ten in the country under the umbrella of the National Harbours Board. Taking over the waterfront, the Board made Scott chairman of the local port authority and earmarked $5 million for development. It was none too soon, for fire destroyed the Ocean Dock at dawn one morning, plunging 6000 tons of copper concentrate destined for Japan into the deep waters of the harbour and causing lumber and minerals to be diverted to Vancouver over BC Rail lines.

Work to replace the Ocean Dock began on the foreshore, where, as on most of the mainland coast of British Columbia, there was so little level ground that some forty acres had to be created by blasting rock out of the foothills of the mountain named after the Grand Trunk's Charles Hays. As the first ceremonial charge was detonated, Graham Lea, provincial minister of highways and legislative member for Prince Rupert, pronounced: "This day should go down in history as Joe Scott day." Built in four years by federal and provincial funds, Fairview Terminal was to handle lumber, mineral concentrates, fish and a small amount of grain. But a $25-million dock, no matter how efficient, does not make a major port, and the events that would transform Prince Rupert were occurring elsewhere.

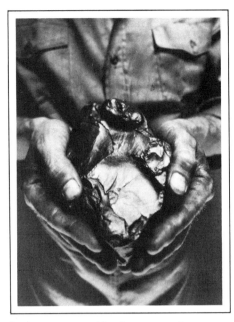

In recent years coal has become a major export. British Columbia possesses reserves of 4.5 million tonnes, enough to satisfy world demand for many generations. *Courtesy CN*

One of the many ingredients in the transformation of Prince Rupert was the OPEC oil price crisis of 1973. Japanese steel mills, which depended on Middle East oil for their blast furnaces, converted to coal and cut back oil consumption by 80 per cent. They were buying ten million tons a year by now from three mines in the southern Rockies, served by the CPR through Roberts Bank, and a mine at Grande Cache, Alberta, served by CN through Neptune Terminal in Vancouver's inner harbour. Coal exports had tripled in five years but the Japanese, who had helped develop the existing mines, were eager for more sources. British Columbia was in a position to oblige.

That large coal deposits existed in the northeast corner of the province had been known since 1793 when the explorer Alexander Mackenzie reported great chunks sticking out of the ground. The area was so remote that it had never been developed, except for a small mine that opened near Hudson Hope after World War I. The provincial and federal governments were eager to open up the virgin resources of the north, an unpopulated region stretching north of the CN line and east to the Alberta border on the far slopes of the Rockies, and now the prospect of coal sales to Japan provided motivation for investment in what came to be called the Northeast Coal Project.

After decades of disappointment it appeared as if Prince Rupert would get the opportunity it was waiting for, and CN would be able to turn its northern line into a paying proposition. Ronald E. Lawless, then vice-president of marketing, had already been to Tokyo the previous year to promote the advantages of the northern route. He recalled:

> When it became apparent there would be a major shift in Japan from oil to coal, and that Canada would play a significant role, the CN already had a good start. It had been supplying coal through Vancouver, liaising between the Canadian coal companies and the Japanese steel companies, and we believed we had a major role to play in the development of Prince Rupert. We were able to demonstrate early in the game that Prince Rupert, the closest west coast port to Japan other than Vancouver, had a major opportunity to become a viable port and that the CN was prepared to upgrade its track, and that these were factors Japan should consider in the future movement of coal, grain, and petrochemicals.

Whereas ports in the past had usually provided services only after they were actually demanded by potential customers, it had become necessary to get out and sell cost and efficiency. The Prince Rupert case was helped by what had become by this time a problem of congestion at Vancouver. By the mid-seventies the CN Mountain Region, which includes Alberta, British Columbia and part of Saskatchewan, had seen its freight tonnage double in a decade, and at least half the volume of twenty million tons was flowing through Vancouver in the form of grain, potash, sulphur and coal. The five grain terminals were frequently hard-pressed to keep up with the ships waiting at anchor in English Bay for their turn at the docks. Since neither Japan nor China had large storage facilities, and delivery schedules were crucial, and since waiting ships ran up heavy demurrage charges — the penalties imposed by shipping companies when cargo is not ready — the prairie grain companies were getting restive. Led by Dr. Hugh Horner, Alberta's minister of agriculture, they agreed that an alternative port was needed.

In Prince Rupert they found an ally in Dr. Hick, whose privately financed waterfront study had helped get Ottawa moving to build the Fairview Terminal, soon to open for business. As head of the city's grain co-ordinating committee Hick was lobbying Ottawa and many of the 150,000 prairie grain farmers, telling them the northern CN line and the port of Prince Rupert could solve their problems in getting wheat to consumers on time and on budget. His seventy-page study, written in 1975 and later submitted to the Hall Commission on Grain Transportation, was a classic of its kind.

Since CN's seminal report in 1965 suggesting a Ridley Island development and a local port authority, there had been so many studies that according to Mayor Lester they "make a stack four-feet high." A report by the Centre for Transportation Studies at the University of British Columbia concluded that routing northern coal and wheat through Prince Rupert "has a cost advantage under virtually every condition." One of the most powerful arguments for opening Prince Rupert to the world came from the National Harbours Board, which concluded that as many as nine new bulk terminals would be needed on the west coast by the year 2000. After checking sixteen possible sites, from Port Simpson in the north to Roberts Bank in the south, it stated: "The combined development of Robert's Bank and Ridley Island stands out as clearly the optimum choice."

9 CANADA'S PACIFIC RIM

ON A SUNNY DAY, Prince Rupert, which stretches over green hills between the Pacific and a snow-topped backdrop of mountains, shares with Vancouver a claim to being one of the handsomest harbours in the country. On one such day there in June 1985 Joe Scott leaned back in his chair at the Prince Rupert Port Corporation and recalled the decades of effort to create a modern port.

Down the hill at Fairview Terminal a dozen forklifts hustled stacks of yellow lumber aboard two freighters. Wood product markets, which account for half of every dollar British Columbia earns, were on the upswing again after one of their frequent slumps. The terminal had been open seven years now and had contributed to the stability of the town. At Ridley Island, south of the city's new housing development, scores of concrete silos, crammed with northern prairie wheat for China, clustered around a forty-five-storey "work house," the tallest building on the north coast. Three years earlier Ridley Island had consisted of 1000 acres of trees, muskeg and tidal flats; now it was what the brochures called "a superport." A few hundred yards from the grain terminal, tall bucketwheels, which look from a distance like fairground equipment, were piling metallurgical coal brought down from the northeast in 98-car unit trains. Coal, which accounted for two thirds of all Prince Rupert's traffic, had boosted exports one and a half times during the past two years to eight million tonnes. Although this was hardly a sixth of the traffic flowing through Vancouver, it was a great improvement from earlier years, and the Prince Rupert port office predicted it would increase to thirteen million tonnes in another five or six years. Hardly any of it consisted of imported goods.

Present-day Prince Rupert, a city of 18 000, with Tuck Inlet stretching into the distance and Fairview lumber terminal in the foreground. Photographer, Brian Mycroft. *Courtesy Prince Rupert Port Corp.*

"Charles Hays was really seventy years ahead of his time," observed Scott, who was one year old when the first man to attempt to make Prince Rupert into a port was drowned at sea. "But for Hays the big thing was imports. He wanted to import silk. What with the shorter sailing time from Japan to Prince Rupert he figured that even if the rail haul was a bit longer from Vancouver or Seattle he could get silk faster to New York."

At the age of seventy-four, and on the verge of retirement, Scott had the air of a man who has lived to see his hopes overcome frustration and take solid form. A few months earlier, as chairman of the port authority, he had packed his audiovisual slides, with a sound track dubbed in Japanese, and headed for Tokyo, accompanied by a group of government and business officials that included CN marketing vice-president John H. D. Sturgess, who would describe CN's track improvement program on its routes to Vancouver and Prince Rupert:

> By 1980 CN Rail had already exceeded the capacity of some of the portions of its main line between Winnipeg and Vancouver. Traffic projections indicated we would face a crisis situation of mammoth proportions before the end of the decade unless we launched an all-out effort to expand capacity. However, some years before 1980 the impending crisis had been foreseen. In the mid-1970s, CN Rail began a plant improvement program, but well before the program was completed revised traffic projections told us much more would have to be done. . . . Looking ahead to 1990 we can see the culmination of more than a decade of hard work and heavy expenditure — a Canadian railway network built to the highest standard, with the capacity to handle all the traffic our customers can offer.

Scott recalled later:

> The port had been growing steadily for a decade but that mission to Tokyo and Seoul, where we talked to hundreds of businessmen, made it clear to me that Prince Rupert had finally arrived and was now a world-class port. Of course I had always believed it was one of the finest natural harbours in the world, and from the beginning it was the terminus of a transcontinental railway with the finest grades and the best winter transportation record of any railroad on the coast.

For the port of Prince Rupert the breakthrough had come in the late 1970s at a time Vancouver's volume of grain shipments

Carved out of a disused island of rock and muskeg, the Ridley Island "superport" boasts the most up-to-date coal and grain terminals in the world. Photographer, Brian Mycroft. *Courtesy Ridley Terminals Inc.*

was expected to triple during the next fifteen years. The Canadian Wheat Board, the federal agency which markets all wheat, barley and oats and controls the grain car movements, decided that Vancouver alone could not handle the anticipated traffic. Congestion had been getting worse, and late in the winter of 1975, during a period of storms in the Rockies, twenty-two grain ships were reported at one time in English Bay, waiting for their turn at the docks and piling up demurrage charges. The grain shippers were worried they would lose markets to the Australians and the Americans, and in its final report Mr. Justice Emmett Hall's grain commission recommended that an alternative port be established.

For Dr. Hugh Horner, the Alberta cabinet minister and former physician from Barrhead, where he owned a wheat and cattle farm, the answer was obvious. In his younger days, as a federal member of parliament, during which he represented the riding of Jasper-Edson which lies athwart the CN northern line, Horner had been a member of the railway committee. He knew all about Prince Rupert, and why it would make a suitable grain port, and in his campaign to see one built had little trouble in gaining the support of Premier Peter Lougheed. He began to discuss the matter with the Alberta Wheat Pool, which maintained the biggest elevator in Vancouver, as well as with grain officials in Saskatche-

Automatic shiploaders at Ridley Island coal terminal filled the *River Star,* one of the world's biggest carriers, with 178 000 tonnes of coal in twenty-nine and a half hours, a North American record. *Courtesy Ridley Terminals Inc.*

wan and Dr. Hick and Mayor Lester of Prince Rupert. He took Lougheed for a firsthand look at Ridley Island in the summer of 1977, checking it out by boat since weather prevented their flying over it. By January 1978 Horner was touring the Far East, realizing that there was no point investing in Prince Rupert without seeing how effective the large grain handling systems were on the receiving end.

Convinced that a terminal at Prince Rupert would be a boon to wheat farmers, particularly those of Alberta, Lougheed agreed to provide risk capital from the swollen coffers of the province's Heritage Fund, which had benefitted when Alberta's oil sales increased during the Middle East oil crisis. By the end of 1978 the major grain companies had swung into line, forming Prince Rupert Grain Ltd., a consortium designed to build a terminal on Ridley Island. In the meantime they purchased the old elevator for the nominal sum of $1, since one of the problems in the past had been the reluctance of the companies which owned the Vancouver terminals to divert their wheat north to the government-owned terminal. With Hick's aid they began negotiations with the National Harbours Board, which controlled Ridley Island and had been charged with the task of preparing it as a port for the Northeast Coal Project.

Whereas the grain terminal was to be a creation of the prairie provinces, the Northeast Coal Project was initiated by the governments of British Columbia and Canada and Canadian and Japanese

Tsuneji Nemoto, president of Kokan Mining, drives a spike in a spur line leading to Ridley Island coal terminal. Looking on are CN president Ronald Lawless, centre, and senior western vice-president Ross Walker. Photographer, J. G. Smith. *Courtesy CN*

coal and steel companies. On 10 February 1981, a year before the National Harbours Board had finished clearing the trees and muskeg off Ridley Island, B.C. premier Bill Bennett had signed the largest contract in the annals of Canadian mining. The other signatories included Denison Mines Limited of Toronto, Teck Corporation of Vancouver, and a large consortium of Japanese steel companies, represented by Tsuneji Nemoto, president of Kokan Mining, a subsidiary of Nippon Kokan (NKK), the world's largest steel company. For the Japanese, coal had become an insurance policy against volatile oil prices, particularly after the second OPEC crisis in 1979 which had increased the cost of oil from a low of $2 to $30 a barrel. They agreed to purchase 115 million tonnes over the next fifteen years and invested $400 million in the Northeast Coal Project, whose two open pit mines would produce nearly nine million tonnes a year. When combined with the output of the Alberta mines and those in southern British Columbia, this would give Canada 25 per cent of the Japanese market.

The larger of the two mines was to be opened by Quintette Coal Limited on behalf of Denison Mines and a consortium of Japanese companies plus the state-owned French company, Charbonages de France. The smaller Bullmoose mine was owned by Teck and Nissho Iwai Corporation of Japan. The governments and the railways — CN and BC Rail, whose main line north of Prince George ran near the mining area — would provide the infrastructure.

(Above and opposite page) By the early 1980s CN was embarking on a $600-million program to upgrade its British Columbia line, laying heavier track to take the strain of 10 000-tonne unit trains. *Courtesy CN*

The Peace River coal field lay in a wild region of tangled old mountains and forested valleys which had changed little since Alexander Mackenzie passed through in the spring of 1793. Intensive coal exploration had begun only in the mid-sixties, and to get out the coal would require a massive effort. Among other things the top of at least one mountain would have to be blown off. Roads needed to be built, including a 92-kilometre paved highway.

BC Rail began fifteen kilometres of tunnelling necessary for a 129-kilometre branch line from Chetwynd on its main line north from Prince George. Between the two mines a town was being built on a forested plateau above a bend in the Murray River, and in less than three years Tumbler Ridge grew from a surveyor's stake and a couple of camp trailers into a community of 5000 people with an airport, a mayor and council, and a little newspaper which attracted attention across the country because it was run by Mark and Derek Stock who were, respectively, aged 11 and "almost 9." The square in front of the town hall, which opened for business in July 1983, was named Nemoto Plaza, after the president of Kokan Mining, in appreciation for his part in the project.

Almost 1000 kilometres away at tidewater, the coal port at Ridley Island was under construction. A joint venture of the National Harbours Board and Federal Commerce and Navigation, the private company that would operate it, the terminal was designed to export twelve million tonnes a year at full capacity and would cost $250 million. The Northeast Coal Project as a whole, embracing two open pit mines, a new town, two railways, roads, and the terminal at Ridley island, was undoubtedly the largest industrial venture in the province's history and would cost $2.5 billion or more.

In April 1982 Ronald Lawless, now president of CN Rail, signed a fifteen-year contract, the largest deal of its kind the company had ever negotiated, to haul the coal to Prince Rupert from Prince George, the connection point with BC Rail. The two railways purchased nine big unit trains that would carry the coal between Tumbler Ridge and Ridley Island, a round trip the trains would be required to complete in seventy-five hours, and CN got on with the job of upgrading a track used mostly to move lumber.

More than half of Canada's entire gross national product was moving by rail, and CN with a total of 36,000 kilometres of track spanning all ten provinces and employing some 48,000 people was the nation's largest carrier. Whereas fifty-car trains had once been considered large, unit trains hauling 10 000 tonnes of coal or other commodities were now a common sight on the CN main line,

putting a strain on a system that had been designed for lighter traffic. Rails that had been required to handle six or seven trains a day in each direction, east and west, were now carrying three times that number. CN's traffic had doubled in two decades largely because of the growth of bulk traffic in the West. To keep up with this wear and tear, as well as to provide for expansion, the corporation had spent a billion dollars in the western region during the past five years and expected to spend a billion and a half during the next five. (Part of the money for this work would come from the savings achieved as a result of the scrapping of the Crow Rate in 1984.)

In some areas the line was practically rebuilt with concrete ties and heavier rails. No longer were these laid by the rickety-looking "praying mantis" of the Grand Trunk Pacific days, but by modern machines that replace a kilometre of line in four hours. When CN signed the contract in 1982 to carry coal from Tumbler Ridge, it had recently commenced a $600-million, ten-year task of improving its tracks to Vancouver and Prince Rupert. Over the 750 kilometres between Prince George and Prince Rupert this would mean sturdier bridges, one of the most advanced systems in the world known as TRACS (Traffic Reporting and Control system), and new sidings to accommodate the long unit trains. (Since one of those sidings — about a kilometre and a half long — costs $5 million, it is interesting to contemplate the cost if Hays were building the whole line today.) Now with the first load of north-

Joe Scott, left, with federal trade and commerce minister Jean-Luc Pepin and British Columbia cabinet minister Don Phillips at commencement of construction at Ridley Island, February 1982. *Courtesy Joseph Scott*

east coal scheduled for delivery at Ridley Island early in November 1983 the work would have to be concluded with great speed.

"The majority of the construction projects were undertaken during a short period when traffic levels were very high due to booming wood product markets," explained Ross Walker, senior vice-president of CN's Western Region. "The railway had never taken on a project as large as this for a single purpose — a mammoth construction project going ahead in the midst of an operating railway." In fact, the work was completed a month ahead of schedule, allowing the line to handle five times more traffic than before. In January 1984 the *Shoryu Maru* took on the first cargo of coal for Japan; within a few months Prince Rupert had set a record for loading the largest dry bulk cargo ever to leave the west coast, aboard the 187 000-tonne *River Star*, then considered the world's largest coal carrier.

The grain terminal was also nearing completion. With the Alberta government providing $200 million in debt funding, 700 builders had been working on it since 1982. Designed to export 3.5 million tonnes annually of wheat, barley and canola (also known as rapeseed), and with a possibility for expansion, it would have three times the capacity of the existing Prince Rupert elevator and thus would increase the west coast grain export potential by 20 per cent. Whereas in Vancouver the big grain carriers frequently had to move from one dock to another to complete their cargo, here it could all be done in one operation.

The terminal was built in three years at a cost of $275 million, the amount not covered by the Alberta government being made up by the consortium, which included the Alberta Wheat Pool, the largest shareholder, the Saskatchewan Wheat Pool, Manitoba Pool Elevators, United Grain Growers, Cargill Ltd. and Pioneer Grain. The first cargo of wheat was loaded aboard the Hong Kong freighter *World Prize* which set off for China one misty morning in March 1985; two months later the terminal was officially opened by Federal Transport Minister Donald Mazankowski and Premier Lougheed. It was clear that the terminal could not make money during its early years because of the recession, but that thought did little to dampen the celebrations. The terminal was needed, and it was built, like the coal port, to serve for fifty years and more.

In a town of 17,000, which had suffered from unemployment longer than anyone cared to recall, there had been great expectations when construction began. Now that the terminals were built, the hundreds of workers from the south drifted off to other jobs, and people discovered that the export of coal and wheat provided far less employment than it did in years past. At Ridley Island there were no gangs manually handling cargo slings, shovelling coal, trundling sacks of wheat, or even driving forklifts. Machines did most of the work. Fewer than 100 employees were needed at the automated coal terminal, and grain flow had become so computerized that when the terminal was opened and the old elevator closed down, seventy-three jobs were lost to the town. Most of the work was still concentrated in the fishing industry and pulp mill, as it had been for decades. The new jobs were up at distant Tumbler Ridge where 2000 miners had been hired.

No more than 200 jobs have been created in Prince Rupert, but the new terminals have broadened the economic base by creating new business opportunities and generating millions in taxes. "They permit us to make improvements to the town that we could not otherwise afford," says Mayor Lester, whose twenty-eight years in office have encompassed bad times and good. "They make for a stable future."

Certainly the ingredients are there for a promising future. There is plenty of room remaining on Ridley Island for potash and sulphur terminals, and space on neighbouring islands, should Canada follow Japan's example and locate more of its heavy industry at tidewater so as to take advantage of cheap and easy transportation to world markets. While no one any longer believes that Prince Rupert can rival Vancouver, they point to the fact that despite the recession Vancouver handled a record volume of sixty million tonnes in 1984 and the port provides one in every ten jobs in the city. In a year when Canada's business with the Asian Pacific nations for the first time surpassed its traditional trans-Atlantic trade, the chairman of the Science Council of Canada, Dr. Stuart L. Smith, stated: "Never again will Canada's Atlantic trade be even close to that which we will experience with Pacific nations. The sooner we begin to think of ourselves as a Pacific rather than an Atlantic nation, the better we are likely to do." People are predicting a Prince Rupert population of 25,000 within the next decade, which given the large investment in the town seems a modest enough figure. But they also know that for a region, and a nation, that depends so heavily on the cyclical activities of mining, lumbering and growing food for others, the answer must in the end lie out in the distant markets beyond the Pacific.

No region in the world has seen more growth in the past twenty years than the Asian Pacific. During the past decade the average annual growth of Canadian exports to the area has been

Since 1966 CN has maintained an exchange program with Japan Railways. CN's consulting arm, CNAC, supplies services throughout the Asian Pacific. *Courtesy CN*

more than 15 per cent. Two-way trade between Canada and Japan now exceeds $11 billion a year, and so long as Canada is prepared to compete with other resource-rich nations such as Australia or the ASEAN countries or, increasingly, China, the market can be expected to grow, even if not at the pace of recent years. The ASEAN countries, led by Singapore and now including the former British protectorate of Brunei as well as Indonesia, Malaysia, the Philippines and Thailand, are maturing into important producing and trading countries in which Canada has seeded much of the $2 billion it has invested in the Asian Pacific. At present they account for only one per cent of Canada's total exports but, like Australasia, might well become a new market for Canadian manufactured goods in a way Japan and her "little dragons" have not.

South Korea, Taiwan and Hong Kong, who are known as NICS (newly industrializing countries) as well as "little dragons," are like Japan in their paucity of natural resources and maintain a similar trade: manufactured goods in return for raw materials. South Korea's trade with Canada rivals that of France, having increased by 31 per cent during the 1970s. "We are Canada's sixth largest trading partner," said South Korean Consul General Soh in Vancouver recently, "and we anticipate two-way trade will exceed $3 billion by the end of the decade and will double by the end of the century. Canada is important to us because it is stable, and we want to draw closer in terms of economics and culture." Taken together, trade between the NICS and Canada is almost half as big as that of Japan's.

A fishing village in the 1850s, Yokohama grew into Japan's second largest city and one of its major ports during the expansion of Japan's foreign trade. *Courtesy CN*

Then there is China, which as early as Prime Minister Laurier's time Canadians believed would naturally be the biggest market of all. Nowhere on the Pacific Rim is goodwill towards Canada more evident than in the People's Republic, for unlike England and France, Canada had no part in Asian colonialism and unlike the United States it has been no military threat. It was not just a matter of chance that the one foreigner to become an exemplary personage for all Chinese school children was the Canadian Dr. Norman Bethune. But trade so far has been lopsided, and most of the $2 billion a year has been accounted for by Canadian exports of wheat.

"Certainly the elements and conditions for a future relationship between Canada and China are all there," says Dr. Paul Lin in Vancouver, a Canadian-born professor of Chinese studies who has worked in China and maintains strong ties there. He wishes, however, that Canadian responses were more imaginative. "For example, we led the way with recognition of China, but we never took full advantage of that fact to expand our trade and other relationships. I often meet people who say they would like to see more Canadians and hear more about their country. They tell me they know a lot about Americans, Japanese, Germans and French, but little about Canadians."

One institution that may provide the cultural and economic understanding obviously necessary between Canada and the New Pacific is the recently created Asia Pacific Foundation, based in Vancouver and funded by the federal government and various provincial governments. Says Foundation president Raymond Anderson, a former assistant federal deputy minister for international trade development:

> The recent recession caused some self-examination in Canada and made us realize that we had better get involved in areas of growth. Canada is yet to become a mature economy and has great potential for growth compared with the mature economy of the United States. Growth in Europe is going to be relatively flat. One of the first things we want to do is to increase the awareness of Canadians to the potential of the Asian Pacific countries, and an understanding that it is not only the sale of Canadian products in the Far East that is important but also the development of a two-way relationship. This could bring us a greater and broader horizon than we have ever had before.
>
> There have been great changes in attitudes towards Pacific trade, culture and in the academic field, and they have been moving slowly across Canada, starting from British Columbia and Alberta. Canada's relations with the Asian Pacific are becoming institutionalized.

In both government and business the old hit-and-miss methods are disappearing. Ontario and Quebec have been sending out trade missions, and the Japanese are establishing an automobile plant in southwestern Ontario while the South Koreans are doing the same in Quebec's Eastern Townships. Montreal has established a permanent agent in its "sister port" of Shanghai, and Nova Scotia has sent an agricultural mission to Singapore. The Canada-Japan Trade Council in Ottawa reports that more than 1000 Canadian firms are now doing business in Japan. The Canadian International Development Agency (CIDA) has provided assistance in China's efforts to improve farming, forestry, energy resources and manpower training. CN's consulting arm, CANAC, which has worked on railway projects in Indonesia, Malaysia, India, Thailand and Australia, has provided its TRACS computerized system of controlling traffic to China Railway and teamed up with China's Civil Engineering Construction Corporation for joint projects in third world countries. Three B.C. universities, the University of British Columbia, Simon Fraser University and the University of Victoria, are setting up a much-needed Asia Pacific Business Institute. At the seventeenth annual meeting of the Pacific Basin Economic Council in Vancouver in 1984, the chairman of the Canadian advisory board of that organization, John Ellis, assured representatives from 400

Pacific Rim business organizations: "To any of you who have questioned Canada's commitment to the Pacific, let me assure you we are very much a Pacific nation, and more important, that we recognize we are."

Relatively small in population and industrial base, Canada is nevertheless one of the world's great trading nations, ranking sixth. This is largely due to a wealth of natural resources, particularly in the West, which the domestic market cannot begin to assimilate. Canadians would like to export more finished products, particularly from industrialized Ontario and Quebec, but for the foreseeable future Canada appears destined to be a source of raw materials for countries like Japan and South Korea. A president of Nippon Kokan, Hisao Makita, once described Canada's role this way: "Insofar as Canada is one of the world's resource-rich countries and a neighbouring land, while we are provided with human resources rated high in skills and industriousness, Canada and Japan are natural partners in any endeavour for economic advancement. Our two countries can be likened to the two wheels of a cart."

For over a century, the dream of Far East trade has waxed and waned like Prince Rupert's rainbows. After the northwest passage by sea proved impracticable, the railroads were built, though they did more to develop western Canada itself than to provide a route to the Orient. A new nation engrossed in its own affairs and still tied to Europe found little time for economic commitment to the Orient. In the past few years, however, the emergence of the New Pacific has begun to fulfill the old dream of Asian trade. The mills and power plants on the western Pacific Rim will need coal. Growing populations and rising standards of living are expected to maintain Canada's role as a grain exporter.

"We've been cyclical in nature since the beginning," commented Ronald Lawless, whose title as president of Canadian National makes him one of the successors to Charles Melville Hays. "We will go through periods when we have big years, consecutive years, and periods when we don't. We may go through some agonizing times between them, but we are in there for the long haul. Of course anything we can do to reduce the cyclical nature of our business is welcome, but it is not easy to achieve. In the meantime, we are still in the early development stages so far as Prince Rupert is concerned. For many reasons, the fact we now have two major west coast ports will prove that Hays had the right idea."

Appendices

APPENDIX A
TABLE 1

CANADIAN EXPORTS TO SELECTED PACIFIC RIM
COUNTRIES DURING PERIOD OF GREATEST GROWTH
(in U.S. $ millions)

	1971	1981	1983*
Japan	783.8	3,739.5	
China	202.0	840.1	1,190.1
Australia	180.8	684.4	
Philippines	39.4	70.7	445.7
New Zealand	35.1	116.8	
South Korea	24.4	372.4	
Hong Kong	20.1	141.8	
Malaysia	15.4	106.1	
Taiwan	14.0	195.9	
Thailand	13.0	98.2	
Indonesia	10.0	79.7	169.4
Singapore	9.5	129.9	
Totals	1,347.5	6,569.5	
World Totals	17,674.5	68,281.2	

*Nations that registered further growth since 1981

SOURCES: United Nations International Trade Statistics; Statistics Canada

	APPENDIX A	
	TABLE 2	

CANADIAN IMPORTS FROM SELECTED PACIFIC RIM
COUNTRIES DURING PERIOD OF GREATEST GROWTH
(in U.S. $ millions)

	1971	1981
Japan	794.1	3,369.3
Australia	124.4	404.9
Taiwan	79.7	608.2
Hong Kong	79.4	562.6
New Zealand	39.8	121.5
Malaysia	26.6	83.4
China	23.0	183.5
South Korea	19.2	506.6
Singapore	18.2	145.0
Philippines	6.1	90.6
Thailand	2.9	27.5
Indonesia	1.0	30.8
Totals	1,214.4	6,133.9
World Totals	15,458.3	64,897.2

SOURCES: United Nations International Trade Statistics; Statistics Canada

	APPENDIX B			
	TABLE 3			

MAJOR TRADING PARTNERS IN TERMS OF PERCENTAGES OF CANADA'S
WORLD TRADE

	United States	United Kingdom	Japan	China
1971				
Exports	67.5	7.8	4.6	1.1
Imports	70.2	5.3	5.1	—
1974				
Exports	65.5	5.9	6.9	1.4
Imports	67.4	3.6	4.5	—
1981				
Exports	65.9	3.7	5.5	1.2
Imports	68.7	2.9	5.2	—
1983				
Exports	72.7	2.7	5.0	1.6
Imports	71.6	2.4	5.9	—

SOURCES: United Nations International Trade Statistics Year Books

Chronology

1836 British North America's first railway—Champlain and St. Lawrence—opened between Laprairie (Montreal) and St-Jean over a 14.5-mile track.

1841 Act of Union creates Province of Canada (Quebec and Ontario).

1849 Railway Guarantee Act launches railway construction boom. Total main line track in British North America: 66 miles.

1852 Grand Trunk Railway Company incorporated by act of parliament.

1854 Three railways—Great Western, Northern and Midland—built in Ontario.

1856 Grand Trunk Railway completed between Montreal and Toronto.

1857 Parliamentary committee in British House of Commons probes future of Hudson's Bay Company.

1861 Edward W. Watkin appointed Superintending Commissioner of ailing Grand Trunk Railway; as result of railway boom, main line tracks in British North America total 2065 miles.

1862 Grand Trunk Arrangements Act refinances company, divorces government from railway operations. Watkin becomes president; Charles J. Brydges, managing director.

1863 Watkin engineers takeover of Hudson's Bay Company by London-based International Financial Society in an effort to open the West for a telegraph line and railway.

1864 Grand Trunk takes over Champlain and St. Lawrence.

1867 Ontario, Quebec, Nova Scotia and New Brunswick united under British North America Act.

1869 Watkin loses shareholders' support and resigns from Grand Trunk. Canadian government buys out Hudson's Bay Company. Union Pacific in the United States completes first coast-to-coast railway. Suez Canal opens.

1871 British Columbia follows Manitoba into Confederation. Sandford Fleming heads Canadian Pacific Survey.

1872 Fleming reports Yellowhead Pass best route through the Rocky Mountains.

1873 Canadian Pacific Scandal; John A. Macdonald resigns. Capt. Henry W. Tyler chosen president of Grand Trunk; Brydges, general superintendent of Canadian Government Railways.

1879 John A. Macdonald re-elected; after failure to persuade Grand Trunk to build to west coast, he seeks another potential builder.

1880 Government contracts with Canadian Pacific Syndicate to build transcontinental railway. Canada possesses 7194 miles of main line.

1882	Grand Trunk takes over 852-mile Great Western.
1885	Canadian Pacific Railway completed—to Burrard Inlet where a lumber mill village is reborn as the city of Vancouver. Canadian main line tracks total 10 773 miles; total freight carried: 14.6 million tons.
1888	Grand Trunk takes over 492-mile Northern Railway in Ontario.
1889	Japan opens consulate in Vancouver, its first official representation in Canada.
1894	John Larke of Toronto goes to Sydney, Australia, as Canada's first official trade representative in a Pacific Rim country.
1895	Sir Charles Rivers Wilson becomes president of Grand Trunk Railway Company; appoints Charles Melville Hays general manager in Montreal.
1896	Wilfrid Laurier elected prime minister. William Mackenzie and Donald Mann team up to purchase Lake Manitoba Railway and Canal Company. Canadian main lines total 15 977 miles and carry 21.5 million tons of freight a year.
1897	Crow's Nest Pass Agreement subsidizes grain farmers at expense of railways.
1899	Mackenzie and Mann incorporate Canadian Northern Railway Company; plan to extend it from Manitoba to Great Lakes and west to Edmonton.
1901	Canadian Northern takes over Manitoba tracks of American Northern Pacific Railroad, increasing total Canadian Northern trackage to 1285 miles.
1902	Charles Melville Hays of Grand Trunk Railway announces plan for a line to Pacific.
1903	Grand Trunk Pacific Railway Company incorporated with Hays as president; having failed to get Hays and Canadian Northern to co-operate, Laurier gives Hays go-ahead to build from Winnipeg to the coast, Port Simpson being mentioned as possible terminus.
1905	Canadian Northern main line reaches Edmonton. On 29 August Grand Trunk Pacific begins building westward on the prairies; Kaien Island chosen as west coast terminal. Canada possesses 20 487 miles of track; some 50.8 million tons of freight carried.
1906	Construction of town of Prince Rupert begins. Canadian Northern surveys for a line through Yellowhead Pass to Vancouver. Laurier urges Canadians to trade with Asian Pacific nations.
1908	First sod turned at Prince Rupert to begin eastward construction of Grand Trunk Pacific.
1909	Sir Charles Rivers Wilson retires; Hays becomes president of Grand Trunk Railway Company with A. W. Smithers as chairman. Grand Trunk Pacific tracks reach Edmonton.
1910	GTP begins construction into British Columbia via Yellowhead Pass, while crews working out of Prince Rupert push rails six miles east of Terrace. Mackenzie and Mann form B.C. subsidiary, Canadian Northern Pacific, and start building through Yellowhead Pass.
1911	Laurier defeated. Canada and Japan sign trade agreement. GTP track reaches Red Pass Junction in the east; on the Prince Rupert end, 100 miles of track is completed.
1912	Hays drowned on the *Titanic;* E. J. Chamberlin becomes president of debt-ridden Grand Trunk Pacific.
1913	Economic depression undermines Grand Trunk Pacific and Canadian Northern. Canadian Northern signs agreement with City of Vancouver for terminal facilities and establishes ocean steamship company.
1914	On 7 April last spike driven near Fort Fraser to complete GTP line between

Prince Rupert and Winnipeg; first train arrives at Prince Rupert following day. Huge rock slide at Hell's Gate in Fraser Canyon en route to Vancouver slows Canadian Northern progress. Panama Canal opened.

1915 Canadian Northern complete between Montreal and Port Mann, near Vancouver, with driving of last spike, 59 miles west of Kamloops Junction, on 22 January. With 34 882 miles of main line, Canada transports 87.2 million tons of freight. Grand Trunk asks Dominion Government to take over ailing GTP.

1916 Both Grand Trunk Pacific and Canadian Northern in serious financial difficulties; Borden government appoints royal commission which recommends nationalization and amalgamation.

1917 Canadian government takes over Canadian Northern, combining it with government-owned railways in eastern Canada and calling new system the Canadian National Railways Company.

1919 Grand Trunk Pacific and newly formed Canadian Government Merchant Marine come under Canadian National Railways management.

1921 CN opens office in the western Pacific, appointing George E. Bunting general traffic agent for Australasia, based in Auckland, New Zealand.

1922 Having now assimilated Grand Trunk Railway Company, CN operates 22 000 miles of track under presidency of Sir Henry Thornton. Former Vancouver manager August Brostedt opens CN office in Shanghai, its first in the Orient.

1923 Brostedt establishes Asian headquarters in Hong Kong; Gary M. Hemsworth becomes manager in Shanghai.

1925 First CN silk train from Vancouver to New York. Total of Canada's main line tracks now 40 350 miles. Freight totals 111 million tons a year on all lines.

1927 CN office opened in Yokohama by Donald E. Ross and Lawrence E. Lawler, and one in Singapore by William A. Watson. Brostedt named Asiatic traffic manager.

1929 Canada establishes diplomatic relations in Asian Pacific, appointing a Minister to Japan.

1932 Thornton resigns as Depression cuts into CN. Imperial Economic Conference in Ottawa.

1936 Canadian Government Merchant Marine goes out of business.

1937 Japanese overrun China. CN closes Shanghai office. Canada exports scrap metal to Japanese war machine.

1941 Japan and Canada break off relations; CN closes Yokohama office; CN agents Middlecoat and Healey are interned.

1942 Middlecoat and Healey repatriated. Port of Prince Rupert turned into wartime base with population of 20 000.

1946 Canada establishes liaison mission with Tokyo; CN reopens Hong Kong office and establishes an office in Calcutta.

1948 CN offices in Hong Kong and Calcutta closed because of "unsettled conditions."

1950 Donald Gordon succeeds R. C. Vaughan as CN president.

1951 Japan peace treaty signed; first post-war Japanese freighters arrive at Vancouver. Canada adheres to Colombo Plan to aid Far Eastern nations.

1954 Louis St. Laurent first Canadian prime minister to visit Japan; signs commercial treaty that restores Japan as Canada's third largest customer.

1955 William H. Neale posted to CN office in Sydney, Australia.

1961	Neale appointed Sales Manager, Orient; Everett Shipping Corporation becomes CN representative in Far East; China buys large quantities of Canadian wheat. Canada's total of main line track reaches its zenith at 44 029 miles.
1963	Neale goes to Peking to establish commercial arrangements with China.
1964	In effort to secure traffic, Prince Rupert Port Commission established with W. J. Scott as chairman.
1965	Japanese exports exceed imports for first time; Canada-Japan committee formed to boost Canadian raw material sales to Japan. CN study recommends Ridley Island as Prince Rupert bulk terminal.
1966	Donald Gordon, first CN president to visit Orient, goes to Hong Kong and Tokyo; signs technical exchange agreement with Japan Railway. Prairie premiers urge development of port of Prince Rupert.
1967	Pacific Basin Economic Council established, with Canada a founding member. Two-way Canada-Japan trade passes $1 billion yearly.
1968	CN's international consulting division, CANAC, established, its first major assignment being study of Korean National Railway.
1970	Canada establishes diplomatic relations with People's Republic of China. Roberts Bank coal terminal opens near Vancouver. CN business through Vancouver doubles in five years.
1972	Prince Rupert proclaimed National Harbours Board port.
1973	OPEC oil crisis causes Japanese industry to convert from oil to coal, providing new market for west coast Canadian coal.
1976	Canada and Japan sign Framework for Economic Co-operation.
1977	Prince Rupert's Fairview Terminal opens for lumber and general commodities.
1978	Prince Rupert Grain Ltd. formed by prairie companies to take over the old elevator and build modern terminal. In Tokyo, Neale retires as Managing Director, Far East and Australasia, and is succeeded by Russell E. Steele.
1979	Second OPEC crisis assures Japanese investment in British Columbia's new Northeast Coal Project.
1981	B.C. Premier Bill Bennett signs contract to supply B.C. coal to Japan. Work begins on Ridley Island coal and grain terminals.
1982	CN Rail president Ronald E. Lawless signs 15-year contract to transport coal from northeastern B.C. to Prince Rupert, and steps up railway's $600-million project to upgrade B.C. tracks.
1983	First trainload of coal leaves Tumbler Ridge, in centre of Northeast Coal Project.
1984	*Soryu Maru* loads first coal for Japan 7 January at Ridley Island. Total annual two-way trade with Japan exceeds $10 billion, coal accounting for $1.3 billion. Crow's Nest Pass Agreement repealed in favour of Western Grain Transportation Act.
1985	*World Prize* loads first prairie wheat to go from Ridley Island, destined for China, 8 March.

Notes

Abbreviations PAC   Public Archives of Canada, Ottawa
               CN/AC   CN Records/Archivist's Collection, Montreal

INTRODUCTION

p.9   "There are a number": Royal Commission on the Economic Union and Development Prospects for Canada (Macdonald Commission), Ottawa, 1985, 1:254.

CHAPTER ONE

Quest for an All-Red Route

p.13   Lord Dorchester (Guy Carleton), Governor of Lower Canada 1786–96.

p.13   Kitten, *see* Myles Pennington, *Railways and Other Ways,* Toronto, 1896, p. 281.

p.14   *Toronto Patriot,* 13 Sept. 1836; *see also* George Johnson, *Alphabet of First Things in Canada,* Ottawa, 1897, p. 27: "One of [Dalton's] favourite ideas was that much time would not lapse before the teas and silks of China would be transported direct from the shores of the Pacific Ocean to Toronto by canal, by river, by railway, and all the way by steam."

p.14   Sir John Smyth: *Railroad Communication: A West Proposed Line of Steam Communication from London in England to China and the East Indies,* Toronto, 1845.

p.14   "We shall yet": Col. Robert Bonnycastle, *Canada and the Canadians in 1846,* 2:138.

p.15   "This national highway": Robert Carmichael-Smyth, *The Employment of the People and Capital of Great Britain in her Own Colonies,* London 1849, p. 2

p.17   "I am neither a prophet": Howe, 15 May 1851, Mason's Hall, Halifax, *Speeches and Public Letters of Joseph Howe,* Halifax, 1909, 2:61.

p.20   "The American railroads": *Prospectus,* Grand Trunk Railway Company, London, 12 April 1853.

p.21   *Railway Times:* 7 May 1853.

p.21   "Nothing would serve": *Morning Chronicle,* Halifax, April 1858, cited in *Canadian Historical Review,* 1953, 34:224.

p.21   "a good, broad, open": Ross, Evidence, Select Committee, Hudson's Bay Company hearings, London, England, 1857.

p.21   "Practical Observations": Sandford Fleming's Appendix to *A Sketch of an Overland Route to British Columbia* by H. Y. Hind, Toronto, 1864.

p.22 "will completely shut": C. P. Ellerman, English railway promotor, to Macdonald, 27 July 1858, Sir John A. Macdonald Papers, v. 127, C-1556, pp. 5224–44.

p.23 "England is suddenly": *New York Herald,* 2 Dec. 1858.

p.23 "While Congress is postponing": *Boston Evening Transcript,* 5 June 1858.

p.23 "a great chain": quoted in R. A. Russell, *Importance of Communications with the Pacific Coast,* Cedar Rapids, Iowa, 1948, p. 267.

p.23 "His Excellency": Minutes, Executive Council of Canada (E), State Book, 18 Feb. 1857, PAC.

p.24 "I hope to see": Select Committee, Hudson's Bay Company hearings, London, 1857.

p.24 "I am quite satisfied,": quoted in G. R. Stevens, *Canadian National Railways,* Toronto, 1962, 2:289.

p.25 "The whole property": Anthony Trollope, *North America,* London, 1862, p. 62.

p.25 "We consider ourselves": quoted in G. R. Stevens, *History of CN Railways,* New York, 1973, p. 57.

CHAPTER TWO

A Northwest Passage by Rail

p.27 "Neither of us": Edward Watkin, *Canada and the States,* London, 1887, p. 3.

p.28 "Our augmenting interests": *Illustrated London News,* Feb. 1861.

p.29 "This line [The Grand Trunk]": quoted in R. G. Trotter, *Canadian Federation,* London, 1924, pp. 179–81.

p.30 "I found Mr. Tilley": Watkin, p. 2.

p.31 "Certainly, in 1861": ibid.

p.33 "We have attempted": Milton and Cheadle, *The Northwest Passage by Land,* London, 1865, p. 396.

p.34 "What! Sequestor our very tap-root": quoted in Watkin, p. 120.

p.34 "It is essential": Report, Hudson's Bay Company Hearings, London, 1857.

p.35 "If the Duke": quoted in Watkin, p. 124.

p.35 "You must really help": Watkin to Baring, 4 Nov. 1862, Baring Papers (Grand Trunk), PAC.

p.35 "The room was the Courtroom": Watkin, p. 124.

p.35 "Your Pacific scheme": quoted in ibid.

p.36 "a gentleman of great experience": Newcastle, House of Lords, 24 Dec. 1863.

p.36 "Thus, after a long and continuous period": Watkin, p. 144.

p.36 "At that time, 1863": ibid., p. 451.

p.37 "safe in saying that negotiations": Brydges to J. W. Taylor, U.S. consul, Winnipeg, 24 Dec. 1863, quoted in A. W. Currie, *The Grand Trunk Railway of Canada,* Toronto, 1957, p. 301.

p.37 "The country itself": Macdonald to Watkin, 25 March 1865, in Joseph Pope, *Correspondence of Sir John Macdonald,* Toronto, 1921, p. 43.

p.38 "Enough is known": Brief of the Northern Pacific Railroad to [U.S.] Congress, 2nd Session, 17 Dec. 1867.

p.40 "I have no belief": Brydges to David L. Macpherson, 11 March 1872, Macdonald Papers, v. 123, C-1555, pp. 50499–556.

p.41 "connect with the splendid": The year Waddington's pamphlet appeared, *London Engineering* reported that such a scheme could see goods shipped "from Liverpool to Canton for $78.25 a ton, compared with the $101.30 it cost to ship entirely by sea." Cited in *U.S. Railroad and Mining Register,* August 1868.

p.42 "that there is": Brydges to Macdonald, 26 Jan. 1870, Macdonald Papers, Letter Book 13, C-28.

p.42 "The line of the Northern Pacific": U.S. Senate Report on Pacific Railroads, 1869.

p.42 "It is quite evident": Macdonald to Brydges, 28 Jan. 1870, Macdonald Papers, Letter Book 13, C-28.

p.43 "We are satisfied": G. M. Grant, *Ocean to Ocean,* Montreal, 1877, p. 356.

p.43 "All this country": ibid., p. 17.

p.46 "Until this great work": Macdonald to Sir Stafford Northcote, in Pope, *Correspondence of Sir John Macdonald,* pp. 240–41.

p.46 "an Imperial Highway": Tupper, House of Commons Debates, May 1879, p. 1919.

p.47 Tyler refused: Sir Charles Tupper, *Recollections of Sixty Years in Canada,* London, 1914, pp. 139–40; Currie, p. 307.

p.47 "A mad undertaking": *Toronto Bystander,* August 1880, p. 403.

p.47 "the pauper": quoted in *Daily Witness,* Montreal, 18 Sept. 1880.

p.47 New York Herald: cited in *Ottawa Free Press,* 2 Oct. 1880.

p.48 "an object of perennial promise": *Canadian Monthly and National Review,* April 1873.

p.48 "So long as the Grand Trunk": semi-annual shareholders meeting, 25 May 1883, quoted in Currie, p. 311.

p.48 "The most serious troubles": quoted in H. A. Lovett, *Canada and the Grand Trunk,* Montreal, 1924, p. 117.

p.49 "This will probably": *Montreal Gazette,* 14 Sept. 1886.

p.49 "The old Grand Trunk": Watkin, p. 52.

p.50 "until we have": Stephen in his first annual CP Syndicate Report, 1881, quoted in W. Kaye Lamb's *History of Canadian Pacific Railway,* New York, 1977, p. 148.

CHAPTER THREE
A Struggle for Supremacy

p.53 "very self-possessed": *Railway Age Gazette,* vol. 47, no. 18, p. 808.

p.54 "Don't you find": *Canadian Magazine,* August 1903, p. 13.

p.55 "The Grand Trunk is": Hays to shareholders, 8 March 1904, quoted in H. A. Lovett, *Canada and the Grand Trunk,* Montreal, 1924, p. 151.

p.57 "We began with two engines": David B. Hanna, *Trains of Recollection,* Toronto, 1924, p. 142.

p.57 "From a series": ibid., p. 174.

p.58 "I believe they may": Rivers Wilson to Hays, 29 July 1903, Charles M. Hays Papers, 1:241.

p.58 "My own preference": Hays to Rivers Wilson, 14 April 1902, ibid., 1:6–7.

p.59 "You know, and I think": Rivers Wilson to Hays, quoted in G. R. Stevens, *Canadian National Railways,* Toronto, 1962, 2:129.

p.59 "We would hail": Van Horne in *Manitoba Free Press,* 13 Nov. 1902.

p.60 "The time is now ripe": Calgary Board of Trade, 6 Dec. 1902, Laurier Papers, p. 68201; also similar letters from Victoria, Regina, Prince Albert, etc., pp. 68203–205.

p.60 "We want all": *Manitoba Free Press,* 3 Nov. 1902.

p.61 "To those who": Laurier, House of Commons Debates, 30 July 1903, p. 8396.

p.62 "Sir Wilfrid Laurier talked": Hays to Rivers Wilson, 24 Oct. 1902, Hays Papers, 1:37.

p.63 "regarded with some little surprise": *Vancouver Daily Province,* 24 Nov. 1902.

p.64 "premature, ill-conceived": cited by Sir John Willison in *Sir W. Laurier,* Makers of Canada Series, Toronto, 1926, 2:360.

p.64 "The United States has": Hill, *Vancouver Daily Province,* 26 Jan. 1903.

p.64 "You appear to be mapping": Rivers Wilson to Hays, 4 Nov. 1902, Hays Papers, 1:43.

p.64 "honest broker": Rivers Wilson to Hays, 10 July 1903, Hays Papers, 1:82.

p.64 "We offered": Evidence given by Mann, Canadian Northern Arbitration, Ottawa, 1918, p. 2683.

p.66 "That mad route,": *Montreal Star,* 23 Jan. 1904.

p.66 "I am greatly vexed": Rivers Wilson to Hays, 10 July 1903, Hays Papers, 1:211–12.

p.67 "Pray believe me": Rivers Wilson to Hays, 14 July 1903, quoted in Stevens, 2:142.

p.67 "It seems clear that": *Robert Laird Borden, His Memoirs,* Toronto, 1938, 1:116.

p.67 "I am well aware that": Laurier quoted in Willison, 2:364.

p.68 "The idea which": Rivers Wilson to shareholders, Oct. 1903, quoted in Stevens, 2:147.

p.69 "We consider it alike": Rivers Wilson to shareholders, special meeting, 8 March 1904, London, quoted in Lovett, Canada and the Grand Trunk, Montreal, 1924, p. 131 et seq.

p.69 "[The west] is the only direction": Hays to shareholders, ibid., p. 151.

p.70 "There is that old fogy": Smithers to shareholders, ibid., p. 158.

p.70 "You know, we expected": Mann, *Toronto Globe,* Dec. 1904, quoted in Stevens, 2:44.

p.72 "I think that it is very generally": Hays to Rivers Wilson, 26 Sept. 1906, ibid., p. 178.

p.72 "The interest on the cost": *Winnipeg Free Press,* 5 Dec. 1908.

p.76 "Railroads are not now built": Hays, *Victoria Daily Times,* 23 Dec. 1908.

p.76 "Words fail me": Rivers Wilson to shareholders, 1909, quoted in Stevens, 2:185.

p.77 "The shortest, most direct": Hays to Laurier, 29 Jan. 1907, Laurier Papers, p. 118716.

p.78 "To grasp its significance": *World's Work,* New York, April 1910.

p.79 "It is merely": quoted in F. A. Talbot, *The Making of a Great Canadian Railway,* London, 1912, p. 189.

p.81 "a thoroughly Canadian system": *Canadian Annual Review,* 1909, p. 587.

p.82 "A wanton waste": Graham to Laurier, 20 Sept. 1909, George Graham Papers, pp. 19445–46, PAC.

CHAPTER FOUR
The Last Frontier

p.85 "I do not approve": *Vancouver Daily Province,* 5 Jan. 1903.

p.87 "We heard very little": Aural History, NW 971.108, B.C. Archives, Victoria.

p.91 "surprised to find flowers": 20 Sept. 1904, Hays Papers, p. 691.

p.93 "hundreds of people": *Victoria Daily Colonist,* 18 July 1906.

p.94 "The opening of Prince Rupert": *Vancouver World,* 15 April 1909.

p.96 "One could hardly": *British Columbia Magazine,* Nov. 1911.

p.98 "The temporary employment": Rivers Wilson, *Winnipeg Free Press,* 13 Oct. 1909. At one time 21,000 men worked on the National Transcontinental Railway, including the Grand Trunk Pacific from Winnipeg to Prince Rupert and the government-owned half from Winnipeg to Moncton, New Brunswick.

p.99 "A port without adequate": *Victoria Daily Colonist,* 15 Jan. 1907.

p.100 "We have first of all": *Victoria Daily Times,* 23 Dec. 1908.

p.100 "To this new port": quoted in *British Columbia Magazine,* August 1912.

p.101 "within 18 months": *Vancouver News Advertiser,* 24 Dec. 1911.

p.103 "beyond question the greatest": Laurier, *Railway Age Gazette,* v. 2, no. 18, p. 8.

p.103 Flavelle: "The leadership of Charles M. Hays for a period gave promise of independent effort. His faulty judgement, however, committed his company to a trans-continental enterprise which could bring no advantage to the Grand Trunk and which established losses that forced it into liquidation." Flavelle to Prime Minister Mackenzie King, 27 Jan. 1922, CN/AC.

p.105 "inexpressibly bitter disappointment": Smithers to Borden, 10 Dec. 1915, quoted in Lovett, p. 177.

CHAPTER FIVE

The Asian Dream

p.107 "Up to the present": Laurier, *Toronto Globe,* 22 Feb. 1906.

p.108 "There is no doubt": Col. James Strange, East India Company, 1786, quoted in Donald MacKay, *Empire of Wood,* Vancouver, 1982, p. 4.

p.111 "One of the principal": Canadian Trade and Commerce Department, 21 Nov. 1891, RG.2, S2, v. 24, PAC.

p.111 "Some come over": Larke to Deputy Minister J. G. Parmelee, 17 April 1895, Trade and Commerce Records, vol. 1117, file 2569, PAC.

p.112 "we would be blind": Laurier, *Toronto Globe,* 22 Feb. 1906.

p.112 "tea to the Orient": ibid., 25 April 1905.

p.116 "have a better route": Laurier 20 Feb., quoted in *Canadian Annual Review,* 1906, p. 542.

p.117 "was one of the greatest": Preston to Laurier, 15 Jan. 1908, Laurier Papers, MG 26, Reel C-857, pp. 135208–16.

p.117 "The Orient is awakening": *Vancouver Daily Province,* 21 Sept. 1911.

p.119 "We have hoped": Chamberlin to Borden, 1916, Borden Papers, Reel C-4211, p. 9232, PAC.

p.119 "at the end of our tether": Smithers, 10 Dec., quoted in G. deT. Glazebrook, *A History of Transportation in Canada,* Toronto, 1938, 2:151.

p.120 "The Canadian Northern": Royal Commission Report on Railways and Transportation, 1917.

p.121 "The Canadian National was": quoted in *Canadian Railway and Marine World,* Nov. 1922, p. 559.

p.123 "The day is not far distant": quoted in ibid., Oct. 1920, p. 18.

p.125 "We tried very hard": Brostedt, "The Opened Door in China," *Canadian National Railways Magazine,* July 1922. Hanna, *Trains of Recollection* (Toronto, 1924, p. 333), describes how CN representatives also were responsible for CGMM traffic.

p.126 "Hong Kong is considered": Brostedt to CN Head Office, 21 April 1930, CN/AC.

p.126 "It will be realized": ibid.

p.128 "I should say we ought": Thornton, Select Committee Report, Canadian National Railways and Shipping, Ottawa, June 1924, p. 50.

p.129 "the foundations which": quoted in *Canadian Railway and Marine World,* March 1927, p. 142.

p.129 "matter of building up": Thornton, in Annual Report, Canadian National Railways, 1922, p. 10.

CHAPTER SIX
Silk Trains and Scrap Iron

p.131 sealed (silk) trains: David B. Hanna, *Trains of Recollection,* Toronto, 1924, p. 310.

p.134 Docked 7:25 A.M.: CN Report, 19 Oct. 1927, File Y-7330-6, CN/AC.

p.136 "I was working": Coté, *Canadian Rail,* August 1976, p. 232.

p.136 "We had five express cars": Scott, letter to author, 7 Feb. 1985.

p.137 "There is a rise": Scott, ibid.

p.137 "In December 1928": Coté, *Canadian Rail,* August 1976.

p.139 "Two miles westward": quoted in "There was never a signal set against a silk train," *Railroad,* April 1965, pp. 13–24.

p.139 "taken all in all": *Port of Vancouver News,* Oct. 1929.

p.140 "Flour King" of Japan: *Canadian National Magazine* vol. 2, no. 1, July 1929.

p.141 "Practically all the travellers": Brostedt to Head Office, CN/AC.

p.141 "As you are aware": ibid. CN's revenue from Far East Traffic in 1929 was $3 million.

p.142 CN decided: The CGMM pulled out of the Orient in 1931, though it did not disband completely for another five years; meantime, CN developed Canadian National Steamships, a service which continued until well into the 1950s.

p.142 "The whole country": Feb. 1930, MacKenzie King Papers, C-2320, p. 151492.

p.142 "The greatest expansion": Stevens in *Industrial Canada,* Sept. 1931, p. 86.

p.142 "Many have expressed regret": ibid., June 1933, p. 29.

p.143 "a very disappointed man": Marler to Stevens, 15 Oct. 1930, Stevens Papers, vol. 22, File 40, PAC.

p.144 "It is abundantly clear": Stevens in *Industrial Canada,* Sept. 1931, p. 86.

p.144 "in an outburst of enthusiam": RG 30, vol. 11933, PAC.

p.148 "I have received word": Healey, Hong Kong, to Foreign Freight Manager, Montreal, 9 Oct. 1941, CN File 3615-131 C, CN/AC.

p.150 "Boarding the *Shanghai Maru*": ibid.

p.150 "I am sorry to have to report": Fraser to Vaughan, 29 Dec. 1941, CN/AC.

CHAPTER SEVEN
The New Pacific

p.155 "This is the beginning": Suzuki, "The Coming of the Pacific Age," speech at the East-West Centre, Hawaii, 15 June 1982. Suzuki was Prime Minister from 1980 to 1982, during which period he visited Canada twice.

p.156 "The present is not": G. R. Fairhead, General Freight Traffic Manager, 16 Jan. 1946. CN/AC.

p.156 S. S. *Windermere Park:* Few silk ships arrived after the war, since nylons and other synthetics dominated the market.

212

p.156 "every pound of cargo": Memo, F. J. Stock, Traffic Manager, Montreal, 28 Oct. 1947 (CN Oriental Organization), CN/AC.

p.157 "It may be that": Gordon, File 385, G662/1950, CN/AC.

p.160 "general impression I have gained": Middlecoat to Head Office, 16 March 1956, CN/AC.

p.160 "I visited Hong Kong": Neale memo, 28 March 1984, CN/AC. Also personal interviews with author.

p.162 "I checked my notes": Craig memo to Montreal from Colombo, 4 Nov. 1960, CN/AC.

p.163 "I encountered all the problems": Neale memo, 28 March 1984, CN/AC.

p.165 "There were virtually": Neale, ibid.

p.168 "Since Japanese oranges": Neale, ibid.

p.172 "enhance the CN presence": Hart, interview with author, London (Eng.), Dec. 1985.

CHAPTER EIGHT

The City of Rainbows

p.177 "If Donald Gordon's wish": G. B. Casey in the *Prince Rupert Daily News,* quoted in CN Daily Report, 22 April, 1954, CN/AC.

p.178 "CN is too conscious": Scott in *Prince Rupert Daily News,* 4 Nov. 1964.

p.178 "Such a project": *Vancouver Province,* 28 Dec. 1965.

p.178 "We wanted to get": Hick interview with author, Nov. 1985.

p.179 "During my recent trip": Manning to Pearson, 13 July 1966. Thatcher sent a similar letter, 29 March 1967. CN/AC.

p.179 "We were getting": Scott quoted in *Port of Prince Rupert Tenth Anniversary Review,* National Harbours Board Publication, 1982.

p.180 "The government had already": Scott interview with author, Prince Rupert, June 1985, CN/AC.

p.182 "When it became": Lawless interview with author, Nov. 1985.

p.183 Hick's waterfront study: *The Case for Expanded Grain Facilities in Prince Rupert,* Grain Coordination Committee. CN/AC.

p.183 "make a stack four feet high": Lester quoted in *Harbour and Shipping,* Oct. 1977, p. 43.

p.183 "has a cost advantage": *Vancouver Sun,* 22 Nov. 1977.

p.183 "the combined development": ibid.

CHAPTER NINE

Canada's Pacific Rim

p.185 "Charles Hays was really": Scott interview with author, June 1985, CN/AC.

p.186 "By 1980 CN Rail": Sturgess address, Oct. 1984, CN/AC.

p.186 "The port had been growing": Scott interview with author, June, 1985, CN/AC.

p.192 "The majority of the construction": Walker quoted in *Movin,* Feb. 1984.

p.193 "They permit us": phone conversation with author, Nov. 1985.

p.193 "Never again will Canada's": Smith, "Canada and the Pacific Challenge," Empire Club of Canada, Toronto, 29 March 1984.

p.194 "We are Canada's sixth largest": Soh interview with Ashley Ford, Vancouver, June 1985, CN/AC.

p.195 "Certainly the elements": Lin interview with Ashley Ford, Vancouver, July, 1985, CN/AC.

p.196 "The recent recession": Anderson interview with Ashley Ford, Vancouver, June, 1985, CN/AC.

p.196 "To any of you": Pacific Basin Economic Council Report, Vancouver Meeting, 1984, p. 2.

p.197 "Insofar as Canada is one of the world's": In *Japanese Economic Mission to Canada 1976*, Symposium on the Results, published by Commission of the Japanese Economic Mission, Tokyo, 1977.

p.197 "We've been cyclical": Lawless interview with author, Nov. 1985.

Select Bibliography

Berton, Pierre. *The Great Railway.* 2 vols. Toronto, 1970, 1971.

Biggar, E. B. *The Canadian Railway Problem.* Toronto, 1917.

Bonnycastle, Sir Richard H. *Canada and the Canadians in 1846.* 2 vols. London, 1846.

Borden, Henry, ed. *Robert Laird Borden, His Memoirs.* 2 vols. Toronto, 1938.

Boulnois, L. *The Silk Road.* New York, 1966.

Bowman, Phylis. *Muskeg, Rocks and Rain.* Prince Rupert, 1973.

Currie, A. W. *The Grand Trunk Railway of Canada.* Toronto, 1957.

Glazebrook, G. deT. *A History of Transportation in Canada.* 2 vols. Ottawa, 1964.

Grant, G. M. *Ocean to Ocean.* Montreal, 1877.

Hanna, David B. *Trains of Recollection: Drawn from Fifty Years of Railway Service in Scotland and Canada.* Toronto, 1924.

Hays, A. J. *Japan and the Pacific Community.* Ottawa, 1981.

Hind, H. Y. *A Sketch of an Overland Route to British Columbia.* Toronto, 1862.

Hyde, F. E. *Blue Funnel.* London, 1956.

Innis, Harold. *A History of the Canadian Pacific.* Toronto, 1923.

Irving, Leonard B. *Pacific Railways and Nationalism in the Canadian American Northwest, 1845–1873.* New York, 1968.

Lamb, W. Kaye. *History of the Canadian Pacific Railway.* New York, 1977.

Large, R. G. *Prince Rupert, a Gateway to Alaska.* Prince Rupert, 1960.

Lovett, H. A. *Canada and the Grand Trunk.* Montreal, 1924.

Lower, J. A. *Canada on the Pacific Rim.* Toronto, 1975.

Marsh, D'Arcy. *The Tragedy of Sir Henry Thornton.* Toronto, 1935.

Milton, Viscount, and Cheadle, W. B. *The Northwest Passage by Land.* London, 1865.

Pope, Sir Joseph. *Memoirs of the Right Hon. Sir John Alexander Macdonald.* 2 vols. Ottawa, 1894.

Regehr, T. D. *The Canadian Northern Railway.* Toronto, 1976.

Rich, E. E. *Hudson's Bay Company 1670–1870.* 3 vols. Toronto, 1960.

Rivers Wilson, Sir Charles. *Chapters from My Official Life.* London, 1916.

Skelton, O. D. *Life and Letters of Sir Wilfrid Laurier.* 2 vols. Toronto, 1965.

Stevens, G. R. *Canadian National Railways.* 2 vols. Toronto, 1960, 1962.

————. *History of the Canadian National Railways.* New York, 1973.

Talbot, F. A. *The Making of a Great Canadian Railway.* London, 1912.

Trotter, R. G. *Canadian Federation, its Origins and Achievements.* London, 1924.

Tupper, Sir Charles. *Recollections of Sixty Years.* London, 1914.

Watkin, Sir Edward. *Canada and the States.* London, 1887.

Acknowledgements

HAVING COMMISSIONED THIS BOOK, CN was generous in providing information and assistance during the researching and writing process. Nevertheless, its content is solely the work of the author who assumes responsibility for any error in fact or interpretation.

I would like to thank the following persons, both in CN and elsewhere, for their help. In particular my gratitude goes to Bill Neale, now of Los Angeles, whose idea was the generating spark for the project, and who generously provided notes, recollections and photos of his years as CN managing director in the Orient, as well as submitting to many long interviews. Ilene Kardashinski-Watt, former Systems Manager, Industrial Development and Marketing Communications, Montreal, provided co-ordination, information and support for the project. The enthusiasm, knowledge and generosity of Dr. Kenneth S. Mackenzie, corporate archivist, lightened my task considerably, and his guidance through Canadian railway history helped me avoid various pitfalls.

In addition I would like to thank the following: Anthony Clegg for researching and drawing the originals of the maps; J. Norman Lowe, veteran CN history research officer; J. D. Poirier, general sales manager, Overseas Markets; P. S. Murray, assistant sales manager, Far East; Henry Au, manager, Hong Kong; Tadashi Kunita, manager, Japan, Korea & Taiwan; Donna Lafleur, word processor; H. B. Weinstein, manager, Financial Planning; J. H. D. Sturgess, former vice-president, Marketing and now vice-president at Toronto; CN president Ronald E. Lawless; senior western vice-president Ross Walker, Edmonton; and corporate vice-president A. R. Williams in Vancouver. Other Vancouver contributors were Connie Hill, Emily Anne Courtright and Ashley Ford, and in Prince Rupert were T. E. Woodcock of CN, Joe Scott and other members of the port authority, and officials of the coal and grain terminals at Ridley Island. Paul Goldring, information officer at the Japan consulate general in Montreal, was unfailingly helpful as were James Shields and David Jones of CPR and R. Lorne Seitz, director general of the Canadian Committee, Pacific Basin Economic Council. Some of the former CN employees, now retired or in other employment, who also contributed include Dr. Robert Bandeen, A. H. Hart, R. R. Latimer, A. R. Steele, S. F. Dingle, Henry Craig, Alan Wynn, Harvey Shute and Sheila Caldwell. My appreciation also extends to the staff of the CN library and photo archives in Montreal. I would also like to thank Marilyn Sacks for her patience and skill in editing this book.

Index

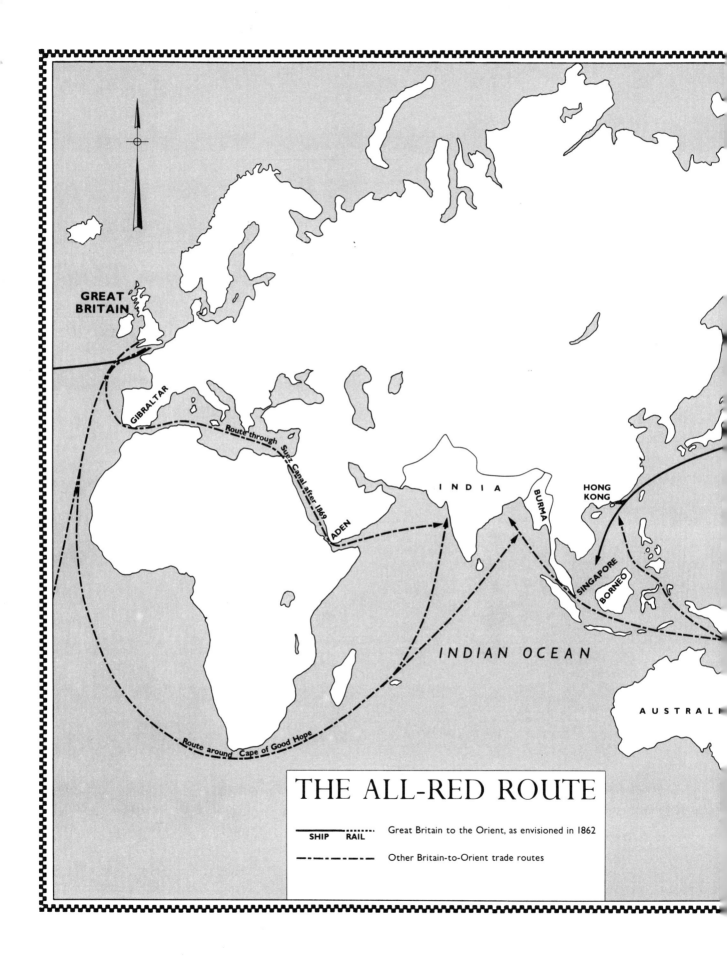

GREAT
BRITAIN

GIBRALTAR

Route through

Suez Canal after 1869

ADEN

I N D I A

BURMA

HONG
KONG

SINGAPORE

BORNEO

INDIAN OCEAN

AUSTRALI

Route around Cape of Good Hope

THE ALL-RED ROUTE

SHIP   RAIL   Great Britain to the Orient, as envisioned in 1862

Other Britain-to-Orient trade routes